# Children and Childhood
# in American Religions

**The Rutgers Series in Childhood Studies**

The Rutgers Series in Childhood Studies is dedicated to increasing our understanding of children and childhoods, past and present, throughout the world. Children's voices and experiences are central. Authors come from a variety of fields, including anthropology, criminal justice, history, literature, psychology, religion, and sociology. The books in this series are intended for students, scholars, practitioners, and those who formulate policies that affect children's everyday lives and futures.

Edited by Myra Bluebond-Langner, Distinguished Professor of Anthropology, Rutgers University, Camden, and founding director of the Rutgers University Center for Children and Childhood Studies

*Advisory Board*
Joan Jacobs Brumberg, Cornell University
Perri Klass, New York University
Jill Korbin, Case Western Reserve University
Bambi Schiefflin, New York University
Enid Schildkraut, American Museum of Natural History and Museum for African Art

# Children and Childhood in American Religions

EDITED BY DON S. BROWNING AND
BONNIE J. MILLER-McLEMORE

RUTGERS UNIVERSITY PRESS

NEW BRUNSWICK, NEW JERSEY, AND LONDON

LIBRARY OF CONGRESS CATALOGING-IN-PUBLICATION DATA

Children and childhood in American religions / edited by Don S. Browning and
Bonnie J. Miller-McLemore.
p. cm.—(The Rutgers series in childhood studies)
Includes bibliographical references and index.
ISBN 978–0–8135–4480–9 (hardcover : alk. paper)
ISBN 978–0–8135–4481–6 (pbk. : alk. paper)
I. United States—Religion. 2. Children—Religious aspects. 3. Children—United
States. I. Browning, Don S. II. Miller-McLemore, Bonnie J.
BL2525.C47 2009
200.83'0973—dc22                                                          2008026184

A British Cataloging-in-Publication record for this book is available from the
British Library.

Visit our Web site: http://rutgerspress.rutgers.edu

Manufactured in the United States of America

# CONTENTS

# PREFACE

This book is the result of efforts by many individuals and organizations. First, every book must be preceded by a vision. This came from the fertile mind of John Witte, the Jonas Robitscher Professor of Law and director of the Center for the Study of Law and Religion, School of Law, Emory University. He conceived and ably directed the two-phase research project that stimulated and supported the development of this book. These were the Sex, Marriage, and Family in the Religions of the Book project (2001–2003) and the Child in Law, Religion, and Society project (2003–2006). Both of these were located in the Center for the Study of Law and Religion in the School of Law at Emory. Appreciation as well must go to his great staff—Eliza Ellison, Amy Wheeler, Anita Mann, Janice Wiggins, and April Bogle—who all do countless important things to move projects along to completion. Christian Green, formerly on the faculty of Harvard Divinity School and now with Emory School of Law, did some of the early conceptualizing of this volume. But then there are the organizations. First, deep thanks must be expressed to the Pew Charitable Trusts for the significant grant that made all these projects, including this book, possible. The Pew grant was generously supplemented by Emory University as part of its long-term commitment to investigating the relation of religion to culture, including law.

Then there were the managing editors of this volume, who did much of the day-to-day work of organizing, communicating, and providing significant stimulation and feedback. This book unfolded over three years and was moved along by the able management skills of Kevin Jung (now on the faculty of Lake Forest University School of Divinity), Sarah Schuurman, and Antonia Daymond, all at one time or another graduate students at the Divinity School, University of Chicago, where much of the work on this volume was done. Their contributions were both vital and outstanding. Appreciation must go to Dean Richard Rosengarten of the Divinity School at Chicago for providing our office, phone, and other supports. Miller-McLemore expresses her appreciation to Vanderbilt Divinity School for its continuing support of her research. We both wish to say thank you very much to our respective spouses and children for help, goodwill, and acceptance of the inevitable preoccupations on our part generated by moving a project like this to completion. Finally, we want to thank Adi Hovav, our helpful Rutgers editor, who ably saw this volume through to completion.

# Children and Childhood
# in American Religions

# Introduction

## Children and Childhood in American Religions

BONNIE J. MILLER-McLEMORE AND DON S. BROWNING

How do religious traditions in the United States understand children today? Religion and children have proved to be challenging subjects to study. Many people consider religion primarily a matter of personal belief, leaving little to be learned about it beyond proclamation and confession. Social scientists have included religion as part of their work on children in the past several decades, but generally speaking have not studied religious texts or history with regard to children and have not seen the field of religious and theological studies as a significant resource. Meanwhile, scholars in religion have been oddly adultcentric, abdicating their role in understanding children over the past century to those in the social sciences and largely neglecting children as a valid subject matter.[1]

As a consequence, a lacuna surrounds knowledge of the particular beliefs and practices of religions in the United States with respect to children.[2] This gap sparks the primary question behind this book and the question put before its contributors, who are scholars in different areas of religious and theological studies: How do different religious traditions in the United States today understand children, and how do people in these religions interpret, reconstruct, and mediate these traditions to support and guide children in light of the prominent threats and opportunities of American life?

*Children and Childhood in American Religions* investigates the many ways in which a variety of religions in the United States understands childhood and guides children. In inviting a closer reading of a diversity of religious traditions, it takes the public discussion of children and religion beyond the stale opposition of the Christian Right against secular society that dominates so much of the popular media as well as a great deal of academic and clinical study of children. It also hopes to add an important perspective to a common approach to children's studies in the social sciences. In contrast to social scientists, authors of the chapters in this book do not focus as much on children's experience of religion as on what religious texts, traditions, communities, and practitioners have said about children. The authors are interested in children, but they also see childhood as indelibly interconnected with families, rituals, and institutions and naturally spend time exploring these. Careful examination by scholars of religion of primary religious texts and doctrines, historical developments in religion, and communal practices in families and congregations can both enrich the discussion of children and show how these religions respond to the challenges of contemporary life as they guide parents and work directly with children, youth, and young people. In other words, the book hopes to provide the kind of foundational knowledge that those who explore children's experiences of religion empirically through ethnography, for example, might find useful in their analysis.[3] The book invites ongoing collaboration between social science and religious studies and hopes to point the way for a rich cross-disciplinary analysis of children and religion as an important direction for further study.

## Definitions

By *American religions*, we do not mean religions that have originated in the United States. Only Native American religions have started indigenously on these shores. We point instead to the variety of increasingly visible religions that are working out their identities in special ways because of the nature of U.S. culture and society. Although Christianity and Judaism are older and more established in the United States, it is now time to recognize that other religions are an important part of the landscape. All the religions in the book have adapted and taken on a particular cast, such that they are now different from how they appear in their countries of origin. In addition to various Christian groups, including the Church of Jesus Christ of the Latter-day Saints and expressions of Black Christianity, we study Native American religion, Judaism, Islam, Confucianism, Hinduism, and Buddhism. This list does not exhaust the American religions, but these are among the major ones, each wielding significant influence and illustrating the evolving issues that arise in the interaction between a particular religious tradition, other religious traditions, and broader social trends. We have also included in the volume two chapters that are not on specific traditions but instead stand back and look at these religions as they cut across broad social issues and interact with the major social institutions of education and law.

By using the terms *children* and *childhood* in our title, we intentionally point toward the plural and diverse understandings found within religious traditions. *Children* refers to a particular segment of the population and *childhood* refers to a particular developmental period, both organized around the common rubric of being young in all societies, although the exact ages, turning points, and meanings assigned to childhood, adulthood, children, and adults vary from one tradition and community to another. For most religious traditions, the term *children* includes youths or those considered more advanced in age but still underage, as defined in contemporary society by national and international institutions and bodies, such as the insurance business and the United Nations. The whole matter of defining children opens the issue of how childhood is socially constructed, a topic we discuss more in the paragraphs below. We choose *children* and *childhood* explicitly over *the child* because this last term often implies a predetermined set of universal or essential qualities. However, this preference in our title does not rule out the usefulness of *the child* in capturing particular patterns through which religions view the child. Religions do make broad generalizations about the child or the nature of childhood and qualities all children share (such as agency, vulnerability, and sacredness or the child as agent, vulnerable, sacred, and so forth).

## Enriching Understanding of Religion and Children

This book hopes to broaden and deepen understanding of religious perspectives on children and childhood in American life. We asked authors to examine their religion's reigning approach to U.S. culture as it influences children. We asked them to consider the question of how religious traditions in the United States have responded to American-style culture, modernization, and democratic polity with respect to their views of childhood in light of two prominent frames of interpretation on contemporary childhood in present-day human sciences: the family modernization hypothesis and the social constructionist hypothesis. The family modernization hypothesis, widely employed in sociology and anthropology, suggests that the spread of technical rationality (the use of efficient means to gain short-term satisfactions) injects various separations into society that affect the lives of children.[4] These include weakened parental supervision; the disconnection of children from inherited religious authority; and the separation of public education from religion, home, and parental supervision. In modern societies, the argument goes, norms governing the socialization of children, education, employment, sexuality, and life's purpose become increasingly oriented around market values, individual rights, self-actualization, and secularism.

A second hypothesis, also widely used in the social sciences and particularly influential in the field of childhood studies, focuses on the cultural construction of childhood. It argues that even though childhood has distinct biological parameters, societies and social groups construct the meaning and nature of childhood to a considerable extent around powerful economic, political, and religious ideas. It traces this construction historically across premodern, modern, and postmodern times and socially across divergent locations, communities, and contexts. In Europe and the United States, constructions of children have evolved, according to some scholars, from that of the depraved child of premodernity to the innocent child of modernity to the knowing or more complex child of today.[5] These two closely related social-systemic and cultural views interact with, and sometimes appear to contradict, traditional religious views of childhood.

We do not present these prominent human-science perspectives as measuring rods against which to judge these religions. Some of these religious traditions have quite different views of their situation in relation to childhood in the United States than would be predicted by these theories. Our authors are asked to consider these frameworks only as possible interpretive *stimuli* in their search for how these religions view American cultures of childhood and how they develop strategies for retrieving and communicating their traditions about children.

To guide our authors as they addressed the question of how the religion they study understands childhood and children and deals with wider cultural and social influences, we spelled out several subquestions that cluster around four major themes: formal doctrinal and institutional beliefs and practices, relationship between parents and children, formational and developmental growth, and relationship between religions and the wider culture. Our authors examined their religion's views and strategies about childhood with this general framework in mind. Some religions make it possible to answer the individual questions directly. Other traditions address these issues more indirectly. One way or another, however, most religions and most of the chapters address basic questions ranging from the fundamental textual and ritual resources of the tradition and its beliefs and practices to its specific view of development and spiritual formation to the appropriate connections between children and adults and between families, children, and the wider culture, as described below:

- *Questions concerning formal doctrinal institutional beliefs and practices*:
  What are the core metaphysical or theological beliefs about children and childhood? What is the ontological and moral status of children before the divine or sacred? What are the central religious,

ritual, and cultural practices as they relate to children? What specific institutions has the religion evolved for children?

- *Relationship between adults and children*:

     Who has authority over children? To what extent do children have a voice in religion and in society? What are the parental and social obligations to children and children's obligations to parents and community?

- *Questions of development and religious formation*:

     What is the meaning of birth and childhood dependency? What is the attitude toward children's sexuality? What are the stages of growing up? How does the religion value certain stages more than others?

- *Relationship between religion and culture*:

     How does the religion assess the resources for children of institutions outside its religious life—public schools, government, citizenship, media, and the marketplace? How does it interpret and respond to the threats and opportunities of U.S. society as they bear on children and youth? How has it reinterpreted its childhood traditions? In what ways are children viewed as important resources for assuring generational continuity for the religion?

To address these questions and accomplish our goal of enriching general understanding of religious perspectives on children and childhood in American life, we assembled top scholars from several disciplines in religion who have been trained in theological studies, religious studies, or the social scientific study of religion and are specialists of one of the major religions present in the United States. As is evident in the notes on contributors at the back of the book, we have brought together historians of Christianity and religion (such as Margaret Bendroth and Jeffrey Meyer), social scientists of religion (such as David Dollahite, Cheryl Townsend Gilkes, and John Bartkowski and Chris Ellison), and religious ethicists and theologians (such as Jennifer Beste). We believe this diversity of approaches and methods within the study of religion is a virtue. Since subareas within religious study presume particular methods and approaches to the subject matter at hand, the careful reader should ask what is being learned, and perhaps not learned, depending on the perspective and methodology used by these experts.

     One key question to keep in mind is the position of authors in relation to the tradition they study. Some authors, such as Dollahite on the Latter-day Saints or Gilkes on the Black Church, locate themselves as confessional insiders and advocates of the tradition they study. Others, such as Raymond Williams on Hinduism or Bartkowski and Ellison on Evangelical Christianity, see themselves ostensibly as objective outsiders to a religion or do not locate themselves at all. The reader will want to assess what difference these episte-mological starting points make. In many ways, our broader cultural conver-sation in the United States reflects the tensions between so-called objective and subjective perspectives on what these religious contribute.

Another difference in approach concerns how authors handle the ques-tion of breadth and depth in covering a particular religion. Some authors choose specific entry points into the subject matter, such as Meyer's focus on filial piety in Confucianism or Bartkowski and Ellison's exploration of discipline in Evangelical Christianity. In this case, authors focus on one par-ticularly prominent characteristic of a religious tradition as a lens through which to consider the whole. Others attempt a more comprehensive cover-age, addressing a broad range of subjects, such as Roger Iron Cloud and Ray Bucko on Native American religions. They discuss not only discipline and piety, for example, but a wide range of topics, such as religious rituals across the life span and stages of spiritual development.

Authors also differ over whether they subject their tradition to cultural and religious criticism or describe the ideal or hoped-for vision of religious life with children as depicted in religious laws, writings, and doctrines. Some, such as Elliot Dorff on Judaism and Dollahite on the Latter-day Saints, primarily describe practices with children as they should happen under the best circumstances. Other authors, for example, Beste on Roman Catholi-cism and Bendroth on mainline Protestantism, analyze and evaluate the suc-cess and failure of a tradition's approach to children, noting the mistakes, oversights, and problematic consequences for families and society.

None of the chapters intends to stand as the definitive statement on a particular religious tradition. Each chapter represents one scholar's view. Just as religion as a whole has many shapes and forms—some of which are represented by the chapters in this volume—so also does each religion have many interpretations. Indeed, some religions, among them Hinduism and Buddhism, are harder to treat in a comprehensive manner than others. Even for those seemingly monolithic traditions, such as Judaism or Evangelical Protestantism, one chapter does not suffice. A chapter written largely from the perspective of Conservative Judaism does not address the many differ-ences of Reform and Orthodox Judaism, for example, or even the complexity of Conservative Judaism. Nor does one chapter on white Evangelical Protes-tantism cover the many shapes Christian evangelicalism assumes in other ethnic communities, for instance, or among charismatic Catholics.

Indeed, readers may actually find themselves most dissatisfied or in the greatest disagreement with the chapter on the religious tradition they know best or most intimately. This is actually not a bad reaction if it pro-vokes greater exploration, conversation, and insight about the relationship between a religious tradition and its attitudes toward and practices with children. Understanding other religions beyond the reader's experience should also serve to enhance understanding of self, society, and religion. The book will have accomplished its goal if it incites engagement, debate, questions, and further exploration among its readers.

## Children in the Social Sciences and Childhood Studies

This book contributes to the growing field of childhood studies that has emerged in the past few decades in a number of academic disciplines. It is helpful and important to understand the book in relationship to this development. Over the past century, scholars and researchers in education and the social sciences increasingly have made children and childhood a primary subject matter. Psychology deserves mention for sparking general intellectual and social interest in the needs and desires of children in the early years of the twentieth century. Sigmund Freud drew heated debate precisely because he dared to suggest that adults had had important emotional needs when they were children—needs adults should take more seriously.[6] Later analysts and psychologists, from Freud's own daughter Anna to Erik Erikson to Robert Coles in more recent years (to mention only a few), made children's inner life and outer behavior prominent matters for public reconsideration.[7] Child psychology especially grew after World War II. Children became a central subject of laboratory study in major universities, and academic journals devoted to child development multiplied. Child experts grew to include not only psychologists and psychiatrists but also pediatricians and educators, and psychoanalytic and psychological ideas about children made their way into the general public through child-care manuals.[8] Although Freud often equated children in limited ways with the "primitive" and irrational and later developmental theorists cast children primarily as little adults-in-the-making, psychology planted a seed for a new way of perceiving children and childhood that has taken deeper root today in an emerging field, identified as "childhood studies," that has garnered strength in the past decade.

Other disciplines besides psychology, however, should be credited with the development of childhood studies as an area of research. Sociology and anthropology in particular have played an important role. A key characteristic of childhood studies, as it has appeared in sociology and anthropology as well as in history, education, and, most recently, religion and theology, is the view of children as important subjects in and of themselves and not just a place where adult pathology first develops, a stage to leave behind, or a space where socialization and religious rituals get enacted. In other words, in childhood studies children move from peripheral vision to the center. This shift in focus is often sparked by a commitment to their fuller participation in society and political advocacy on their behalf. They are

commonly dubbed "agents," a term that has become especially prevalent
in the literature. For example, this term organizes the major sections of
a recently edited text in the field, Peter Pufall and Richard Unsworth's
*Rethinking Childhood* ("Children's Voice and Agency," "Voice and Agency in
Education").[9] The term is also widespread in religious studies. It appears
in chapter titles of Bonnie Miller-McLemore's book *Let the Children Come*
("Feminism and Faith: Children as Agents")[10] and in recent titles of a new
program unit on childhood offered by the American Academy of Religion
("Children as Agents of Good and Evil," "Children as Moral and Religious
Agents in Literature and Film"). In the chapters in this volume, the rubric of
the child's agency is investigated, but generally from the perspective of how
a particular religion did or did not represent and acknowledge it in the tradition's teachings about childhood. Traditions vary in the degree to which
they recognize the subjectivity, feeling, intentionality, and decision-making
capacities of children. Most of them, however, do address the issue.

Although the exact definition of childhood studies as a field remains
unsettled, one foundational text, *An Introduction to Childhood Studies*, suggests
several elements that characterize it: an interdisciplinary interest, a contex-
tual methodology or a "more integrated approach to research" on children,
a recognition of the multiple social constructions of childhood, and an
"emphasis on recognizing children as social actors." The field, the editor
argues, was "born out of frustration with the narrow versions of 'the child'
offered by traditional academic discourses and methods of inquiry" that do
not give adequate representation to the voices, experiences, and social con-
textual location of children.[11] The field gained more formal self-conscious-
ness slightly earlier in the European context but today has established itself
as a distinct presence in a number of disciplines in the United States. So, for
example, the International Sociological Association established a "Sociology of Childhood" research section in 1998 after several years of study as a
working group. The American Sociological Association has recently formed
a similar research section. Such developments coincide with the establishment of new journals on children and new academic programs in childhood
studies in the United States and abroad.[12] New scholarship on children has
appeared in many fields, from sociology and anthropology to history, art theory, literature, and philosophy.[13] Children's spiritual development has most
recently become the subject of many major studies in the social sciences,
including, for example, the National Study of Youth and Religion project.
Recent and emerging research from sociologists and anthropologists shed
important light on the lived experiences of youth as they relate to religion
and spirituality in the United States and around the world.[14] A similar development has occurred among scholars in child development, developmental
psychology, and counseling and clinical psychology.[15]

Even as some disciplines, such as sociology and anthropology, initiated more directed research on children and included religion and spirituality, they tended to concentrate on religions in simpler societies; on religious acts, rituals, and behaviors; or on faith as a generic category in stage development theory. Less attention was given to the study of the so-called axial religions—Judaism, Christianity, Confucianism, Hinduism, and Buddhism—and their core texts, traditions, doctrines, and practices. Thus far, prominent texts in childhood studies have paid insufficient attention to religious studies as a partner in this interdisciplinary field and often do not include treatment of religion. For example, *Rethinking Childhood* has one chapter by a Christian church historian among its fourteen chapters by psychologists, anthropologists, and sociologists. *An Introduction to Childhood Studies* does not contain a chapter on religion at all. A recent reader, *Childhood in America*, edited by historian Paula Fass and law and social welfare professor Mary Ann Mason, contains in its seven hundred pages 178 selections on various aspects of childhood.[16] None of these selections contains religious perspectives on children.

## The Study of Children in Religion

The responsibility for this omission of religious scholarship is, of course, widely shared. Religious scholars have only come to the table of childhood studies in the past few years. As emblematic of this new development, in 2003 the American Academy of Religion also accepted a new program unit, a Consultation on Childhood Studies and Religion, initiated by Marcia Bunge, Bonnie Miller-McLemore, and several other interested scholars. Leaders chose the term *childhood studies* for pragmatic, strategic, and political reasons more than out of explicit intentions to contribute to a new field in the academy at large. Academic clout accrues around the term *studies*, and other areas, such as women's, gender, and African American studies, set an example, paved the way, and made progress under the same rubric. Many of those involved in this development had participated in a Lilly Endowment–funded project on children, contributing essays to the first major work on children in Christian theology, *The Child in Christian Thought*, edited by Marcia Bunge.[17] Many have gone on to publish additional essays and books on children.[18] Perhaps inadvertently at first, therefore, but now by greater design, these scholars lend support to establishment of the field of childhood studies and, as important, to religious study as a key player and participant.

A growing number of scholars, especially within the Christian tradition, have joined this development, building an expanding corpus of literature supporting the growth of childhood studies as a legitimate and important

area of study in religion. Several scholars have focused on religious constructions of children and childhood and their social, cultural, and political
implications.[19] Others have contributed to a growing body of literature on
the spiritual experience of children and the role of families and other adults
in their religious formation.[20] A select number of books have focused on historical investigation of children and childhood.[21] A group of sociologists of
religion have also begun to study children's participation in religious communities and the impact of religion on children.[22] As an additional mark of
the expanding interested in scholarship on children and religion, children
and childhood have also been the theme of several prominent journals in
religion in the past several years.[23] Although only the most recent journal
refers explicitly to the field of "childhood studies," all these efforts contribute to religion's participation in this endeavor.[24]

*Children and Childhood in American Religions* takes one further step in the
recognition of the importance of the study of children and religion to the
growing field of childhood studies, not only within Christianity but also among
other religions. Most of the scholarship thus far has focused on Christianity,
and few books attempt to address more than one religious tradition around
the question of children and childhood.[25] Although the various Christian traditions are still evident in American life, it is now time to understand more
fully the childhood traditions of other prominent religions. There has been a
general neglect in academic circles of how American religions have shaped,
and still shape, our children and our images of childhood. This book hopes to
clarify and begin to remedy this neglected childhood-religion connection.

At the same time that the religion-childhood connection was often
overlooked by scholars, the need to attend to religion in the public sphere
intensified on at least three fronts. First, critics and public intellectuals in
the past decade have often agreed, despite divergent political positions, that
popular culture and market forces exploit children. Often, in response to
broad social and cultural problems, they move beyond the usual boundaries
of their scientific disciplines and delve into normative or prescriptive solutions. The solutions, however, are often unsatisfying because of a limited
understanding of religion and culture. The problem is not just being "more
explicit about the interaction of religious belief and psychology" or any
other field, as one scholar has urged.[26] It is a matter of gaining greater knowledge and understanding of specific religious traditions. Creating new public
norms or challenging a dominant morality of materialism and big business
is difficult without addressing the particularities of the many religious traditions and beliefs that shape morality. In the United States, religion is still
one of the most powerful culture-shaping institutions.

This underscores a second area calling for greater understanding of
religion. Ann Hulbert, in *Raising America: Experts, Parents, and a Century of*

*Advice about Children*, observes that the new child experts for many parents—replacing established psychologists and psychiatrists—are actually religious advisors, such as the evangelical James Dobson.[27] This observation suggests that scholars may be neglecting to study religion's impact on children, but many parents, it appears, do not ignore the religious factor themselves. Nor do children avoid its influence. In a recent large-scale survey of American youth, sociologists of religion Christian Smith and Melinda Denton demonstrate that religion measurably influences more than 50 percent of U.S. children and youth and is, in fact, correlated with a number of positive outcomes. The "differences between more religious and less religious teenagers in the United States," they argue, "are actually significant and consistent across every outcome measure examined: risk behaviors, quality of family and adult relationships, moral reasoning and behavior, community participation, media consumption, sexual activity, and emotional well-being."[28] These studies suggest that contemporary society needs to take religious formation seriously as a force that is still functioning in the lives of many children, youth, and their families. Furthermore, we need to go beyond raw statistics about religion's impact on children and come to better understand the content of religion's teachings, beliefs, practices, and rituals pertaining to children.

Finally, the United States is struggling over the question of what children need or deserve, and it necessarily does so as an increasingly ethnic and religiously diverse nation, perhaps one of the most diverse in the world. Among the concerns brought to the debate over what is good for children and what harms them is the question of the impact of religious traditions. Even if some Americans are convinced that their own religion is good for the young, they may not be certain at all that other religions are constructive influences. There is a great deal of distrust both among and within religions and between religions and secular society about what is right, just, and beneficial for children.

This review of the recent history of childhood studies, the longer history of the study of children, their relative oversight in religion and other fields, the neglect of religion in childhood studies, and the current unrest in society's efforts to understand and care adequately for all children make clear why the question that sparked this book—How do religious traditions today understand children, and how do people interpret, reconstruct, and mediate these traditions to support and guide children in light of the dominant threats and opportunities of American life?—deserves more concentrated attention. In the past, and even today, the meaning, value, goals, socialization, and construction of children in the United States has been massively shaped by their various religious heritages and contexts. Time has come to understand this influence with greater sensitivity, insight, and knowledge.

## Seeing Religions in a New Way

The neglect of children in the academic study of religion has not only robbed us of a deeper understanding of them, it has deprived us of an important angle of vision on understanding these diverse religions themselves. Readers of this volume will therefore gain a twofold learning: they will learn more about how religious traditions understand children and they will see values and accents in these religions that scholarship has often overlooked. This will be true not only for the branches of traditional American religions of Judaism and Christianity but also for the other world religions, such as Islam, Confucianism, Hinduism, and Buddhism. In other words, this book is as much about religion as it is about children.

One learns something unique about religion—something special and profound—when one views it from the perspective of what it says about children. It is, in effect, looking at a religion from an entirely fresh angle. Of course, we are not saying that these articles look at religion from the child's point of view or through the experiences of children of being involved in religious institutions or developing a religious identity. That would require empirical methodologies, among them interviews with children, not featured in this volume. Rather we are saying that these chapters not only examine religions from the perspective of their dogmas, moral teachings, and official rituals as understood by and for adults and adulthood, they view them from the angle of what these elements mean for the rhythms, goals, and needs of children. It is from the perspective of the formation of children that we learn something fresh about what is important to a particular religious tradition—what it truly cares about. It is at the level of children that a religion touches the most vital and profound aspects of life. Furthermore, from the viewpoint of what a religion says about childhood, we most deeply learn how it sees the wider society and its institutions, opportunities, and threats. From the perspective of its teaching about children, we learn how those in religious traditions support, ignore, criticize, or reject the social and secular world around them and how raising children functions as part of the reproduction of religious communities and social worlds.

## Seeing Children in New Ways

Of course, the primary goal remains seeing children in new ways through the lens of a variety of religious perspectives and approaches, as revealed by scriptural texts, written and oral traditions, community practices and rituals, historical study, and, in a few cases, empirical observation. A careful investigation of religions in a comparative analysis can significantly advance

contemporary attitudes toward children and provide a richer basis for concerted public action on their behalf.

### Children as Sacred

Several intriguing themes emerge when one takes both the study of religion and the study of children more seriously. One of the most striking and
important is the realization that all religions have some way of speaking
about children as sacred, perhaps even divine. Those people nourished
by Judaism and Christianity are familiar with the idea that humans, even
children, are created "in the image of God" (Gen. 1: 27) and are indeed "gifts
of God." But a view of the child as sacred is also shared by Islam, which is
informed by the Hebrew scriptures and their doctrine of creation.

Other religions have ways of saying something similar. Rita Gross tells us
that Buddhism sees children as reflections of Buddha himself. Native American religions, especially that of the Lakota, whom Roger Iron Cloud and Ray
Bucko study, also see children as showing forth the divine. In Confucianism
and Hinduism, however, the sacredness of children refers less to the individual child and is more fused or identified with the sacred importance of
the larger kinship group and children's importance to the mutual support
passed on from generation to generation.

Even when a religion grants sacredness to children, it does not mean it
is necessarily child centered. Both Hinduism and Confucianism have often
spoken of parents as gods or demigods. It is the task of the child to mature
and serve his or her parents and honor, and perhaps directly assist, deceased
ancestors as well. Even the monotheistic religions of Judaism and Christianity hold that children should honor their mother and father (Deut. 5:16),
though this injunction sometimes can be distorted to support punitive and
oppressive parental behavior.

Affirmation of the sacredness of children is extremely important, however, for the relation of religion to some aspects of modernity. If modernity is
defined, in part, around market capitalism, technical reason, efficiency, and
short-term goals and goods, modernity can function to reduce all humans,
especially vulnerable children, to means for the ends of production and
consumption. The witness in these religions to the sacredness of children
constitutes a moral and ontological affirmation that children should not be
reduced to means for the advancement of technical ends, be they commercial, medical, or economic. This fundamental affirmation that each child is a
child of God has been absolutely central, as Gilkes demonstrates, to the survival and flourishing of African American children confronted by economic,
political, and social racism. It is not clear that there are sufficient resources
outside these religions for affirming, both morally and ontologically, that
children, and humans in general, must be treated as sacred ends, never to

be reduced to means or utilities for the increase of collective wealth or the power and prestige of corporate and governmental entities.

### Children as Innocent, Culpable, and Morally Neutral

Closely related to the inherent worth of children are various assertions in different religions about children's sinfulness or innocence. Certain strands of Christianity especially stand out as proclaiming the sinfulness of the child. Although the Augustinian doctrine of original or inherited sin may not be present in either the Old or New Testament, it has been a substantial part of Roman Catholicism and portions of Protestantism. In fact, teachings about both the graced *and* sinful nature of children have coexisted in major branches of Christianity. The idea of the original sin of children, however, is far less prominent today in almost all expressions of modern Christianity. By contrast, Raymond Williams and Rita Gross reveal that classically both Hinduism and Buddhism held views analogous to the Christian teachings about sinfulness. The Hindu and Buddhist concept of karma was understood as the evil deeds of ancestors communicated to newborn children in the family line, giving them a kind of original and inherited taint from the misdeeds of those who preceded them.

Not all religions view children as innately sinful. Despite their many other differences, Judaism, the Latter-day Saints, and the Lakota all see children in a largely positive light. All three view the inclinations and deeds of infants and young children as morally neutral. For these religions, sin, or moral and spiritual fault, comes with freedom of the will and only gradually emerges in the lifespan of children. Most liberal Protestant groups also downplay the concept of original sin, acknowledging but not dwelling on the idea that humans, including children, inevitably sin.

One way or the other, however, all these religions share a degree of realism about the nature of children. Children embody or reflect the sacred, are ends in themselves, but sooner or later have capacities for evil for which they must be held responsible. Articulating this tension between the ontological or inherent goodness of children and their emerging capacity for evil seems to be a perennial goal of the world religions, even as they struggle with American life. In this, these religions simultaneously show both a higher and lower, or perhaps more realistic, image of children than can be found in more secular or strictly modern pragmatic and utilitarian views of childhood.

### Discipline and Parental Responsibility

In light of beliefs about children's essentially mixed nature, religious traditions have created widely varying ways of orchestrating parental authority and the discipline of children. On this question, Judaism, Buddhism, Native

American religions, and some streams of Christianity depart significantly from conservative Protestantism, which requires children to submit to the parent's will. Adults are sometimes encouraged to discipline them physically, as instructed by a particular interpretation of scriptures in Proverbs, so they will learn to submit in turn to God.

By contrast, Native Americans are represented by Iron Cloud and Bucko as giving children considerable behavioral latitude within an extended kinship network, never hitting them and relying heavily on adultlike conversation to convey right and wrong. Some streams of liberal Christianity couple the demand for obedience with scriptural views in the Synoptic Gospels rather than Proverbs of children as called and blessed by Jesus—a conviction that encourages a process of guiding children rather than ruling over them as the most beneficial way to develop children's faith and personhood. Judaism expects children to honor parents but does not say that the children must agree with them. Honor does not necessarily entail compliance or obedience. Judaism's vitality lies in debate and engagement, a practice that has implications for a parental style of modeling and teaching. For Buddhism, karmic inheritance shapes children. Consequently, parents do not have the right, as Gross comments, to "reproduce in them their own cultural and religious prejudices." Emphasis falls instead on providing the kind of environment that will allow their true nature to emerge.

### The Relationship with and Role of Other Social Institutions

In this complex process of shaping, forming, and raising children, these religions vary significantly, especially in the United States, on whether they assume support or opposition from surrounding institutions. Bendroth points out that mainline Protestantism until recent decades could assume continuity between its values and those of surrounding educational, legal, cultural, commercial, and governmental institutions. This made it possible for Horace Bushnell, a major nineteenth-century influence on mainline Christian education theory, to teach that socialization into Christianity should be a smooth process brought about simply by surrounding children with the Christian way of life. This came more easily, she observes, when Protestant Christianity, as the dominant religious force in U.S. society, was itself shaping schools, legal institutions, commerce, and government. But when these institutions differentiated and gained more autonomy from religious influence, Protestant Christianity faced the challenge of raising children in the Christian faith as a minority religion in a complex market economy that no longer supported all its values.

Paul Numrich helps us understand what happens when a religion does not trust the influence on its children of surrounding secular institutions, especially public schools. One strategy is to create alternative educational institutions. As Gilkes points out, African American churches put considerable energy and resources into the support of educational institutions that were designed to promote the growth and success of its children in a culture that was often hostile to them. Today, Islam is a leading religion creating alternative school systems for its children and youth in the United States. This strategy reflects characteristics of both U.S. society and the traditions and beliefs of Islam. As Jane Smith shows, Islam historically has believed that the teachings of the Qur'an, formulated gradually into a body of law called Shar'ia, should apply rigorously to all of life—family, marriage, education, commerce, and government. This effort by much of Islam to shape the totality of social life differs from what exists in many modern manifestations of Christianity.

Religions with detailed prescriptions, laws, and regulations for how to live are more likely to want to control the educational formation of their children by establishing alternative schools systems. Because of its strong canon law and liturgical traditions, Roman Catholicism did that in the United States in the nineteenth and twentieth centuries. Bartkowski's and Ellison's description of Evangelical patterns of child discipline helps us understand why in recent decades conservative Protestant denominations have done more to establish their own parochial schools as well as cultivating a homeschooling movement.

Williams points out, however, that Hindu parents are equally skeptical of aspects of U.S. culture, but are more inclined to use their temple life and home-based religious practices to shape their children. When resources for schools were lacking, Black Christians also turned to the congregation to nurture children. Immigrant Buddhist parents are likely to center their formation of children in the home, whereas converted Buddhists who may not have the support of ethnic communities are now establishing specialized religious education for their children that is analogous to the Protestant Sunday school. Nevertheless, Buddhists, like Hindus, have not developed parochial schools. As legal scholar Emily Buss indicates, these different strategies for the formation of children bring up issues pertaining to the secular law of families and the relation of religion to the state, especially state-mandated guidelines for the education of children. Furthermore, laws affecting religious freedom and the regulation of parochial schools will affect some religious traditions more than others. Buss helps us understand present and emerging tensions between religion and secular law as our society becomes increasingly pluralistic.

### The Role of Scriptural Texts and Traditions

Care of children is also shaped by the proclamations of inherited texts and traditions. Religions in the United States vary on whether they define themselves around a single text and official body of commentary or around more diffuse literary traditions and systems of interpretation. This makes a difference in how they express their claims on the lives of children and negotiate with a complex society such as that of the United States. Judaism, Confucianism, Hinduism, and Buddhism are religious traditions with many texts and multiple authoritative traditions of interpretation. Islam has its Qur'an as its central text and an authoritative body of commentary called the hadith. Latter-day Saints have the Book of Mormon, which is their revealed, and therefore authoritative, commentary on the Christian Bible.

Religions with the most compact textual resources are also more inclined to insist that children learn and follow these texts. Christianity has its Bible, but it is made up of many books written by numerous known and unknown authors at different times and places over hundreds of years. Protestant groups are more likely to view the New Testament as their authority, although as Bartkowski and Ellison point out, conservative Evangelicals get much of their understanding of child discipline from the Book of Proverbs, a book in both the Hebrew Scriptures and in what Christians call the Old Testament. Roman Catholicism honors the Christian Bible, but grants a great deal of interpretive authority to its councils and popes. It has definite dogmas and moral teachings developed by this tradition of interpretation. It is a religion of a Book—like Judaism, Islam, and Protestantism—but also functions as an evolving tradition, like Confucianism, Hinduism, Buddhism, and Judaism. Since Roman Catholicism carries its tradition through the judgments of authoritative councils and popes, its teachings are more compact and specific than other more freely evolving traditions. Hence, its differences with the dominant culture on the formation of children are more apparent, as is the case with Islam and in recent decades has become the case with conservative Protestantism.

### The Role of the Extended Family

The extent to which religions value the continuity between the generations of the extended family affects how they regard the social role of children and how religions cope with American life. All the world religions consolidating around the axial age from 800 to 200 B.C.E. (Confucianism, Hinduism, Buddhism, and Judaism) valued lineage and family continuity, generally defined around the patriarchal line. The continuity over the generations of the extended patriarchal family was the world's first welfare system. Consequently, in these traditions children, especially older sons, have a huge obligation to care for their parents, and perhaps even their dead ancestors, out of appreciation for their own birth and nurture. Judaism, Confucianism, Hinduism, Native American religion, and even Buddhism, in its own way, assume and sanction this family continuity. Children, as we noted above, are often defined in close association with their place in this cycle of the generations. Islam also highly values this intergenerational family continuity even though it is a younger religion founded in the seventh century C.E. Even the Church of Jesus Christ of the Latter-day Saints—a distinctively American and in many ways quite modern expression of Christianity—values and promotes family continuity as part of its entire conception of God's purpose in preserving families and actively involves its young in learning their genealogies, even going so far as to keep meticulous historical records to help them do this.

Christianity and Buddhism may be exceptions to this ancient, yet still visible, emphasis on intergenerational continuity. Both traditions developed strong monastic movements and drew clear distinctions between celibate religious orders and family life, sometimes seeing the latter as a hindrance to spiritual pursuits. Christianity warns against idolatry of the family, recognizes the Christian community as a new family in Christ, and sees pursuit of God's will as a legitimate justification for resisting parental demands. At the same time, both traditions also have sought ways to bridge the distance between families and the practice of faith. Lay Buddhism in the United States, established outside monastic orders, has created a great need for integrating family life and Buddhist practice. Reform movements in Christianity, going back to the Reformation itself, also have attempted to reclaim parenting as a religious practice.[29] Scholars tell us, moreover, that early Christianity did not so much oppose the antique extended and intergenerational family as insist that it not function to block individuals from becoming disciples of Jesus and serving the kingdom of God.

This stance in early Christianity, however, still gave the individual, even the individual child and youth, more independence from extended family. But only occasionally did Christianity's subordination of the extended family to the kingdom of God lead to its total repudiation. Often, in the early days of the Christian movement, entire families converted. In Buddhism, the call to renounce mundane worldly pursuits and surrender to the authority of the Buddha in monastic life may have functioned to endow the individual person, even the child, with more independence from the extended family. At the same time, as Alan Cole has recently argued, complex patterns of mutual support and intergenerational benefit often developed between monastic sons and their families as the latter supported the monasteries and their sons prayed, and thereby created merit, for their families.[30] Religions that emphasize the individual person may be able to adapt to modernization and American individualism more smoothly. They also may have more difficulty socializing their children to resist the more negative aspects of these social and cultural trends.

### The Value and Role of the Parent-Child Relationship

Finally, along the same track, religions differ in whether they make the parent-child relationship or the husband-wife relationship central to the family. Confucianism, Hinduism, and Buddhism are key examples of the centrality of the parent-child (most noticeably the father-son) relationship. Christianity, by contrast, has elevated the husband-wife relation just as it has weakened its emphasis on the importance of the extended, intergenerational family. Some commentators have wondered whether this impulse in Christianity has now developed to the place where the family is more and more defined around the intimate relation of the adults in contrast to the ancient emphasis on the tie between parent and child. Whether this is true or not, we see evidence of the power of Asian families—significantly shaped by a cultural ethos stemming from Confucianism and Hinduism and the importance of honoring the family and pleasing prior generations—to produce children and youth disciplined to excel in institutions of higher education at higher rates than their proportions in the general population.

The fruitful lines of inquiry and comparison go on and on. There is little doubt that in the future, U.S. society will become more and more involved in a great conversation about how these traditions should work out their values, commitments, and logics about childhood in the context of the American styles of modernization, democracy, and religious pluralism. These religions will transform aspects of the U.S. culture of childhood even as they also will be changed themselves. This book, we believe, will make a contribution to the ongoing process of interpretation, clarification, debate, and negotiation.

## The Order and Audience of the Book

We consider this book an exercise in cultural self-interpretation and self-understanding, influenced by the hermeneutic philosophies of Hans-Georg Gadamer and Paul Ricoeur.[31] From this perspective, it is good to begin self-reflection by coming to understand the history that has shaped us. Hence, the chapters are ordered roughly around the historical entry and prominence or visibility of each religion on the U.S. scene. Of course, any linear ordering cannot do justice to the complex historical and social interaction among traditions and the ambiguous ways in which dominant religions have supplanted, repressed, and transformed other traditions. Nonetheless, roughly speaking, we order the chapters to facilitate hermeneutical understanding of the evolving influence of different religious forces on children.

Native American religion is perhaps the hardest to place. Historically it predates all other religions in terms of its presence but not in terms of its influence, since it was subjected to the destructive exploitation of Christian hegemony. Renewed appreciation of Native American religion in recent years reveals how it both sustained distinct elements that predate Christianity and incorporated the latter. We start the book instead with what has been called mainline Protestantism not because it is the most important but because of its early and ongoing influence. Broadly speaking, it was the dominant religious influence on schools, legal institutions, and civil society from the seventeenth to early twentieth century. We then turn to Evangelical Protestantism, which emerged as a distinct voice toward the end of the nineteenth and early decades of the twentieth century, gaining its present cultural influence mainly in the past fifty years. The next religions in the book—Judaism, Roman Catholicism, the Black Church, Latter-day Saints, and Native American religion—all suffered repressions of various kinds over the past few centuries. Judaism and Roman Catholicism, although present as minority religions from the beginning of U.S. history, gained social and political visibility and gradually grew in numbers and influence during the twentieth century. The Black Church functioned for four centuries of slavery and segregation as a powerful institution sustaining community, families, and children against the dehumanization of racism and injustice. The Latter-day Saints, although regarded with deep suspicion from their earliest origins in the nineteenth century until recently, has also grown in numbers and influence since the mid-twentieth century. Finally, we turn to religions outside the Jewish and Christian traditions later in the book, but not to suggest their lesser importance. In fact, one of the main messages of the book is that these religions are, will, and should have increasing visibility in American life and deserve to be more deeply understood and appreciated.

In its effort to raise awareness and enhance knowledge about children and religion, this volume should have relevance for students, professionals who work with children, scholars in a range of disciplines, and laypeople interested in children in all walks of life. Not only should those in the social sciences and humanities understand more profoundly the influence and impact of these religions on childhood, but also those pursuing or already active in the professions should gain from the insights of the book. Doctors, nurses, lawyers, psychotherapists, and teachers of all kinds more and more will confront the variety of American religions and what they teach and value about children. Even parents are increasingly discovering that their children are meeting and becoming friends with children raised in other traditions. We all need to understand children in light of the new religious situation and the challenges of contemporary culture. This book hopes to contribute to that task by recognizing the study of religion and its rich and sometimes controversial resources as an important conversation partner in the effort to enrich understanding of children and promote their welfare in society at large.

## NOTES

1. See Todd David Whitmore with Tobias Winright, "Children: An Undeveloped Theme in Catholic Teaching," in *The Challenge of Global Stewardship: Roman Catholic Response*, ed. Maura A. Ryan and Todd David Whitmore (Notre Dame: University of Notre Dame, 1997), 161–185; Marcia J. Bunge, ed., introduction to *The Child in Christian Thought* (Grand Rapids, MI: Eerdmans, 2001), 3–4; Bonnie J. Miller-McLemore, "Children and Religion in the Public Square: 'Too Dangerous and Too Safe, Too Difficult and Too Silly,'" *Journal of Religion* 86, no. 3 (2006): 385–401; Bonnie J. Miller-McLemore, "Whither the Children? Childhood in Religious Education," *Journal of Religion* 86, no. 4 (2007).

2. In the title and throughout the book, authors follow common practice of using "America" and "American" interchangeably with "the United States," while recognizing that the former terms include other parts of both continents—Canada and America's southern hemisphere.

3. In recent years a few scholars in religion have begun to explore more seriously children's own experiences of religion. See, for example, Carol E. Lytch, *Choosing Church: What Makes a Difference for Teens* (Louisville, KY: Westminster John Knox, 2004); Susan Ridgely Bales, *When I Was a Child: Children's Interpretations of First Communion* (Chapel Hill: University of North Carolina, 2005); Christian Smith and Melinda Denton, *Soul Searching: The Religious and Spiritual Lives of American Teenagers* (Oxford: Oxford University Press, 2005).

4. Faith Robertson Elliot, *The Family: Change or Continuity?* (Atlantic Highlands, NJ: Atlantic Press International, 1986), 35–38.

5. See, for example, Allison James and Alan Prout, eds., *Constructing and Reconstructing Childhood: Contemporary Issues in the Sociological Study of Childhood*, 2nd ed. (Washington, DC: Falmer Press, 1997); Anne Higonnet, *Pictures of Innocence: The History and Crisis of Ideal Childhood* (New York: Thames and Hudson, 1998); Steven Mintz, *Huck's Raft: A History of American Childhood* (Cambridge: Harvard University Press, 2004). Philippe Ariès first suggested that childhood has a history in his widely read and contested book, *Centuries of Childhood: A Social History of Family Life* (New York: Vintage Books, 1962).

6. Freud's interest in children (mostly to understand adult pathology) is most evident in his work on psychosexual development. See Bonnie Miller-McLemore, *Let the Children Come: Reimagining Childhood from a Christian Perspective* (San Francisco: Jossey-Bass, 2003), 27–30.

7. Anna Freud, *The Writings of Anna Freud*, 8 vols. (New York: International Universities Press, 1966–1980); Erik H. Erikson, *Childhood and Society*, 35th anniversary ed. (1950; New York: Norton, 1963); Robert Coles, *Children of Crisis*, 5 vols. (Boston: Little, Brown, 1967–1977); Robert Coles, *The Moral Life of Children* (Boston: Atlantic Monthly Press, 1986); Robert Coles, *The Political Life of Children* (Boston: Atlantic Monthly Press, 1986); Robert Coles, The *Spiritual Life of Children* (Boston: Houghton Mifflin, 1990).

8. See A. Michael Sulman, "The Humanization of the American Child: Benjamin Spock as a Popularizer of Psychoanalytic Thought," *Journal of the History of the Behavioral Sciences* 9 (1973): 258–265.

9. Peter B. Pufall and Richard P. Unsworth, eds., *Rethinking Childhood* (New Brunswick: Rutgers University Press, 2004).

10. Miller-McLemore, *Let the Children Come*, chap. 6.

11. Mary Jane Kehily, *An Introduction to Childhood Studies* (London: Open University Press, 2004), x–xi.

12. See, for example, the new journal *Childhood: A Global Journal of Child Research*, published in association with the Norwegian Centre for Child Research. New programs in the United States have begun at Rutgers University (http://childhood-studies. camden.rutgers.edu/) and Case Western Reserve University (http://www.case. edu/artsci/childstudies/) and at the Open University in the United Kingdom. New international organizations have also arisen, such as Childwatch: International Research Network.

13. The following are some of the many books contributing to this new field. In sociology: James and Prout, *Constructing and Reconstructing Childhood*; Chris Jenks, *The Sociology of Childhood: Essential Readings* (London: Batsford, 1982); Chris Jenks, *Childhood* (London: Routledge, 1996); Allison James, Chris Jenks, and Alan Prout, *Theorizing Childhood* (New York: Teachers College Press, 1998). In anthropology: Nancy Scheper-Hughes and Carolyn Sargent, eds., *The Cultural Politics of Childhood* (Berkeley and Los Angeles: University of California Press, 1998); Helen B. Schwartzman, ed., *Children and Anthropology Perspectives for the 21st Century* (Westport, CT.: Bergin and Garvey, 2001). For history, see Karin Calvert, *Children in the House: The Material Culture of Early Childhood, 1600–1900* (Boston: Northeastern University Press, 1992); Hugh Cunningham, *Children and Childhood in Western Society since 1500* (New York: Langman, 1995); Colin Heywood, *A History of Childhood: Children and Childhood in the West from Medieval to Modern Times* (Malden, MA: Polity Press, 2001); Steven Mintz, *Huck's Raft: A History of American Childhood* (Cambridge: Harvard University Press, 2004). In art theory: Anne Higonnet, *Pictures of Innocence: The History and Crisis of Ideal Childhood* (New York: Thames and Hudson, 1998). In philosophy: Gareth B. Matthews, *The Philosophy of Childhood* (Cambridge: Harvard University Press, 1994). In literature: Patricia Holland, *Picturing Childhood: The Myth of the Child in Popular Imagery* (London and New York: Taurus, 2004).

14. See, for example, Smith and Denton, *Soul Searching*. The National Study of Youth and Religion, funded by the Lilly Endowment, is under the direction of Dr. Christian Smith and Dr. Lisa Pearce (http://www.youthandreligion.org/)

15. See, for example, Elizabeth M. Dowling and W. George Scarlett, eds., *Encyclopedia of Religious and Spiritual Development* (Thousand Oaks, CA: Sage, 2005); See also the work of the Search Institute (http://www.search-institute.org/) and its recent publication, Eugene C. Roehlkepartain, Pamela Ebstyne King, Linda Wagener, and Peter L. Benson, eds., *The Handbook of Spiritual Development in Childhood and Adolescence* (Thousand Oaks, CA: Sage, 2006).

16. Paula S. Fass and Mary Ann Mason, *Childhood in America* (New York: New York University Press, 2000).

17. Marcia Bunge, ed., *The Child in Christian Thought* (Grand Rapids, MI: Eerdmans, 2001).

18. Margaret Lamberts Bendroth, "Children of Adam, Children of God: Christian Nurture in Early Nineteenth-Century America," *Theology Today* 56, no. 4 (2000): 495–505; Margaret Bendroth, *Growing Up Protestant: Parents, Children, and Mainline Churches* (New Brunswick: Rutgers University Press, 2002); Marcia J. Bunge, "Children, the Church, and the Domestic Church: Supporting Parents in the Task of Nurturing the Moral and Spiritual Lives of Children," *New Theology Review: An*

American Catholic Journal of Ministry 14, no. 3 (2001): 5–15; Dawn DeVries, "Toward a Theology of Childhood," *Interpretation: A Journal of Bible and Tradition* 55, no. 2 (2001): 161–173; Miller-McLemore, *Let the Children Come*; Bonnie J. Miller-McLemore, *In the Midst of Chaos: Care of Children as Spiritual Practice* (San Francisco: Jossey-Bass, 2006); Barbara Pitkin, "Are Children Human?" Theology and Worship Occasional Paper 12, Presbyterian Church, Louisville, KY, 2000; Martha Ellen Stortz, "Whither Childhood?" *Dialog* 37, no. 3 (1998): 162–163; Cristian L. H. Traina, "Learning from the Tradition: The Religious Lives of Children," *New Theology Review: An American Catholic Journal of Ministry* 14, no. 3 (2001): 17–25.

19. Avner Gil'adi, *Children of Islam: Concepts of Childhood in Medieval Muslim Society* (New York: Macmillan, 1992); Robert Jackson and Elanor Nesbitt, *Hindu Children in Britain* (Staffordshire, U.K.: Trentham Books, 1993); Herbert Anderson and Susan B. Johnson, *Regarding Children: A New Respect for Childhood and Families* (Louisville, KY: Westminster John Knox, 1994); Pamela D. Couture, *Seeing Children, Seeing God: A Practical Theology of Children and Poverty* (Nashville, TN: Abingdon, 2000); Pamela D. Couture, *Child Poverty: Love, Justice, and Social Responsibility* (St. Louis, MO: Chalice, 2007); Bunge, ed., *The Child in Christian Thought*; Miller-McLemore, *Let the Children Come*; David H. Jensen, *Graced Vulnerability: A Theology of Childhood* (Cleveland: Pilgrim, 2005); Joyce Ann Mercer, *Welcoming Children: A Practical Theology of Childhood* (St. Louis, MO: Chalice, 2005); Kristin Herzog, *Children and Our Global Future* (Cleveland: Pilgrim, 2005).

20. See, for example, Catherine Stonehouse, *Joining Children on the Spiritual Journey* (Grand Rapids, MI: Baker, 1998); Abu Merboob and Bin Faiz, *Rearing Children and Islam* (Riverside, CA: Fatima, 1992); Ariela Keysar, Barry A. Kosmin, and Jeffry Scheckner, *The New Generation: Jewish Children and Adolescents* (Albany: State University of New York Press, 2000); Elizabeth F. Caldwell, *Making a Home for Faith: Nurturing the Spiritual Life of Your Children* (Cleveland: Pilgrim Press, 2000); Elizabeth F. Caldwell, *Leaving Home with Faith: Nurturing the Spiritual Life of Our Youth* (Cleveland: Pilgrim Press, 2002); Muhammad Habilullaah Mukhatar, *Bringing Up Children in Islam* (New Delhi: Islamic Book Service, 2002); Bradley J. Wigger, *The Power of God at Home: Nurturing Our Children in Love and Grace* (San Francisco: Jossey-Bass, 2003); Karen-Marie Yust, *Real Kids, Real Faith* (San Francisco: Jossey-Bass, 2004); Miller-McLemore, *In the Midst of Chaos*; Roehlkepartain et al., *The Handbook of Spiritual Development*; Karen Marie Yust, Aostre N. Johnson, Sandy Eisenberg Sasso, and Eugene C. Roehlkepartain, eds., *Nurturing Child and Adolescent Spirituality: Perspectives from the World's Religious Traditions* (Lanham, MD: Rowman and Littlefield, 2006). Of course, when we refer to scholarship on children, we are not including the many publications of curricular and educational materials by religious bodies or denominational presses.

21. See, for example, Gil'adi, *Children of Islam*; Diana Wood, ed., *The Church and Childhood* (Oxford, U.K.: Blackwell, 1994); John Cooper, *The Child in Jewish History* (Northvale, NJ: Aronson, 1996); Bunge, *The Child in Christian Thought*; Bendroth, *Growing Up Protestant*; O. M. Bakke, *When Children Became People: The Birth of Childhood in Early Christianity* (Minneapolis: Fortress, 2005).

22. See, for example, Lytch, *Choosing Church*; Bales, *When I Was a Child*; Smith and Denton, *Soul Searching*; Christopher Ellison and Darren F. Sherkat, "Obedience and Autonomy: Religion and Child-Rearing Orientation Reconsidered," *Journal for the Scientific Study of Religion* 32 (1993): 313–329; John Bartkowski and Christopher

Ellison, "Divergent Models of Childrearing in Popular Manuals: Conservative Protestant vs. the Mainline Experts," *Sociology of Religion* 56 (1995): 21–34.

23. *Theology Today* 56, no. 4 (2000): 451–460; *Interpretation: A Journal of Bible and Tradition* 55, no. 2 (2001); *New Theology Review: An American Catholic Journal of Ministry* 14, no. 3 (2001); most recently, *Journal of Religion* 86, no. 4 (2006).

24. For helpful overview essays in *Journal of Religion* 86, no. 4 (2006), see especially Catherine A. Brekus, "Special Issue: Religion and Childhood Studies," 521–522; John Wall, "Childhood Studies, Hermeneutics, and Theological Ethics," 523–548; Marcia J. Bunge, "The Child, Religion, and the Academy: Developing Robust Theological and Religious Understandings of Children and Childhood," 549–579.

25. There are a few important exceptions to this rule, such as Joseph M. Hawes and N. Ray Hiner, eds., *Children in Historical and Comparative Perspective: An International Handbook and Research Guide* (New York: Greenwood Press, 1999); Harold G. Coward and Philip Cook, *Religious Dimensions of Child and Family Life: Reflections on the UN Convention on the Rights of the Child* (Waterloo, Ontario: Wilfrid Laurier University Press, 1996); and Yust et al., *Nurturing Child and Adolescent Spirituality.*

26. Stanton L. Jones, "A Constructive Relationship for Religion with the Science and Profession of Psychology: Perhaps the Boldest Model Yet," *American Psychologist* 49, no. 3 (1994): 184–199.

27. Ann Hulbert, *Raising America: Experts, Parents, and a Century of Advice about Children* (New York: Alfred A. Knopf, 2003), 14.

28. Smith and Denton, *Soul Searching*, 20.

29. See Miller-McLemore, *In the Midst of Chaos.*

30. Alan Cole, "Buddhism," in *Sex, Marriage, and Family in the World Religions*, ed. Don Browning, Christian Green, and John Witte (New York: Columbia University Press, 2006), 301.

31. Hans-Georg Gadamer, *Truth and Method* (New York: Crossroad, 1982); Paul Ricoeur, *Hermeneutics and the Human Sciences* (Cambridge: Cambridge University Press, 1981).

# 1

# Mainline Protestants and Children

MARGARET BENDROTH

One day, when William Ellery Channing was a little boy, his father took him to hear a famous preacher. That in itself was not unusual: in the early nineteenth century, many New England Congregationalists considered a rousing sermon a good day's entertainment. But this was no ordinary diversion. The afternoon fare was a full-tilt fire-and-brimstone sermon, laying out in lurid detail the lost state of humanity, its abandonment to evil, and its exceedingly dim prospects outside the grace of God. As the future founder of Unitarianism later recalled, "A curse seemed to rest upon the earth, and darkness and horror to veil the face of nature." The thoroughly horrified child left the sanctuary convinced that all of life's trivial amusements would have to go. His resolve grew even stronger as he heard his father's gruff words of approval to a fellow congregant as they passed out the door: "Sound doctrine, Sir."

The return trip began in silence, with young Channing so "absorbed in awful thoughts" that he could not speak. But then his father began to whistle! And when they arrived home, the elder Channing casually sat down, took off his boots, and began to read the evening newspaper, apparently unmoved by the prospect of hell and all its demons yawning below his feet.

The truth began to dawn: "His father did not believe it; people did not believe it! It was *not* true!" As Channing later wrote in his memoirs, the incident was a watershed in his spiritual life; he would be forever after wary of religious emotionalism and of cynical adults. He vowed always to listen to sermons with an attitude of doubt, for "he had received a profound lesson on the worth of sincerity."[1]

Channing's story has all the elements quickly associated with the experience of children growing up in liberal churches: dutiful attendance in Sunday service, early faith slowly undercut by a cheerfully agnostic parent, and then a moment of dawning cynicism. The prevailing picture of this tradition is that it simply cannot—or will not—transform its youngest members into churchgoing adults. Indeed, of all the adherents of religious traditions discussed in this volume, mainline Protestants seem the least apt to insist on specific parameters of belief and practice. They stand in stark contrast to Evangelical Protestants and Mormons, who take great care to impart deference to adults and the didactic content of faith; they cannot begin to rival Catholics and Jews in reverence for text and tradition; and in comparison with many believers in immigrant faiths, where family religion provides a vital protective barrier against the full press of American culture, mainliners seem very lightly anchored by cultural or theological distinctives. Within the scope of this volume, they very ably hold down one end of a spectrum of approaches to the universal problem of modern American child rearing.

This problematic picture of mainline churches is rooted in many different sources. The demographic evidence is particularly striking: over the past fifty years, the general departure of teenagers and young adults has left many congregations filled with elderly people. Indeed, by the 1980s, the mean age of members in the United Church of Christ was more than fifty, thereby identifying it as one of the oldest denominations in the United States.[2] Critics have also noted the virtual absence of children from the past half century of ethical debates in national denominational circles, where adult-oriented concerns about divorce, homosexuality, and abortion gradually assumed center stage. Although, theoretically at least, children's welfare should have figured prominently in these family-related discussions, younger church members found few active advocates. By the 1970s and 1980s, the silence of mainline churches loomed larger still as conservative Evangelical churches stepped quickly into the breach, spinning off a variety of family-based ministries across the age span, many of them specifically aimed at young parents with school-age children.[3]

But that bleak picture is hardly the full story; closer inspection reveals far more vitality and awareness than the current stereotype generally suggests. Indeed, as this chapter explains in some detail, over the course of the past two centuries, liberal and moderate Protestant churches have evolved a variety of understandings of childhood.

The "liberal child" was a construct developed most fully by theologian Horace Bushnell in the mid-nineteenth century, as an alternative to the punitive emphasis on original sin characteristic of many Evangelical churches. Bushnell's assertion that children could come to faith without psychological trauma assumed that they were morally pliable and, in the proper circumstances, thoroughly amenable to the good. Following in Bushnell's path, many liberal Protestant thinkers argued that each child was endowed with an authentic religious sensibility commensurate with age and understanding.

The advent of "scientific child rearing" in the early twentieth century would affirm this fundamentally optimistic view of children, even as it added a layer of mystery to the task of Christian parenting. During that time, a growing cadre of psychological experts and education professionals began to warn well-meaning mothers and fathers that their adorable young offspring were complex mechanisms easily ruined by insensitive handling. The "modern child" in mainline Protestant churches was still naturally attuned toward faith, but just as easily turned from it, and for reasons that few ordinary parents would be able to fathom.

By the late twentieth century, as mainline churches encountered severe reverses in numbers and financial support, their traditional optimism toward childhood began to erode. The "problem child" of the liberal denominations was in many ways a creature of those hard times, as resources shifted away from family-oriented programs to socially relevant ones aimed primarily at adults. But the times themselves took a toll. From the 1960s onward, old and untested assumptions about children as inherently amenable to religion collapsed under the weight of mounting statistics on juvenile delinquency and family dissolution. The long-standing mainline emphasis on happy, well-rounded families as the seedbeds of childhood faith began to look dangerously glib in the face of wrenching social conflicts around race, class, and gender. The mainline problem child thus emerged as a mass of contradictions: basically good but deeply rebellious, accessible to reason but fundamentally irrational, open to God but thoroughly secular.

But that picture is changing. Especially in recent years, many local mainline churches have demonstrated enormous creativity in integrating children into worship and educational programs. Moreover, many mainline denominations, perhaps atoning for past neglect, have begun to embrace "children's issues" within a larger span of social justice concerns. And all these efforts have been supported by a growing body of scholars and religious leaders, who have established a legitimate intellectual platform for family concerns within the liberal mainline agenda.

In doing so, they are not simply playing "catch up" with Evangelical Protestants; they are recovering their own tradition. Across the long span of their history, as this chapter will illustrate, mainline Protestant churches have paid a great deal of attention to the religious formation of children. The story of the past fifty years, when many mainline churches have recoiled from what was perceived as an overemphasis on children during the 1950s, is, to say the least, ironic. Moderate and liberal Protestant churches have a long history of valuing children and the religion of childhood, though much of that older conversation has been lost within the present-day rhetoric of religious polarization.

My purpose in this chapter, therefore, is to provide a brief historical reminder—to tell the story of the changing understanding of children and their church role as these have unfolded over the past century and a half—and to draw a general picture of mainline churches and children in the present day. Neither end of the story makes complete sense without the other. Indeed, taken as a whole, both suggest that the liberal Protestant tradition has plenty of theological resources for creative thinking about children. Recent fears about religious "familism," especially as it has been politicized in the past several decades, have obscured a long and productive stream of liberal thought that has profoundly shaped contemporary understanding of who children are and what they might justly expect from adults.

## Defining the Mainline

The first hurdle to clear is the term *mainline*. Certainly in terms of membership statistics and degree of public attention, burgeoning Evangelical churches are far more mainline their more liberal cousins. The old religious establishment that dominated American culture for most of its history has been failing for decades, and once-proud denominational institutions now struggle to meet their annual budgets. But the term persists, sometimes in ironic quotation marks, more for what it says about the general outlines of American religious culture than in regard to its current configuration.

In simplest terms, mainline churches represent the moderate-to-liberal stream of the American Protestant Christian tradition. The typical definition usually includes a list of relatively old, mostly white, northern denominations: United Methodists, the Presbyterian Church (USA), American Baptists, Episcopalians, the Evangelical Lutheran Church in America, and the United Church of Christ. By the end of the twentieth century, these denominations represented nearly 22 million American Protestants.[4]

Despite their denominational differences, these churches share some general characteristics. They emphasize tolerance toward other faiths and have often taken public stands on issues of social justice. Many mainline churches are the products of denominational mergers, reflecting a long-standing theological commitment to nonsectarian cooperation and ecumenical outreach. Although critics often point out the disparity between mainline leadership and its more conservative constituency, dislike of religious dogma is often evident in the pews. According to one recent study, more than 80 percent of mainliners agreed that their church teachings offered the best means of relating to God, but an equally strong proportion believed that all religions contained genuine spiritual truth.[5] The negative reading of these surveys is that moderate and liberal Protestants are simply unschooled and inarticulate about their core beliefs, which is a difficult charge to refute. But the more positive interpretation is that they are religious in a particular sense. The so-called Golden Rule Christians who populate many mainline churches tend to measure their faith by acts of social compassion—in marked contrast to Evangelical Protestants, who would place verbal proclamation at the top of the list.[6]

Yet despite their much-publicized differences, mainline churches share many similarities with their Evangelical cousins. In many conservative, moderate, and liberal congregations across the country, the basic order of Sunday service and sacramental rituals are all but indistinguishable. All Protestants, whatever their theology, practice only two sacraments (baptism and communion) and they draw their beliefs from the Bible. They may, of course, differ vastly in their interpretation of these rituals or their understanding of the nature of biblical authority; mainline Protestants are, on the whole, less committed to a high standard of biblical inerrancy—that is, without any factual error—than are Evangelicals. In fact, in the same recent study, only about a quarter (28 percent) of mainliners held to an inerrant Bible, though a full 92 percent held that it was, in a more general sense, the inspired word of God.[7] They may also differ in their choice of music or the length of the Sunday sermon. But in the larger scheme of things, it is important to remember that all Protestants share a basic family resemblance in their approach to worship, use of the sacraments, and understanding of the broad themes of Christian theology.

Moreover, in terms of their basic sociological profile, the "average" mainline Protestant and the "average" Evangelical are more similar than different, especially when compared with other groups, such as Roman Catholics or the nonreligious. Both have relatively high levels of education and income and are more likely to be married than the general population.[8] Neither group is socially oriented toward political radicalism. Mainliners in fact tend toward the higher end of the occupational ladder: 72 percent of the church members in Robert Wuthnow's recent study described themselves as professionals, managers, or in some other white-collar profession.[9]

The more basic distinguishing factor among mainline Protestants is in their historic stance toward modern American culture. The label itself emerged in the early twentieth century in reference to the cultural dominance of certain types of Protestants. By definition it excluded smaller sectarian groups, immigrant denominations, and culturally isolated fundamentalists and Pentecostals. The mainline was the religion of the Protestant "establishment," the ready provider of prominent educational and benevolent institutions and nationally influential authors, educators, and politicians.[10]

In practical terms this dominance meant two things. First, mainline Protestants were to some extent adapted to modernity. By the late nineteenth century, the core principle of liberal theology was that God was to be found within the created order, not through an exclusive special revelation; God was immanent in the real world, not removed and transcendent. Truth might be found therefore in the everyday experiences of life, and, of course, in the laboratory, library, or lecture hall. Thus, mainline Protestants were historically open to insights from psychology or sociology, and beginning in the 1920s and 1930s, they readily applied the advice of expert professionals to church programs for children and families.

The second implication of the "establishment" status of mainline churches was that they experienced the late twentieth century as a harrowing and humbling time. The 1960s and 1970s saw a steady blossoming of conservative Evangelical influence and prestige and a rapidly building stream of loss in the mainline. By the 1980s and 1990s, the positions of the two were almost reversing, with Evangelicals enjoying political power, a strengthened cultural voice, and local congregations bursting at the seams with new members. Within the mainline, the language of marginality and alienation, once the sole property of conservative religious separatists, began to make increasing sense.

This recent history is, of course, extremely pertinent to understanding the role of children in mainline churches. Many observers have tied the weakness of liberal mainline churches to their overconcern with children in the 1950s and have linked the resurgence of Evangelicals with their ability to attract children, teenagers, and parents.[11] One variant of that argument suggests that the relative strictness of such groups as the Evangelicals and Mormons described in this volume, especially on family life, made them the preferred destination for younger spiritual seekers. But this may not be the whole story: the most recent sociological study of church growth traces a good deal of mainline decline and Evangelical resurgence to the simple matter of different birthrates. Thus the loss of liberal membership in the 1960s and beyond may be more a function of middle-class family planning than slow religious apostasy. Some scholars have stressed that the jury is still out on this argument, but the basic issue still seems clear: churches ignore their youngest members at their demographic peril.[12]

## The Liberal Child

The liberal strain in Protestant thinking about childhood dates back to the early nineteenth century, a time when the revivalistic emotion that terrified William Ellery Channing also inspired a wave of innovative theological reflection. The undisputed leader of this new thrust was Congregational theologian Horace Bushnell, for most of his life the busy pastor of a church in Hartford, Connecticut. When his seminal work *Christian Nurture* went to press in 1847, Bushnell found himself at the center of intense controversy. To many conservatives, his antirevivalist arguments appeared to suggest that a decent Protestant upbringing obviated the need for an experience of Christian conversion. In Bushnell's memorable phrase, a child was "to grow up a Christian, and never know himself as being otherwise."[13]

But, in fact, Bushnell never saw children as sinless in the way that Romantic poets and Rousseauean educators often advocated; in his view, children were endlessly pliable spiritual beings. He therefore worried deeply about the negative influences that faithless parents might exercise over helpless infants. If parents were "carnal, coarse, passionate, profane, sensual, [and] devilish, then [the child's] little plastic nature takes the poison of course," Bushnell warned. "Their very motions, manners, and voices will be distinguishable in him. He lives and moves and has his being in them."[14]

Nor did Bushnell discount children's need for salvation. While recognizing even the youngest infant's capacity for sin, Bushnell believed that they were fully capable of authentic religious belief, from the earliest stages of life. Christ was not "the Saviour of adults only!" he declared, but "a Saviour for infants, and children, and youth, as truly as for the adult age; gathering them all into his fold together, there to be kept and nourished together, by gifts appropriate to their years."[15]

Early nineteenth-century Evangelical Protestants worried a great deal about the spiritual state of young children. Early death was not uncommon and bereavement an expected part of raising a family. To make matters worse, according to strict Calvinist doctrine, even an infant a few hours old was in a state of rebellion against God and liable to eternal punishment. Although by Bushnell's time few New England divines were willing to accept that harsh logic, they nevertheless assumed that all young children required special discipline to help them avoid undue sinning until they were old enough to experience full conversion, usually after the age of seven.[16] By modern standards, the practice of "breaking the will" could be emotionally, if not also physically, abusive; stories circulated about children being locked in closets or kept away from the dinner table for hours, sometimes days, on end.[17] Again, most parents avoided such extremes, but the basic assumption that children were intellectually and spiritually unable to practice true religion on their own was a principle rarely held up to inspection. Rare examples of precocious childhood religiosity were exceptions that merely proved the general rule.

In contrast, Bushnell saw children as young, budding plants. Although certainly vulnerable to harm or neglect, they did not need special intervention to grow from seedlings to sprouts. Time and wise husbandry would do all that was required. Thus Bushnell's model of Christian nurture explicitly denied that children had to rebel in order to experience real salvation. "The true problem," he explained, "is not to break, but to bend rather, to draw the will down, . . . to teach it the way of submitting to wise limitations, and raise it into the great and glorious liberties of a state of loyalty to God."[18] Even a wordless infant who was regularly fed, changed, and cuddled was learning to worship God at a later time in life. Full understanding of Christian teaching might not arrive until much later, but the years of childhood were not a spiritual wasteland. Indeed, the daily rituals of family life—everything from mealtime prayers to the kinds of foods served and clothing worn—could have a long-term salvific effect. Parents should take care not to "disturb the simplicity of nature" through excess proselytizing, Bushnell warned. But at the same time, they could gently and consistently make Christian faith the child's logical option. "Dress your child for Christ, if you will have him a Christian," he declared; "bring every thing, in the training, even of his body, to this one final aim, and it will be strange, if the Christian body you give him does not contain a Christian soul."[19]

*Christian Nurture* was a relatively small part of Bushnell's theological work, which justly earned him recognition as one of the nation's leading liberal voices. But it deftly encapsulated some key themes in liberal Protestant dissent from conservative orthodoxy. Bushnell's model of childhood assumed a rational basis of religious belief, yet with due regard for religious emotion; it implied a belief in the immanence of God, that is, in God's presence in and through the daily workings of the world; and it evidenced a firm optimism about the role of human institutions in bringing about a just and humane society. According to Bushnell's scheme, children required, and in fact deserved, the unflagging care of godly parents, acting as God's intermediaries in creating childhood faith. Moreover, using early nineteenth-century New England as a model, Bushnell assumed that those parents would be buttressed by equally righteous social institutions: churches, schools, and even local governments. All these institutions stood together in what Bushnell called an "organic unity," easily envisioned as a series of concentric rings, with parents and children at the center.[20]

Not surprisingly perhaps, some aspects of Bushnell's Christian nurture ideal proved easier to adopt than others. Clearly, the model of a godly home lent itself readily to prevailing social trends of the mid-nineteenth century and to the enshrinement of middle-class domesticity as the highest form of human relationship. In a rapidly urbanizing and market-driven culture, Christian nurture provided a theological rationale for secular desires for privacy and domestic comfort. Moreover, succeeding generations of religious educators found Bushnell's endorsement of childhood religiosity a genuine boon for expanded Sunday school curricula.

But other aspects of Bushnell's thought proved more troublesome. Certainly his ideal of a godly child growing up within a righteous community was rarely if ever realized by most nineteenth-century families. Indeed, as American society became more diverse and complex over the following century and a half, Bushnell's vision inspired more nostalgia than purposeful activity. His view of the child as godly and simple, a seedling bound to grow into a tree with the right amount of care, would not survive the psychological revolution of the next hundred years. Bushnell's theology said little about the deep-seated conflicts that Freud would soon unearth or about the spiritual mysteries posed by teenagers and young adults, who would bedevil American society for much of the following century.

## The Modern Child

Bushnell's model of the spiritually intact, responsible child set the course for Protestant thinking about childhood for decades to come. By the late nineteenth century, even more conservative Evangelical churches, those that had excoriated Bushnell for heresy in the decades before the Civil War, had settled into a regular package of weekly Sunday school instruction and family devotions, not dire warnings about infants being consumed by the fires of hell. Moreover, by the early twentieth century, Bushnell's assumptions about childhood religiosity had gained important allies in the newly developing social sciences. Spurred by Freud's so-called discovery of the subconscious mind and by the work of philosopher and psychologist William James on the mental phenomena of religious experience, the developmental processes of faith became an important object of study.

Led by such well-known and influential figures as G. Stanley Hall, the child study movement of the early twentieth century sought to plumb the mysterious world of childhood and to delineate the psychological mechanisms that prodded the growing child to move from one stage to the next.[21] Hall in fact introduced the American public to the idea of "adolescence" as a discreet period of life—an insight that reflected the complexity of growing up in a modern world where children no longer automatically followed the occupational paths laid out for them by their fathers. Developmental psychology, as explained by Hall, the dutiful son of a pious mother, seemed to substantiate Bushnell's insistence on the integrity of every stage of childhood experience. But it also drove a wedge between parents and children. The fundamental implication of Hall's view was that children were basically different from adults, not mere miniatures; they saw the world in odd and sometimes startlingly different terms, and they had remarkably different perceptions of God.

This meant that adults had to approach children with spiritual caution; simple formulas and short-answer catechisms would longer suffice for religious education. The rote memory of Bible verses that formed the backbone of the nineteenth-century Sunday school were almost worse than nothing at all. In fact, some experts warned that the careless telling of vivid Bible stories or displaying lurid pictures of heaven or hell could actively harm children. Well-known religious educator Sophia Lyon Fahs told the cautionary tale of a young boy who had been taught to think of God as a "white-bearded, stern old man" and who had turned to "stealing and sex-play with little girls."[22] Early twentieth-century religious educators—they were no longer just "Sunday school teachers"—used all the psychological training they could muster to create age-appropriate materials, to be used not so much by parents in the home, but by trained professionals in the Sunday morning hour.

By midcentury, contradictions had multiplied. At bottom, the majority of Protestants assumed that Bushnell was right and that children were essentially capable of religious faith with relatively little prodding, certainly not with the didactic or punitive methods favored during Channing's time. But growing doubts about the efficacy of the "Christian home" in producing knowledgeable, committed believers became difficult to put aside, especially as many families struggled to chart a moral course during times of massive social upheaval and rapid change. Privately, and sometimes publicly, religious educators of the 1930s and 1940s worried that the old Bushnellian model was fundamentally unworkable for producing godly children in the modern world.

## The Problem Child

All these doubts found substance in the waning years of the 1950s and in the early 1960s. Although the picture of the postwar years as a time of uncritical "familism" among mainline churches is certainly true, it is not the whole story. The pliant young Christian imagined by Bushnell and his followers seemed to have little relevance to a world dominated by rebellious juvenile delinquents and broken homes. To their growing dismay, many Protestant educators discovered that the long-standing fascination with the earliest stages of childhood religion had ill prepared them for dealing with problems of adolescent sexuality. Indeed, the experience of many middle-class parents, whose acquiescent grade-schoolers were transformed almost overnight into sullen teenage agnostics, contradicted every textbook truism about the steadily unfolding religiosity of childhood.

The relatively quick abandonment of child-centered church programs in the late twentieth century has been well documented. Sociologist Bradford Wilcox has found that the proportion of articles about children and the family in the *Christian Century* and two other mainline Protestant journals declined by 55 percent between 1950 and 1975.[23] The changing subject matter reflects not just a declining interest in child welfare, but also the rise of tacitly competing concerns about adult fulfillment. The spate of study groups, pronouncements, and resolutions issued by mainline churches during this time often introduced radical new policies about sexual ethics that were oriented primarily toward adults. As in the wider culture, mainline discussions emphasized the need for personal expression and for the emotional and sexual needs of people who were unmarried by fate or by choice. Thus, a controversial 1970 report by Presbyterians questioned whether "society has the right to impose celibacy or celibate standards on those who do not choose them." The report further emphasized the church's obligation to "explore the possibilities of both celibate and non-celibate communal living arrangements as ethically acceptable and personally fulfilling alternatives for unmarried persons." Nowhere in this controversial redrawing of traditional Protestant understandings of family and sexual morality was there discussion of its impact on children.[24]

Even religious educators, long devoted to issues around childhood religiosity, began to emphasize the need for more sophisticated, critical approaches to the Christian faith. One Presbyterian educator described what used to be the business of "Sunday school" as an "adult search" for meaning. Although "children also share in it," the primary focus was on the maturing thought of young adults, designed around an open-ended process of questions without ready answers. "The teacher does not talk *about* Bible or theology, but initiates the student into the material itself—with complete openness toward the questions, problems, and meanings," avoiding a dogmatic need to "propagandize" questing students.[25]

The seamless net of Christian institutions that had theoretically protected childhood since the late nineteenth century also sustained major damage during this time. In the early 1960s, a series of highly symbolic U.S. Supreme Court decisions prohibiting prayer in public schools shocked parents of every theological background. Although most Americans would have readily attested to the impartiality of public education, they had along assumed that some low level of Protestant religiosity was acceptable to all. The sudden disenfranchisement of a mainstream faith from a major social institution signaled the decisive end of an old Protestant consensus, which had in fact been unraveling for many decades. The integrated moral program of home, church, and school long ago imagined by Bushnell faced a difficult, uncertain future.

In some quarters, cultural disestablishment brought an almost visible sense of relief. It was difficult for earnest mainliners who traveled to Appalachia or the Deep South to reconcile their child- and family-oriented church programs with the needs of the alienated and illiterate poor. As one Presbyterian official confided to another, the traditional approach was "crashingly middle class" and thoroughly irrelevant to many of the communities they hoped to reach. Even the most popular family programs of the postwar era were, as a fellow colleague agreed, "simply impossible" to implement in an inner city neighborhood or a backwoods community.[26]

The rise of the Religious Right further entrenched the growing assumption that "family values," now understood in both Evangelical and mainline camps as a cluster of issues related to sexuality, were antithetical to a prophetic social agenda. Even in the wider culture, *family* became a code word for middle-class behavior: a "family film" or a "family restaurant" was by definition bland and dull, of clearly limited interest to any adults without children in tow.

## Mainline Future

Despite the political changes of the past decades, many local mainline churches would be surprised to hear that they are no longer "child centered." In thousands of congregations across the country, children are visible—and audible—every Sunday, as they rush to the front of the sanctuary for the "children's sermon" and then noisily file out for Sunday school classes. Children are even physically present throughout the week. Many of the large and otherwise empty buildings of old mainline churches become day-care centers from Monday through Friday, often subsidizing church budgets or functioning as a formal church ministry in themselves. In fact, the prevalence of day-care centers is one factor that distinguishes mainline Protestants from their conservative cousins, signaling perhaps an acceptance of working mothers that is not always mirrored among Evangelicals.[27]

The liturgical creativity of many intentionally liberal, or so-called practicing congregations, also belies the frequent assumption that effective religious formation requires conservative theology. One good example— out of many—is a medium-sized New England church with a program in "children's worship and arts," designed and run largely by laypeople. Every Sunday morning, the congregation's younger members gather in their own space for worship, a special cloth laid out in the fellowship hall and covered with symbols of the faith—light, Word, and cross. As the children sit together, they learn to "feel at home with the elements and flow of Reformed worship" and "rehearse traditions" peculiar to their congregation. Simple worship leads into art projects designed to follow the liturgical calendar or focusing on Christian practices around prayer, hospitality, the sacraments, and social justice. Children, working with adults, have created giant saint-puppets (complete with names and life stories), an altar-cloth quilt, and music for the adult choir to sing. In good Bushnellian tradition, the church sees the children as "belonging fully—not as guests in a grown-up church; not as building blocks for its future, valuable only when they reach adulthood; not as holy and very cute photo ops." The radical inclusion of children is fundamental to the congregation's own ethic of Christian hospitality.[28]

In recent years, children have also reappeared within public denominational forums. Beginning with the International Year of the Child in 1979, issues of child abuse and exploitation have gained worldwide attention; in 1996, an enormous public rally, called Stand for Children and sponsored by the Children's Defense Fund, cemented these issues in the national consciousness. Mainline denominations quickly took up the cause. That same year, United Methodists announced their intention of "putting children and their families first," and in 1997, Episcopalians proclaimed a "Children's Charter for the Church." In 2001, Presbyterians declared a "Decade of the Child," acknowledging that "the future well-being of our church and nation depends on the healthy nurture of our children spiritually, physically, emotionally, intellectually, psychologically, and socially." Within the United Church of Christ, concern for children touches almost every point of the denomination's robust social agenda: poverty, health, sexuality, public schooling, and peacemaking.[29]

Mainline churches have also begun to focus more purposefully on religious education. New educational models, describing human learning as a diverse, multifaceted process involving various types of "intelligences," allowed religious educators to open new conversations about religious formation. Freed from a narrow focus on cognition, they began to imagine children's faith development as a wide-ranging, creative endeavor, engaging all the senses and every part of the brain. Robert Fowler's popular *Stages of Faith*, published in 1991, added theological heft, emphasizing the importance of stories in childhood religion and recentering the biblical text as an educational tool. Popular new curricula such as Godly Play engaged children in ritual, in an unfolding array of age-appropriate and spiritually evocative activities, and a spate of new books invited mainline parents to become thoughtful guides in their children's spiritual quest.[30]

All these new efforts have been undergirded by a growing body of critical scholarly literature, making the case for a liberal mainline ethic of family care. During the 1990s, the Religion, Culture, and Family Project, based at the University of Chicago, produced an influential series of books by leading biblical scholars, theologians, sociologists, and historians, all insisting that a "pro-family" stance was not necessarily a conservative one.[31] In recent years, scholarly advocacy for children and the family has continued to grow, as has the literature for parents and caregivers.[32]

In mainline circles, theological creativity is usually not a problem. Nor is a basic willingness to respond to human need. But as one recent study of local church programming has found, change stalls quickly when financial resources lag behind these other factors, and with the demographic downturn of the past decades, the issue is far from theoretical. For all the public awareness of divorced and blended families, working parents, and the economic pressures on poor and working-class families, most mainline (and Evangelical) churches still offer an antiquated regimen of Sunday morning religious education, weekday women's groups, and evening family programming. Below the regular hubbub of controversy about gay marriage, abortion, and divorce, the average local church follows a fairly mundane "standard package" of activities. The issue is not really theological; in churches, as in the larger world, creativity flows in large, well-funded institutions where money is simply not an issue.[33]

Larger questions still loom as well. The reintroduction of children as a denominational concern has, as some critics have noted, stressed their social "plight" more than their positive spiritual role in the larger church family. It is one thing for churches to minister to children as clients, it is another to recognize both the need and the gift they offer their local congregations. The old Bushnellian model of the child as an authentic church member, albeit temporarily limited in understanding, might provide a useful balance.

The more dubious side of Bushnell's legacy has been a tendency to sentimentalize children, to believe they are somehow more pure and unspoiled than adults. Although his Christian nurture theory dealt with infant sinfulness in a fairly nuanced manner, later generations worried less about the effects of original sin and concentrated instead on the possibilities for raising truly exemplary children. In practical terms, this has meant that churches have often felt no pressing need for early religious teaching and have historically encouraged parents not to unduly "proselytize" their children or teenagers into a particular faith choice. But, in fact, some of the most recent research on teenagers, a perennial challenge for all religious traditions, demonstrates the powerful effect of a self-aware church community, where adults regularly articulate and practice their faith. Conservative or liberal theology alone does not make the most crucial difference; in the end, as Bushnell might have predicted, there is no substitute for consistent parental involvement and daily Christian nurture.[34]

Raising liberal children is not an easy task, and it is perhaps not surprising that mainline churches have lately become fairly reticent within the spiraling social debate about children and childhood. Certainty is a powerful tool, for both theologians and parents. But it is best wielded with caution, as a stream of recent political events in the United States and around the world has amply demonstrated. There is no current oversupply of religious tolerance. Within that global context, it seems entirely possible that mainline churches may well have an important contribution to make toward the nuanced and careful understanding of childhood that families need and our times require.

## NOTES

1.  *Memoir of William Ellery Channing, With Extracts from His Correspondence and Manuscripts, in Three Volumes*, vol. 1, 2nd ed. (Boston: William Crosby and H. P. Nichols, 1848), 34–35.

2.  Wade Clark Roof and William McKinney, *American Mainline Religion: Its Changing Shape and Future* (New Brunswick: Rutgers University Press, 1987), 152–155.

3.  On the general topic of mainline Protestants and children, see Margaret Bendroth, *Growing Up Protestant: Parents, Children, and Mainline Churches* (New Brunswick: Rutgers University Press, 2002); Bonnie Miller-McLemore, *Let the Children Come: Reimagining Childhood from a Christian Perspective* (San Francisco: Jossey-Bass, 2003).

4.  Robert Wuthnow, introduction to *The Quiet Hand of God: Faith-Based Activism and the Public Role of Mainline Protestantism*, ed. Robert Wuthnow and John H. Evans (Berkeley and Los Angeles: University of California Press, 2002), 4. See also Roof and McKinney, *American Mainline Religion*; Randall Balmer, *Grant Us Courage: Travels Along the Mainline of American Protestantism* (New York: Oxford University Press, 1996).

5.  Wuthnow, introduction to *The Quiet Hand of God*, 8–10. Peter Thuesen describes them as "universalists" in their understanding of human sin and redemption. See his article "The Logic of Mainline Churchiness: Historical Background Since the Reformation," in *The Quiet Hand of God: Faith-Based Activism and the Public Role of Mainline Protestantism*, ed. Robert Wuthnow and John H. Evans (Berkeley and Los Angeles: University of California Press, 2002), 27–53. The other possible interpretation of this data is that mainliners are, on the whole, less active churchgoers than evangelicals. See, for example, Christian Smith, *American Evangelicalism: Embattled and Thriving* (Chicago: University of Chicago Press, 1998), 51–63.

6.  Nancy Ammerman, "Golden Rule Christianity: Lived Religion in the American Mainstream," in *Lived Religion in America: Toward a History of Practice*, ed. David D. Hall (Princeton: Princeton University Press, 1997), 198.

7.  Wuthnow, introduction to *The Quiet Hand of God*, 10.

8.  Smith, *American Evangelicalism*, 75–82.

9.  Wuthnow, introduction to *The Quiet Hand of God*, 13.

10. See, for example, the essays in *Between the Times: The Travail of the Protestant Establishment in America, 1900–1960*, ed. William R. Hutchison (Cambridge: Harvard University Press, 1989).

11. Dennison Nash and Peter Berger, "The Child, the Family, and the 'Religious Revival' in Suburbia," *Journal for the Scientific Study of Religion* 2 (1962): 85–93; Dennison Nash, "A Little Child Shall Lead Them," *Journal for the Scientific Study of Religion* 7 (1968): 238–240; Benton Johnson, Dean R. Hoge, and Donald A. Luidens, "Mainline Churches: The Real Reason for Decline," *First Things* 31 (March 1993): 13–18; W. Bradford Wilcox, "For the Sake of the Children? Family-Related Discourse and Practices in the Mainline," in *The Quiet Hand of God: Faith-Based Activism and*

*the Public Role of Mainline Protestantism*, ed. Robert Wuthnow and John H. Evans (Berkeley and Los Angeles: University of California Press, 2002), 287–316.

12. Michael A. Hout, Andrew Greeley, and Melissa J. Wilde, "The Demographic Imperative in Religious Change in the United States," *American Journal of Sociology* 107 (September 2001): 468–500. For a good overview of current debate, see James A. Mathisen, "Tell Me Again: Why Do Churches Grow?" *Books and Culture*, May 1, 2004.

13. Horace Bushnell, *Christian Nurture* (New York: Charles Scribner, 1861; rpt. Cleveland: Pilgrim Press, 1994), 10.

14. Ibid., 107.

15. Ibid., 83.

16. For a full accounting, see H. Shelton Smith, *Changing Conceptions of Original Sin* (New York: Charles Scribner's Sons, 1955); Peter Slater, *Children in the New England Mind* (Hamden, CT: Archon Books, 1977).

17. See, for example, William McLoughlin, "Evangelical Child-Rearing in the Age of Jackson," *Journal of Social History* 9 (1975): 35–39.

18. Ibid., 245.

19. Ibid., 276, 293.

20. Howard A. Barnes, *Horace Bushnell and the Virtuous Republic* (Metuchen, NJ: ATLA and Scarecrow Press, 1991), 39.

21. G. Stanley Hall, "The Content of Children's Minds," *Princeton Review* 11 (1883): 249–272.

22. Sophia Lyon Fahs, "The Beginnings of Religion in Baby Behavior," *Religious Education* 25 (1930): 896–897.

23. Wilcox, "For the Sake of the Children? Family-Related Discourse and Practice in the Mainline," 296–297.

24. "Excerpt from the Report 'Sexuality and the Human Community' (1970)," in *The Churches Speak On: Sex and Family Life; Official Statements from Religious Bodies and Ecumenical Organizations*, ed. J. Gordon Melton (Detroit: Gale Research, 1991), 127. On the "new morality" more generally, see Roof and McKinney, *American Mainline Religion*, 209–217.

25. Quoted in Bendroth, *Growing Up Protestant*, 128.

26. uoted in ibid., 127.

27. Eileen W. Lindner et al., *When Churches Mind the Children* (Ypsilanti, MI: High/Scope Press, 1983). See also her article "Ecumenical and Interdenominational: Private and Public Approaches to Family Issues," in *Faith Traditions and the Family*, ed. Phyllis Airhart and Margaret Bendroth (Louisville, KY: Westminster/John Knox, 1996), 157–172.

28. J. Mary Luti, "Where Are the Children?" in *From Nomads to Pilgrims: Stories from Practicing Congregations*, ed. Diana Butler Bass and Joseph Stewart-Sicking (Herndon, VA: Alban Institute, 2005), 35–45.

29. W. Bradford Wilcox, "Churches' Witness on the Family: Mixed Messages," *Christian Century*, February 21, 2001, 16–19; "Committee Approves Recommendation Proclaiming 'Decade of the Child,'" http://www.pcusa.org/ga213/news/ga01032.htm, accessed March 25, 2006.

30. Catherine Stonehouse, "Knowing God in Childhood: A Study of Godly Play and the Spirituality of Children," *Christian Education Journal*, n.s., 5 (Fall 2001): 27–45.

31. Information, including lists of books and other materials, is available at http://marty-center.uchicago.edu/research/rcfp/.

32. See, for example, Miller-McLemore, *Let the Children Come*; J. Bradley Wigger, *The Power of God at Home: Nurturing Our Children in Love and Grace* (San Francisco: Jossey-Bass, 2003); Elizabeth Caldwell, *Making a Home for Faith: Nurturing the Spiritual Life of Your Children* (Cleveland: United Church Press, 2000); Herbert Anderson and Susan B. W. Anderson, *Regarding Children: A New Respect for Childhood and Families* (Louisville, KY: Westminster/John Knox Press, 1994); Karen Marie Yust, *Real Kids, Real Faith: Practices for Nurturing Children's Spiritual Lives* (San Francisco: Jossey-Bass, 2004).

33. Penny Edgell, *Religion and Family in a Changing Society* (Princeton: Princeton University Press, 2006), 139–143.

34. Christian Smith and Melinda Lundquist Denton, *Soul Searching: The Religious and Spiritual Lives of American Teenagers* (New York: Oxford University Press, 2005), 265–271.

# 2

# Conservative Protestants on Children and Parenting

JOHN P. BARTKOWSKI AND CHRISTOPHER G. ELLISON

For nearly fifteen years now, scholars have expended a great deal of energy studying the contours of conservative Protestant (or Evangelical) parenting. Given the distinctive aspects of conservative Protestant child discipline, much of this scholarly attention has explored how and why Evangelical parents discipline their children. This chapter provides a review of this body of scholarship, thereby distilling the key insights that have surfaced from research using textual sources (best-selling conservative Protestant parenting manuals) and nationally representative survey data.

The chapter proceeds as follows: We begin by outlining the contours of the conservative Protestant worldview, an essential starting point from which to understand the contours and underlying logic of conservative Protestant child rearing. Conservative Protestants are distinguished from other groups by their distinctive epistemological commitment to the Bible as the inerrant word of God, as well as their beliefs about the nature of sin and salvation. We then distill the key elements of elite Evangelical advice on the topic of parenting. Leading conservative Protestants, including Focus on the Family's James Dobson, have written advice manuals for Evangelical parents that have sold millions of copies through Christian bookstores while providing an Evangelical alternative to child-rearing manuals written by secular parenting specialists. We unpack what we call the "layered logics" embedded in Evangelical parenting texts. On the one hand, such texts advocate a hierarchical family structure and strongly endorse the use of corporal punishment as a means of child discipline. These distinctive orientations are rooted largely in beliefs about the inherent sinfulness of children who, like all human beings, are construed as innately rebellious to authority (a product of original sin). Conservative Protestant parenting experts cite a series of biblical passages in support of this distinctive disciplinary strategy and recommend a scriptural methodology for such discipline (such as physical punishment with a "rod of chastisement"). Yet, on the other hand, elite Evangelicals place a strong emphasis on emotional bonding between parents and children through affirmative parenting. To this end, parents are urged to provide frequent displays of affection to their youngsters and to avoid harmful practices such as yelling at children or disciplining youngsters in anger. Moreover, paternal involvement in child rearing is strongly advocated by such Evangelical specialists.

After outlining the layered logics that constitute this conservative Protestant child-rearing ideology, we review empirical research concerning the parenting practices used in Evangelical households. These layered logics give rise to paradoxical child-rearing practices in which an emphasis on children's submission to parental authority and caregivers' use of corporal punishment is coupled with progressive child-rearing orientations such as less parental yelling, more affectionate child rearing, and higher levels of paternal involvement. Current evidence links spanking to positive developmental outcomes among Evangelical youngsters, a finding that challenges totalizing condemnations of corporal punishment typically advanced by sociologists. We conclude by identifying the implications that stem from extant research and suggesting directions for future research.

## Scripture, Sin, and Salvation: Anatomy of a Worldview

Any meaningful analysis of conservative Protestant parenting must begin with an appreciation of the underpinnings of the conservative Protestant worldview. By way of brief summary, Evangelicals are distinguished from other Christian groups by their unique epistemological, ontological, and soteriological commitments.[1] The conservative Protestant epistemology is rooted in a "high view" of scripture, one in which the Bible is treated as the inerrant word of God. Thus, biblical injunctions to "train up a child" and specific references to the corporal punishment of children cannot be dismissed by conservative Protestants as a product of the traditional or "backward" cultures from which the Bible emerged. From a conservative Protestant perspective, the Bible contains divinely ordained propositional truths that believers can apply in their everyday lives, including in family relationships. Conservative Protestants take seriously the injunction in 2 Timothy 3:16 that states: "All scripture is God-breathed and is useful for teaching, rebuking, correcting and training in righteousness."

The ontology of conservative Protestantism (that is, this subculture's vision of human nature and the state of the world) stems from a particular interpretation of the book of Genesis. Genesis describes Adam and Eve as the first parents of all humankind and conservative Protestants view these first parents' "original sin" as rebellion against the laws of God, leading to their banishment from the Garden of Eden and to the "fall of man." From this vantage point, Adam and Eve's progeny (all human beings) are viewed as having a predisposition to sin (selfish, willful rebellion against God's laws) and as occupying a world characterized by evil (separation from God, temptation of Satan). The Evangelical soteriology (conceptualization of human salvation) places a premium on the reconnection of human beings with God through an acceptance of the atonement of Jesus Christ. As Evangelicals understand it, Jesus Christ was literally the Son of God and paid the price through His crucifixion for the sins of all humankind. Salvation is viewed as a product of believers' submission to God's will through a "born again" experience in which the individual recognizes his or her inherently "sinful nature" and accepts Jesus Christ as "personal Lord and Savior." Conversely, those who give into their sinful nature and reject Christ as the Savior of humankind can expect to receive God's punishment in the form of eternal damnation.

## Layered Logics: The Parenting Advice of Elite Evangelicals

Conservative Protestant parenting advice manuals occupy significant shelf space in Christian bookstores across America. Many of these advice manuals have sold more than a million copies. Upon comparison with secular parenting-advice manuals, the most distinctive aspects of Evangelical child-rearing texts are (1) the hierarchical nature of the human family and, in particular, the parent-child relationship, and (2) an endorsement of corporal punishment for the disciplining of children.[2]

### Discipline . . .

At first glance, Evangelical parenting specialists seem to advocate a very traditional brand of parenting, one that outside observers might describe as authoritarian.[3] Elite Evangelical parenting discourse places a premium on obedience to parental authority and control of youngsters' behavior through the use of physical discipline.[4] Evangelical parenting specialists contend that God created the family not as a democratic unit (as most secular parenting experts contend), but rather as an institution defined by clear lines of hierarchy and authority. From this vantage point, just as human beings must learn to submit to God's authority in order to be saved, little children, to develop psychologically, socially, and spiritually, must be taught to submit to the authority of their parents. Evangelical authors therefore emphasize biblical commands for children to honor and obey the authority of their parents under the threat of divine judgment (see, for example, Exod. 20:12, 21:15–17; Prov. 29:15, 30:17). If submission is not learned at an early age, it is believed, the sinful nature that all persons have inherited from Adam and Eve holds sway with ruinous consequences in one's earthly life and eternally. In his best-selling *The Strong-Willed Child*, James Dobson comments that his writings on child rearing "are a product of the biblical orientation toward human nature. We are not typically kind and loving and generous and yielded to God. Our tendency is toward selfishness and stubbornness and sin. We are all, in effect, 'strong-willed children' as we stand before God."[5] Thus, from an Evangelical perspective, parents are charged with the responsibility of "training up a child" and are held accountable by God for "shaping the will" of their youngsters. From this standpoint, children are naturally rebellious to authority and must be taught to cultivate a submissive demeanor toward those who stand in authority over them. Parents are the first and most formative earthly authority in a child's life, the paradigm from which the child will develop an orientation toward other authority figures (teachers later in childhood, workplace supervisors in adulthood, and ultimately God in the eternities).

Just how are parents to go about shaping their youngsters' wills? According to conservative Protestant parenting specialists, the Bible provides clear mandates for child discipline. Parents are expected to use physical discipline to teach young children right from wrong at an early age. Biblical passages that are interpreted by conservative Protestant parenting specialists to support corporal punishment are legion: "He that spares the rod hates his son; he that loves his son chastens him" (Prov. 13:24); "Foolishness is bound in the heart of a child; but the rod of correction shall drive it far from him" (Prov. 22:15); "The rod and reproof give wisdom; but a child left to himself brings his mother to shame" (Prov. 29:15). Thus, Evangelical luminaries charge that the Bible mandates parents to use physical discipline to correct the willful misbehavior of their errant youngsters. As Proverbs 13:24 indicates, spanking is a manifestation of love inasmuch as parents who genuinely care for their children will not shy away from using corporal punishment as a means of correction.

Make no mistake in presuming that conservative Protestant child-rearing specialists interpret scriptural references to "the rod" metaphorically. Quite the contrary: Evangelical parenting experts urge parents to use a literal rod such as a wooden spoon or switch to spank their children, and these authorities propose a detailed methodology for doing so. While the use of a "rod of chastisement" appears to many outside this religious subculture to border on barbarism, Evangelical luminaries view this item as a "neutral object" designed to depersonalize punishment, thereby distinguishing it from the "loving hand" of the parent. The use of a rod is part of a broader orientation toward child discipline that is designed to be deliberate, controlled, and restrained. Dobson, for example, warns against a "'slap 'em across the mouth" approach to authoritarianism and, with other Evangelical specialists, instead recommends the controlled, strategic, delimited use of physical punishment.[6] To wit, parents are expected to administer punishment in response to a child's willful defiance of clearly established household rules. Once parents have ascertained that a child is willfully defiant, they are to inflict sufficient pain immediately with a rod on the child's buttocks to promote behavioral correction. This behaviorist approach to child discipline has its roots in the pragmatic and Puritanical origins of American Evangelicalism.[7] Notably, Evangelical parents are specifically admonished against "lashing out" at children in anger or allowing their tempers to gradually boil over, thus raising the specter of abusive physical punishment. "Slowness to anger" is seen as a biblical virtue (Prov. 16:32). According to conservative Protestant parenting experts, the short-term pain brought about through properly administered physical punishment is a "purifier," one that corrects children's behavior without inflicting injury. As stated in Hebrews 12:11, "No discipline seems pleasant at the time, but [is instead] painful. Later on, however, it produces a harvest of righteousness and peace for those who have been trained by it."

### . . . Yet Cherish

This traditional (and allegedly authoritarian) logic found in conservative Protestant child-rearing advice manuals is interwoven with a countervailing logic that promotes expressive and nurturant parenting. Thus, Evangelical commentary about the importance of children's obedience and parents' use of corporal punishment is overlaid with a strong emphasis on parental affirmative support of children. While parents are expected to shape the will of their children, they are warned against adopting an overbearing demeanor or harming the child's spirit. In this way, the logic of nurturant parenting emphasizes parental tenderness and resonates with Ephesians 6:4, which warns parents, "Do not exasperate your children; instead, bring them up in the training and instruction of the Lord." Consequently, the rather strident tone found in some parts of Evangelical parenting-advice manuals is ineluctably coupled with softer language that highlights the "tender side" of Christian parenting. This turn toward parental tenderness draws considerable force from the integration of key elements of therapeutic culture into conservative Protestantism.

Apart from admonitions concerning disciplinary restraint (noted above), this motif of tenderness is also manifested in frequent references concerning the need for parents to affirm their children through practices sociologists would describe as "positive emotion work" (hugging, praising, expressing affection).[8] Thus, although advocacy for the use of corporal punishment is a key feature of the conservative Protestant parenting perspective, the rearing of children is not to be characterized by emotional detachment or austerity. Dobson's *The Strong-Willed Child* is instructive in just this way. After discussing how parents must "shape the will" of their children and delineating the role of corporal punishment in rooting out human "selfishness and stubbornness," Dobson highlights "the dangers" in misinterpreting his advice. In doing so, he emphasizes the absolutely vital role of parental tenderness in child rearing:

> The reader could assume that I perceive children as the villains and parents as the inevitable good guys. Of greater concern is the inference that I'm recommending a rigid, harsh, oppressive approach to discipline. Neither statement is even partially accurate. . . . I see small children (even those who challenge authority) as vulnerable little creatures who need buckets of love and tenderness every day of their lives. One of my greatest frustrations in teaching parents has been the difficulty in conveying a balanced environment, wherein discipline is evident when necessary, but where it is matched by patience and respect and affection.[9]

Dobson goes on to say that "healthy parenthood can be boiled down to . . . two essential ingredients, love and control. . . . [An] authoritarian and oppressive home atmosphere is deeply resented by the child who feels unloved or even hated."[10]

Here again, the relationship between God and the Christian believer is viewed as paradigmatic for the parent-child relationship. Because God's love is expansive enough to chastise those who have sinned and extend mercy to the penitent (see, for example, Heb. 12:6), parents are expected to couple chastisement with forgiveness. Dobson states outright that parenting must combine "mercy and justice, affection and authority, love and control."[11] In fact, conservative Protestant writers view the disciplinary encounter as an opportunity for spiritual instruction whereby children should be taught to recognize how they erred; experience remorse for their transgression; seek forgiveness from the parent; and be extended mercy, culminating in reconciliation between the loving parent and contrite child. In this sense, children are taught, simultaneously, how to seek forgiveness from their fellow human beings and, ultimately, from a God who is both just and merciful.

Interestingly, as part of the broader Evangelical commitment to parental control and expressive child rearing, caregivers are expressly warned against the negative consequences of uncontrolled outbursts, particularly yelling, directed at their youngsters.[12] Richard Fugate, widely regarded as one of the most ardent Evangelical proponents of corporal punishment, states that "chastisement is not a tongue lashing, threats, or screaming fits of anger; in other words, adult temper tantrums. These [attempts at verbal intimidation] do nothing but support the child's disrespect for his parents' authority and demonstrate the parents' inability to rule."[13] Moreover, because parents are charged with representing God to their children, yelling at children is seen as a misrepresentation of God's nature, an approach that can have particularly harmful—even abusive—consequences for youngsters. For his part, Dobson criticizes yelling on more pragmatic grounds: "Parents often use anger to get action instead of using action [spanking] to get action [compliance]. . . . Trying to control children by screaming is as utterly futile as trying to steer a car by honking the horn."[14]

Strong recommendations for paternal involvement in child rearing also fit within the progressive spectrum of Evangelical parenting. Although conservative Protestant commentators generally endorse a patriarchal family structure, this particular brand of patriarchy places a premium on paternal responsibility and involvement rather than on male dominance.[15] As a result, conservative Protestant parenting advice dovetails quite nicely with the New Father ideal in contemporary American society, a paradigm in which normative expectations encourage greater levels of paternal involvement in child care than was the case in years past. However, the neotraditional language of "leadership" remains a central feature within conservative Protestant child-rearing discourse, perhaps as an incentive to coax men into making their (gender-specific) contributions to children's well-being through paternal involvement.

### What the Research Reveals: Parenting Paradoxes in Evangelical Households

To this point, we have explored the layered logics of elite Evangelical parenting discourse. Leading conservative Protestant child-rearing specialists support an unusual amalgam of parenting practices. On the one hand, elite Evangelicals embrace a parenting orientation that is quite traditional (some would say authoritarian) in its advocacy of children's submission to parental authority and caregivers' use of corporal punishment—using a rod of chastisement—to foster youngster's compliance. Yet, on the other hand, these same commentators argue for disciplinary restraint (the delimited use of corporal punishment) bereft of parental outbursts (yelling). Moreover, they advocate an array of progressive parenting practices that include emotionally expressive child rearing (hugging and praising youngsters) coupled with encouragement for paternal involvement. What does empirical research reveal concerning the actual ideals held and practices used by conservative Protestant parents? The research conducted to date reveals a striking paradox where Evangelical child rearing is concerned, one that resonates with the layered logics of conservative Protestant parenting discourse outlined above.

Current evidence suggests that the apparently authoritarian elements of Evangelical parenting are a key feature of child discipline in conservative Protestant households. Analyses of nationally representative data reveal that conservative Protestants are significantly more likely than their non-Evangelical peers to express attitudinal support for the view that "it is sometimes necessary to discipline a child with a good, hard spanking."[16] Notably, this research reveals that support for corporal punishment is strongly associated with the distinctive Evangelical beliefs in the inerrancy of the Bible, the depravity of human nature, and punishment as a legitimate response to sin. Moreover, conservative Protestants are more apt to value children's obedience to parental authority, whereas their non-Evangelical counterparts tend to value youngsters' autonomy and self-direction.[17] And perhaps most tellingly, Evangelical parents report actually spanking their toddlers and preschoolers much more often than do other parents.[18] This practice is largely rooted in inerrantist beliefs about the Bible. In short, children in conservative Protestant households are more likely to have parents who are committed to children's submission to parental authority, who believe that corporal punishment is justified in the face of children's misbehavior, and who actually administer physical punishment with greater frequency than do their non-Evangelical peers.

Yet despite elite Evangelicals' enthusiasm for upholding parental authority in the home, research reveals that conservative Protestant parents are also attuned to the countervailing logic of expressive caregiving embedded within best-selling Christian advice manuals. Research conducted with nationally representative survey data reveals that Evangelical mothers praise and hug their children more often than do other mothers.[19] What's more, Evangelical fathers are also quite inclined to engage in this kind of expressive parenting.[20] Moreover, consistent with admonitions against verbal outbursts found in conservative Protestant parenting manuals, Evangelical parents are significantly less inclined to using yelling as a means of disciplining their youngsters.[21]

Evidence of progressive parenting practices within Evangelical households is also found in the generally higher level of paternal involvement within such homes. Evangelical fathers have proved to be more involved with their children than proved their peers in other faith traditions.[22] Conservative Protestant fathers report greater involvement with their youngsters across a number of self-reported survey measures, for example, having dinner with their children and volunteering for youth activities such as soccer and Scouts. And, perhaps because elite conservative Protestant discourse charges husbands with family "leadership," Evangelical fathers are also more likely to shoulder the many supervisory tasks associated with raising school-aged children. Evangelical fathers are more inclined to monitor their children's chores, homework, and television viewing than are other fathers. Evangelical fathers are no more or less likely than other fathers to participate in basic child-care tasks such as feeding, clothing, and bathing preschoolers.

Of course, arguments about the paradoxical contours of conservative Protestant parenting would not have much sociological weight if the developmental effects of such child-rearing practices proved to be quite negative. To be sure, a great deal of social scientific research links corporal punishment, broadly defined, with an array of negative consequences (emotional distress, low self-esteem, aggression, academic underachievement) for maturing youngsters.[23] Given the higher rates of corporal punishment found in conservative Protestant homes, are Evangelical youngsters particularly at risk for such developmental problems? Although there is only preliminary evidence available on this front, the unique nature of Evangelical child discipline seems to yield distinctive developmental outcomes.

One study examined the effects of corporal punishment administered by parents of children from two to four years of age.[24] This study compared the incidence of emotional and behavioral problems five years after initial reports of physical punishment (at this five-year point the children were in grade school) for both Evangelical and non-Evangelical children. The study also accounted for recent episodes of corporal punishment by parents of these grade school–age children. Among the Evangelical children, this study found no harmful effects of spanking. Interestingly, Evangelical children who were not spanked at either point in time (that is, as toddlers or in grade school) actually exhibited greater risk of emotional and behavioral problems than that of their Evangelical peers who were spanked. These findings buttress other research that has detected fewer symptoms of emotional distress among children of theologically conservative mothers and those studies that underscore the generally beneficial effects of maternal religiosity and parental religiosity for youngsters.[25]

Why is spanking less harmful—and perhaps not harmful at all—for Evangelical children? Researchers offer several speculative explanations. First, as we have suggested here, corporal punishment is one facet of a broader complex of parenting behaviors. It is possible that any negative effects of physical punishment are offset by positive aspects of Evangelical family life discussed here and analyzed elsewhere. Second, there may be greater social and cultural support for physical discipline within Evangelical communities, that is, from family members, pastors, youth ministers, and fellow congregants. Because of this support, the distinctive parenting culture of conservative Protestantism might lead Evangelical children to expect spanking and, perhaps, to interpret such discipline as a sign of parental love and concern rather than of rejection. Third, Evangelical parents may administer corporal punishment differently from other parents as part of a coherent disciplinary strategy. As described above, James Dobson and other Evangelical writers have offered detailed advice on when, where, and how to administer corporal punishment, with an emphasis on avoiding uncontrolled or abusive discipline. Consistent with much of this counsel, Evangelical parents seem to be more likely than others to employ corporal punishment consistently, in response to disobedience, and to achieve behavioral compliance, moral training, and other socialization goals.[26]

The current research, then, paints a paradoxical portrait of child rearing within conservative Protestant families. Traditional (and some would say, authoritarian) forms of discipline such as the valuation of children's obedience and the more frequent use of corporal punishment have indeed been observed in such families. Yet these practices are coupled with a series of progressive parenting practices, such as more frequent parental hugging and praising of youngsters, less parental yelling, and more robust forms of paternal involvement. Evangelical child-rearing practices, then, seem to confound long-standing sociological typologies that aim to fit parents neatly into "authoritarian," "authoritative," and "permissive" categories. The panoply of child-rearing practices within this subculture can be best characterized as "neotraditional" in form.

## Future Directions and Roads Not (Yet) Taken

Over the past fifteen years, studies conducted mainly by sociologists have cast fresh light on the distinctive child-rearing orientations and practices of conservative (or Evangelical) Protestants. Although these works have answered a number of important questions and debunked an array of unflattering stereotypes, our understanding of many of these issues remains in its infancy. In this final section of the chapter, we outline several of the most promising directions for further inquiry on Evangelical child rearing in the contemporary United States.

First, conservative Protestants do not constitute a monolithic community. Indeed, there are a number of potential sources of disagreement and cleavage regarding child-rearing approaches, even on the subject of corporal punishment. For example, whereas a few conservative Protestant writers endorse physical punishment in response to virtually any childhood misbehavior, a minority camp of elite Evangelicals discourage the use of spanking because they prioritize children's emotional vulnerability over the youngsters' sinful nature.[27] Even Dobson places much less emphasis on physical punishment in more recent work, as compared with the initial version of his best-selling *Dare to Discipline*. This degree of fluidity and difference on the nature of children and child discipline should be investigated further.

No community or population remains static in terms of opinions, norms, and practices, and studies have shown that corporal punishment is slowly but surely losing favor in the general public. Once approved by nearly all (more than 90 percent) of Americans, this practice is now rejected by roughly one-third of U.S. adults, according to recent polls. This raises interesting and important questions about the degree of Evangelical resistance or capitulation to these broader cultural trends, and also the extent to which any shifts in values and attitudes are concentrated in certain subgroups of the Evangelical population. One recent study finds that overall, Evangelicals are maintaining their distance versus non-Evangelicals in approval of the physical punishment of children, but also that this overall pattern masks a widening gap between college-educated conservative Protestants and their less-educated counterparts.[28] Indeed, well-educated Evangelicals are withdrawing their support for this practice at a much faster rate than is the population as a whole; the education gap in attitudes regarding physical punishment has emerged entirely since the mid-1980s. Apart from class-based cleavages, racial differences in conservative Protestant conceptualizations of children and parenting also merit investigation.[29]

Second, the role of religion in the actual decision-making processes related to child discipline remains opaque. How, when, and why do religious factors lead parents to divergent decisions regarding child discipline? It may be fruitful to approach this issue via notions of cognitive schema and information processing that are common in the child development literature.[30] The most basic social information–processing models distinguish between several stages of parental decision making. For example, at the representation-and-appraisal phase, parents seek to apprehend the nature and motivations for child misbehavior, defining and classifying myriad problem behaviors into a limited number of simpler categories. Theological differences may bear upon this categorization process, such that parents whose faith commitments stress the innate sinfulness (selfishness, willfulness) of human nature may be particularly primed to interpret child misbehaviors as expressions of "willful defiance" toward parental authority. By contrast, other parents might chalk the same types of infractions up to inevitable immaturity, childish forgetfulness, or other benign causes.[31]

Finally, surprisingly few studies have explored religious differentials in child outcomes. Given the evidence of distinctive Evangelical child-rearing practices, including the combination of high parental control and high parental support, there are sound reasons to anticipate that children raised in conservative Protestant families may differ from their peers in a host of cognitive, behavioral, and emotional outcomes, in both a short-term and a long-term perspective. To be sure, some critics suspect the worst, worrying that Evangelical children will grow up prone to violence, lacking in empathy, and exhibiting other potential developmental problems.[32] However, the apparent correspondence between the emerging portrait of Evangelical child-rearing and the merits of an authoritative parenting style suggests a more favorable developmental profile.

Children from conservative Protestant families may differ from their peers in (1) different levels of discipline, warmth and nurturance, or other child-rearing factors; (2) different effects of these factors as implemented within Evangelical homes; or (c) the distinctive combination of high levels of control and support advised by Dobson and other Evangelical luminaries.[33] Although we noted one previous study on religious differences in the effects of corporal punishment among young children (toddlers and preschoolers) as they mature into grade school–aged children,[34] a sustained research agenda in this area should distinguish between short-term effects, namely, those lasting a matter of months, or at most a few years, and longer-term effects, those extending into adulthood. Researchers should be particularly attentive to potential variations by age and gender of the child. With regard to corporal punishment, for example, Dobson and other Evangelical defenders of this practice argue that early spanking to "shape the will"—provided that it is curtailed well in advance of adolescence—will tend to yield the most desirable child outcomes. This is especially important because the most compelling evidence of negative effects associated with corporal punishment surfaces in studies of adolescents; by contrast, findings of long-term undesirable effects among very young children are scant.

In this chapter, we have outlined the essential features of Evangelical beliefs and values, discussed their links with child-rearing philosophy and practice, reviewed the growing body of empirical work on this topic, and outlined several fruitful directions for further investigation. Although this list of neglected research topics is far from exhaustive, it may be adequate to suggest the magnitude of the tasks at hand. And until such work is conducted, it is clear that a keen understanding of Evangelical views on the nature of children and their place within family and society are key elements to understanding the paradoxical nature of Evangelical parenting.

## ACKNOWLEDGMENTS

The authors thank Margaret Bendroth, along with other contributors to this volume, for thoughtful comments on an earlier version of this chapter.

## NOTES

1.  John P. Bartkowski, *Remaking the Godly Marriage: Gender Negotiation in Evangelical Families* (New Brunswick: Rutgers University Press, 2001); Christopher G. Ellison and Darren E. Sherkat, "Obedience and Autonomy: Religion and Parental Values Reconsidered," *Journal for the Scientific Study of Religion* 32 (1993): 313–329.

2.  John P. Bartkowski and Christopher G. Ellison, "Divergent Models of Childrearing: Conservative Protestants vs. the Mainstream Experts," *Sociology of Religion* 56 (1995): 21–34.

3.  John P. Bartkowski, "Spare the Rod . . . , or Spare the Child? Divergent Perspectives on Conservative Protestant Child Discipline," *Review of Religious Research* 37 (1995): 97–116; W. Bradford Wilcox, "Conservative Protestant Parenting: Authoritarian or Authoritative?" *American Sociological Review* 63 (1998): 796–809.

4.  See references cited above, as well as the following: Christopher G. Ellison and John P. Bartkowski, "Religion and the Legitimation of Violence: Conservative Protestantism and Corporal Punishment," in *The Web of Violence: From Interpersonal to Global*, ed. Jennifer Turpin and Lester R. Kurtz (Urbana: University of Illinois Press), 45–67; Christopher G. Ellison, John P. Bartkowski, and Michelle L. Segal, "Do Conservative Protestant Parents Spank More Often? Further Evidence from the National Survey of Families and Households," *Social Science Quarterly* 77 (1996): 663–673; Christopher G. Ellison, John P. Bartkowski, and Michelle L. Segal, "Conservative Protestantism and the Parental Use of Corporal Punishment," *Social Forces* 74 (1996): 1003–1028; Christopher G. Ellison and Darren E. Sherkat, "Conservative Protestantism and Support for Corporal Punishment," *American Sociological Review* 58 (1993): 131–144.

5.  James Dobson, *The Strong-Willed Child* (Wheaton, IL: Tyndale House, 1976), 174–175.

6.  Ibid., 74.

7.  Wilcox, "Conservative Protestant Parenting."

8.  Ibid.

9.  Dobson, *The Strong-Willed Child*, 73.

10. Ibid., 52.

11. Ibid.

12. John P. Bartkowski and W. Bradford Wilcox, "Conservative Protestant Child Discipline: The Case of Parental Yelling," *Social Forces* 79 (2000): 865–891.

13. J. Richard Fugate, "What the Bible Says about Child Training" (Tempe, AZ: Alpha-Omega, 1980), 154.

14. James Dobson, *The New Dare to Discipline* (Wheaton, IL: Tyndale House, 1992), 36.

15. John P. Bartkowski and Xiaohe Xu, "Distant Patriarchs or Expressive Dads? The Discourse and Practice of Fathering in Conservative Protestant Families," *Sociological Quarterly* 41 (2000): 465–485; W. Bradford Wilcox, *Soft Patriarchs, New Men: How Christianity Shape Fathers and Husbands* (Chicago: University of Chicago Press, 2004). See also Bartkowski, *Remaking the Godly Marriage.*

16. Ellison and Sherkat, "Conservative Protestantism and Support for Corporal Punishment"; Harold Grasmick, Robert Bursik, and M'lou Kimpel, "Protestant Fundamentalism and Attitudes toward Corporal Punishment of Children," *Violence and Victims* 6 (1991): 283–297.

17. Ellison and Sherkat, "Obedience and Autonomy."

18. Ellison, Bartkowski, and Segal, "Conservative Protestantism and the Parental Use of Corporal Punishment"; Ellison, Bartkowski, and Segal, "Do Conservative Protestant Parents Spank More Often?"

19. Wilcox, "Conservative Protestant Parenting."

20. Bartkowski and Xu, "Distant Patriarchs or Expressive Dads?"; W. Bradford Wilcox, "Emerging Attitudes about Gender Roles and Fatherhood," in *The Faith Factor in Fatherhood*, ed. Don Eberly (Lanham, MD.: Lexington Books, 1999), 219–239.

21. Bartkowski and Wilcox, "Conservative Protestant Child Discipline."

22. Bartkowski and Xu, "Distant Patriarchs or Expressive Dads?"; Wilcox, "Emerging Attitudes about Gender Roles and Fatherhood."

23. Murray A. Straus, *Beating the Devil Out of Them: Corporal Punishment in American Families* (San Francisco: Lexington, 1994).

24. Christopher G. Ellison, Marc A. Musick, and George W. Holden, "The Effects of Corporal Punishment on Young Children: Are They Less Harmful for Conservative Protestants?" (paper presented at the annual meetings of the Society for the Scientific Study of Religion, Boston, 1999).

25. John P. Bartkowski, Xiaohe Xu, and Martin L. Levin, "The Impact of Religion on Early Childhood Development," *Social Science Research*, 2007 (in press); Lisa Miller, Virginia Warner, Priya Wickramaratne, and Myrna Weissman, "Religiosity and Depression: Ten-Year Follow-up of Depressed Mothers and Offspring," *Journal of the American Academy of Child and Adolescent Psychiatry* 36 (1997): 1416–1425.

26. Elizabeth Thompson Gershoff, Pamela C. Miller, and George W. Holden, "Parenting Influences from the Pulpit: Religious Affiliation as a Determinant of Parental Corporal Punishment," *Journal of Family Psychology* 13 (1999): 307–320.

27. See John P. Bartkowski, "Beyond Biblical Literalism and Inerrancy: Conservative Protestants and the Hermeneutic Interpretation of Scripture," *Sociology of Religion* 57 (1996): 259–272.

28. John P. Hoffmann, Christopher G. Ellison, and John P. Bartkowski, "Conservative Protestantism and Attitudes toward Corporal Punishment, 1986–2000" (paper presented at the annual meetings of the Pacific Sociological Association, Vancouver, B.C., Canada, 2002).

29. See Gilkes's chapter in this volume.

30. Christopher G. Ellison, "Conservative Protestantism and the Corporal Punishment of Children: Clarifying the Issues," *Journal for the Scientific Study of Religion* 35 (1996): 1–16.

31. For an intriguing counterpoint to Evangelical child rearing, see Bendroth's chapter on mainline conceptualizations of children and parenting in this volume.

32. Phillip Greven, *Spare the Child: The Religious Roots of Punishment and the Psychological Impact of Physical Abuse* (New York: Alfred Knopf, 1991); Adah Maurer, "Religious Values and Child Abuse," in *Institutional Abuse of Children*, ed. R. Hanson (New York: Haworth Press, 1982), 57–63.

33. Ellison, "Conservative Protestantism and the Corporal Punishment of Children."

34. Ellison, Musick, and Holden, "The Effects of Corporal Punishment on Young Children."

# 3

## The Status of Children within
## the Roman Catholic Church

JENNIFER BESTE

In Roman Catholicism, we find a view of children that simultaneously celebrates them as gifts from God, made in the image of God, endowed early
in life with rationality, capable of initiative and deliberation, carriers of
obligations to parents and society, and themselves sources of grace. But
they are also human creatures in need of the sacraments, grace, and strong
parental and institutional guidance. These views are sometimes in conflict,
especially as the Catholic Church confronts the challenges of American
secularism, mass media, and excessive individualism. In this chapter, I
begin with Roman Catholicism's view of the child within the context of the
family and society and its account of adults' obligations to children.[1] Next,
I examine how the Catholic clergy evaluates and responds to U.S. cultural
influences that threaten children's well-being and their spiritual and moral
development. Last, I highlight certain tensions between Catholicism's official teachings about children and its actual practices. Such tensions present
challenges that Catholics need to address if the Catholic Church wishes to
realize its religious ideals more effectively and serve as the best possible
advocate for children in American culture.

### The Catholic Church's View of Children
### within the Family and Society

How does the Catholic Church perceive children's ontological and moral status? According to canon law, children are from birth accorded equal dignity

with the rest of Christians by virtue of rebirth through baptism.[2] At the heart of the Catholic tradition lies the conviction that God offers Christ to each person and invites all to a life of eternal communion with the divine. With the aid of God's grace, individuals have the freedom to respond to God's self-offer and actualize a "yes" to God throughout their lifetimes by loving God and neighbor. Like adults, children are believed to be affected deeply by the structures of sin present in the world. Both God's grace and the capacity to reason, however, offer hope that children, given adequate formation by their family and church, can grow in their capacity to recognize and strive after what truly fulfills them. Attaining the capacity to reason around the age of seven has thus been theologically significant throughout the Catholic tradition: children at this time are traditionally viewed as personally responsible for living out a "yes" to God's self-offer. Canon law affirms that children share responsibility for "the building up of the body of Christ in accord with each one's own condition and function."[3]

To find further Catholic teachings on the nature of children and their rights and responsibilities, it is necessary to consult Catholic writings concerning the meaning of marriage and the family. The birth of a child within Catholicism signifies God's continual gift and presence within the world. When giving birth to a child, married couples are viewed as co-creators with God as they bring into being new life through love. It is important to underscore how the belief that each child is made in the image of God and created for a life of communion with God functions to qualify parents' rights and desires. Current Vatican doctrine emphasizes that the right to life for each unborn child trumps any possible reason for a woman to abort her pregnancy. Catholic teaching also warns parents against projecting their desires onto their children during their upbringing: parents should foster their children's ability to pursue their God-given interests and gifts and respect children's decisions regarding career, marriage, and so on.[4]

According to Catholic teaching, parents are responsible mainly for the physical, psychological, and spiritual nurturing of their children. Through word and example, they are the primary teachers and evangelizers of faith for their children. The church teaches that consistent love and nurturing by parents during the child-rearing years make it possible for a child to experience security and trust, which in turn provides the foundation for trust and faith in God. Because of the importance of consistent nurturing, the church claims that a child has the right to two parents, which it views as the best chance for a stable family environment. In several documents, the church also emphasizes that children need or even have a right to be cared for by their mother at home.[5]

In their response to the care and love they receive from their families, Catholic children are exhorted to obey their parents and other authority figures unless such counsel violates their conscience. According to Catholic tradition, once children attain their use of reason around the age of seven, they can exercise certain rights apart from the authority of their parents. For instance, they have a right through their own volition to receive the Sacraments of Reconciliation, Eucharist, Anointing of the Sick, and confirmation.[6] Throughout their lives, children are expected to respect their parents, take parental advice seriously, and care for their elderly parents. Catholic children are also expected to reach out to the most marginalized in society, contribute to the common good, and strive for justice and peace.

Noteworthy is the concept that spiritual and moral growth do not flow unilaterally from parents to children: children, too, have a profound impact and contribute positively to the spiritual development of their family members. The teachings of Vatican II recognize that "children contribute very substantially to the welfare of their parents" and "contribute in their own way to making their parents holy."[7] Religious educators Leonard Rochon and Josephine McCarthy describe the distinctive ways in which children mediate grace to their parents, siblings, and extended families:

> Children, too, are in their own way catechizers in the home. Their wonder at the beauty and grandeur of nature, their expressions of welcome, of forgiveness, and of friendship among themselves and with their little friends, their naïve questions, intuitive reflections they voice aloud on the events of the day . . . the lessons, prayers, songs, drawings, projects which they bring home from the class in catechetics . . . the way they sometimes interpret their joys and sorrows, their success and failures, or the way they express their gratitude to their parents in their difficulties—all of this is a bit of the gospel which children write day after day and communicate to their parents.[8]

## Responsibilities of Society to Families

To elucidate the Catholic view of how children, parents, the church, and society ought to relate to one another, it is important to understand the Catholic principle of subsidiarity. According to this principle, the individual and family precede the state, which means that the state and market exist for the benefit of individuals and families. A nation's government and economic system, then, should support rather than undermine the rights and responsibilities of parents in the care and education of their children. In their letter *Putting Children and Families First*, the American bishops exhort the public to reevaluate every policy and program in government and church according to its effects on children and families.[9] The Catholic Church has consistently emphasized that a nation's economy should serve people and foster the stability of family: "Economic and social policies as well as the organization of work should be continually evaluated in light of their impact on the strength and stability of family life."[10] Elsewhere, they state: "Families need workplace policies that promote responsive child-care arrangements; flexible employment terms and conditions for parents; and family and medical leave for parents of newborns, sick children, and aging parents."[11]

## Threats to the Catholic Vision of Healthy Families and Children

While the Catholic Church affirms the distinctive way Christian families are called to embody Christ to one another and to the larger society, it acknowledges that serious threats exist in U.S. culture that undermine the healthy functioning of families and children and the realization of social justice and peace. According to John Paul II and U.S. bishops, the Catholic call to raise children to respond affirmatively to God's self-offer by loving God and neighbor sharply contrasts with U.S. secular culture.[12] The root of the problem consists in American secular culture's rejection of Christian insights about humanity and what constitutes authentic fulfillment. Rather than embracing the truth that happiness lies in our ability to honor our interdependence and freely give ourselves as gifts to each other, secular culture embraces a philosophy of relativism in which each person is free to construct what is good and true and is encouraged to be accepting of all views. Ironically, while espousing relativism rhetorically, secular culture typically defines the good and the true as whatever maximizes utility, productivity, and individual pleasure. Catholic teaching argues that these utilitarian values violate the dignity of persons and their right to be treated as ends in themselves; persons are reduced to being objects of pleasure and profit for the most powerful. John Paul II and American bishops argue that such social values specifically harm children by undermining marriage and family stability; threatening children's physical, psychological, and spiritual well-being; and opposing the central Christian commandments to love God and love one's neighbor as oneself.

According to John Paul II and U.S. bishops, secular values of excessive individualism and the pursuit of pleasure mock and undermine the value of lifelong commitment in marriage and intimate familial bonds. These misplaced values are in part responsible for the high rates of extramarital affairs and divorce, which result in psychological harm and economic hardship, especially for women and children. U.S. bishops also emphasize how economic and social problems such as poverty, unemployment, homelessness, and racism contribute significant stress to families and threaten their stability. The bishops note that, since women and children constitute the highest percentage of the poor, they are most likely to suffer from chronic hunger and victimization and to be denied basic goods such as adequate housing, education, and health care.[13]

Even for those families who manage to stay intact, the economic pressure either to satisfy basic needs for their families or satisfy materialist desires can cause both parents to work long hours away from home. As a result, children spend more of their time unsupervised, and parents and children are deprived of quality time together. Compounding these challenges is that parents who overextend themselves at work obviously compromise their ability to nurture their children physically, psychologically, and spiritually.

The Catholic Church also identifies a number of other cultural threats that harm children's well-being. In addition to the high percentage of physical and sexual violence inflicted upon youth and children directly, media influences such as television, the Internet, advertising, and video games constantly bombard children with images of physical and sexual violence, which desensitizes them and promotes violent behaviors.[14] Catholic clergy and educators also warn that our media's pervasive promotion of sexual pleasure and activity threatens the physical, psychological, and social well-being of children, adolescents, and young adults.

The cultural obsession with materialism and consumerism also harms children and adolescents through its great pressure on young people to conform to societal standards of acceptability. Such focus on materialism, individualism, and relativism often results in a sense of emptiness and meaninglessness and contributes to intense suffering, resulting in addiction to drugs and alcohol, sex, violence, depression, and suicide. As Catholic educator Gerald Grace observes:

> Many young people find themselves in a condition of radical instability. . . . They live in a one-dimensional universe in which the only criterion is practical utility and the only value is economic and technological progress. . . . Not a few young people, unable to find any meaning in life or trying to find an escape from loneliness, turn to alcohol, drugs, the erotic, the exotic, etc. Christian education is faced with the huge challenge of helping these young people discover something of value in their lives.[15]

Furthermore, Catholic leaders soberly recognize that U.S. secular values make it very difficult for Christian families to embrace the core values of the Gospels: social concern, collective responsibility, charity, and justice. A Catholic family that realizes its mission to be a domestic church is by definition countercultural when it attempts to be self-critical about materialist and consumerist values, reaches out with concern to others beyond the confines of family, and seeks to realize greater justice for all members of society.

Because of these challenges, U.S. bishops exhort parents to be critical of how U.S. culture undermines Christian values:

> [Parents] must teach their children the truths of the Faith and pray with them; share Christian values with them in the face of pressures to conform to the hostile values of the secular society; initiate them into the practice of stewardship itself in all its dimensions, contrary to today's widespread consumerism and individualism. This may require adjusting the family's own patterns of consumption and its lifestyle, including the use of television and other media which sometimes preach values in conflict with the mind of Christ. Above all, it requires that parents themselves be models of stewardship, especially by their selfless service to one another, to their children, and church and community needs.[16]

How does the Catholic Church help its members deal with conflicts between mainstream American values and Christian values, and how does it seek to reduce the suffering produced by secular values? There are at least three strategies the Catholic Church has used to respond to threats from secular culture: the development of Catholic parochial school and parish religious education programs designed to inculcate students with a strong faith that enables them to follow Christ; a shift toward greater youth participation in weekly liturgy and the sacraments, which cultivates spiritual strength to help children live out their faith; and advocacy of greater societal support for families and maintenance of charitable institutions and programs to help families and children in need and in crisis.

## Catholic Parochial Schools and Religious Education

As discussed in Paul Numrich's chapter in this volume, the Catholic Church in the nineteenth century created its own private educational institutions in order to counteract hostile threats from U.S. culture. Because of the presence of anti-Catholic prejudice and hostility in a predominantly Protestant American culture and the Protestant influence evident in public education, the bishops commanded all parishes in 1884 to build schools within two years. Catholic parents were now obligated to send their children to parochial schools whenever possible.[17] A central cause driving the establishment of parochial schools was the conviction that the education of children is a primary responsibility of the family and church, not the government. The church rejects the idea of separating religion and education:

> It is . . . the special function of the Catholic school to develop in the school community an atmosphere animated by a spirit of liberty and charity based on the Gospel. It enables young people, while

developing their own personality, to grow at the same time in that new life which has been given them in baptism. . . . Accordingly the Catholic school can be of such service in developing the mission of the People of God.[18]

From the mid-nineteenth century to the 1960s, Catholic schools were regarded as a fortress to "protect children from the 'wolves of the world' and preserve the Catholic faith throughout generations."[19] However, because of Vatican II's call to be more open to the world and learn from it, Catholic culture since the mid-1960s stopped viewing itself as opposed to American culture and instead envisioned itself as active within it; the goal was to be like yeast within the culture—permeating, serving, and prophetically transforming it. As contemporary Catholics have assimilated and internalized American values more deeply than ever before, questions have arisen since the 1970s about the continuing value and need for separate schools. Even so, Catholic leaders and educators still stress the ever-present need for children to be formed and socialized within the Catholic faith. Currently, 16 percent of Catholic children attend Catholic schools and 52 percent of Catholic children participate in parish religious education programs.[20] Catholic schools focus on educating the very "being" of their students, helping them mature in their faith and be confident in their own rational capacities to discern what God desires for them. Schools also seek to inspire students to view themselves as "history-makers," persons capable of making a difference to society.[21]

## The Importance of the Sacraments and Liturgy

According to the Catholic tradition, participation in weekly liturgy and reception of the sacraments play a central role in forming and fostering Catholic children's faith and religious imagination. Since Vatican II, the Catholic Church has been seeking more effective ways to enable children to participate in the liturgy. Not surprisingly, today more than ever, congregations are offering some form of children's liturgy.[22] Children usually leave the church after the opening prayer, discuss the Gospel, and return to their parents for the remainder of the liturgy. This newer practice, however, is not without its critics, as some liturgists oppose the change and argue that "separate but equal" liturgies for children undermine the inclusive nature of the gathered community.

As for reception of the sacraments, Catholic children are expected to have received four of the seven sacraments by adolescence: baptism, the Sacrament of Reconciliation, Eucharist, and confirmation. Baptism is the first sacrament Catholic children receive typically as infants. Through the waters of baptism, a person is cleansed from sin, incorporated into the body of Christ, and invited to share in divine life.

The age of seven is the next significant religious marker in the life of the church because it is at or around this age that children are believed to attain reason. Since the Fourth Lateran Council of 1215, the Catholic Church has taught that reason equips a child with the ability to comprehend right versus wrong, commit mortal sin, and take responsibility for one's relationship to God. While contemporary church teaching does not directly address the question of whether a seven-year-old has the capacity for mortal sin, it is explicit that seven-year-olds can distinguish right from wrong, commit venial (less serious) sins, and desire pardon from God.[23] During the past twenty years, the Vatican has become increasingly insistent that Catholic second graders receive the Sacrament of Reconciliation, during which they confess their sins to a priest, express contrition, receive absolution, and perform a penance as reparation for wrongdoing.[24]

The age of reason also equips children with the ability to recognize the presence of Jesus in the consecrated bread and wine, which gives them the right to receive the Eucharist. By participating in the Eucharistic meal, Catholics enter into the most intimate encounter with Christ and seek deeper communion with God and neighbor. Children at this time also have the right to receive confirmation and are anointed with holy oil and strengthened by the Holy Spirit in their ability to profess their faith and live as true witnesses of Christ. While Roman law traditionally prefers children to receive confirmation prior to the Eucharist, most Catholic dioceses usually choose to confirm children in eighth grade or high school, a decision made at least partly to ensure that Catholic youth continue to form their religious identity. After receiving the three sacraments of initiation—baptism, confirmation, and Eucharist—children and adolescents exercise full membership in the church and share in the communal responsibility of building up the body of Christ.

## The Catholic Church as an Advocate for Children and the Family

American Catholicism also seeks to promote the stability of the family and well-being of children through advocacy. Many lay Catholics and clergy participate in an impressive variety of organizations that seek to respect the sanctity and dignity of human life. They promote human dignity by lobbying for legislation that supports children and families, increases access to affordable housing and health care, and alters unjust labor policies.

Furthermore, Catholic organizations such as Catholic Charities provide a wide range of services to families and children, such as counseling, community health services, employment programs, family assistance, and mental health/substance abuse services. Catholic Charities typically serves 9 million to 10 million people a year.[25] The Catholic Campaign for Human Development (CCHD) also deserves mention in its effort to foster children's and families' well-being. Sponsored by the United States Conference of Catholic Bishops, CCHD focuses on educating the public about the root causes of poverty. It specifically seeks to eradicate poverty by empowering poor people to organize and demand basic rights to participate in society and receive just wages, adequate housing, and quality health care. Since its founding in 1970, CCHD has granted $270 million to more than four thousand community-based self-help projects designed and led by people living in poverty.[26]

## Particular Challenges Confronting American Catholicism's Advocacy of Children

Clearly, the Catholic tradition is theologically rich in its affirmation of children's dignity and its actual service toward children and families. I wish to end this chapter, however, by identifying at least three challenges (by no means exhaustive) confronting the church that arise from discrepancies between Catholicism's teachings about children and some of its actual practices: the challenge to attain justice and closure with respect to the church's own child sexual abuse crisis, the challenge to foster children's moral agency more effectively, and the challenge to evangelize Catholic youth and better convey Catholic social teachings to enable youth to resist secular culture's individualism and materialist consumerism.

The first and most obvious challenge that threatens the church's moral credibility and its ability to be an effective advocate for children involves its own child sexual abuse crisis. While it is unlikely that any religious denomination can claim to be innocent of child sexual abuse, no religious tradition has faced the same staggering number of public allegations and intense media scrutiny as the U.S. Catholic Church. According to self-reports of Catholic dioceses, approximately 4 percent of Catholic priests and deacons active in 95 percent of U.S. dioceses between 1950 and 2002 have been accused of sexual abuse of youth under eighteen years of age. More than 10,667 youth in the United States reported being sexually victimized by Catholic clergy during these years.[27] As if these statistics were not sufficiently damaging, the way in which the Catholic hierarchy responded to reports of abuse is just as, or even more, troubling. When confronted with allegations of sexual abuse, many bishops denied or minimized the abuse; blamed the victims themselves; or sought to silence victims and their lawyers through intimidation, harassment, counterlawsuits, and gag orders in an effort to avoid public scandal.[28]

The Catholic Church has sought to restore trust among its laity by acknowledging its failures to protect children and foster healing for victims. Specifically, the church has committed itself to pursue justice for victims and has implemented child protection policies.[29] However, if it wishes to identify all the factors contributing to the sexual abuse crisis and protect children most effectively in the future, the church must frankly examine how some of its beliefs and attitudes about children may actually have contributed to the climate of clergy sexual abuse. Despite the vast coverage of the sexual abuse crisis and speculation about its causes by commentators inside and outside the church, there is surprisingly little analysis about the underlying beliefs and attitudes concerning children that may have enabled the phenomenon of clergy sexual abuse and influenced bishops' responses to the abuse. Specifically, Catholics need to explore the following questions: What beliefs about children contributed to clergy members' decisions to sexually abuse them? What particular beliefs and practices embedded within the socialization of Catholic culture contributed to the victimization of Catholic youths and their subsequent silence and self-blame? What beliefs and attitudes about children made it possible for bishops to reassign offenders to different parishes and give children's right to bodily integrity such low priority?

In their document *Breach of Trust, Breach of Faith*, the Canadian Conference of Bishops diverge from most commentators about the causes of the child sexual abuse crisis and briefly explore prevailing attitudes about children that contribute to their victimization. These bishops note that children are socialized to respect and obey adults and are thus easily led and controlled by adults: "It appears that many adults teach children to be passive, to be obedient and to be controlled."[30] They argue that obedience and passivity contribute to children's victimization by adults: "Children who are abused sexually are children who don't understand that they have a right to say 'No.' They are children who can be controlled by adults who choose to use their power to exploit those who are most vulnerable."[31]

This heightened awareness of the harm that can result from attempting to control children leads to a second challenge facing the Catholic Church: the church has an opportunity to recommit itself to fostering children's moral agency and equipping them with the resources to say no to sexual abuse and any other practices inside or outside the church that feel threatening or uncomfortable. To address this second challenge successfully, several steps are in order. First, the church needs to probe the way its beliefs and practices have historically constructed adults' and children's perceptions of children as vulnerable, easily manipulated, passive, and powerless. The next task is to explore whether any current religious practices involving children reflect and perpetuate the basic image of children as passive and needing to be controlled. Once identified, these practices must be altered to foster children's moral agency and construct a view of children as resourceful, confident, and capable of resisting harm. Religious historian Robert Orsi argues that an adequate response to the sexual abuse crisis must include a focus on instituting mechanisms "for giving children greater voice in the church"; the church must be committed to finding "ways of making children more authentically and autonomously present in contemporary Christian contexts."[32] The Canadian bishops also affirm this move to foster children's moral agency, arguing that children have "the right to learn how to be actively involved in decisions about their own lives."[33]

Given the Catholic tradition's affirmation of human reason and its emphasis on personal responsibility, it would seem that the practice of promoting children's moral agency and ability to defend themselves and say no to any activities that are uncomfortable to them would be a natural extension of its teaching. However, according to some Catholic educators, an emphasis on the need to form children's religious identity and ensure adequate moral and spiritual formation in Catholicism sometimes overrides any concern in practice to listen to the voices of children themselves about their needs and desires in the process of their religious formation.

To explore more concretely this tension between official teachings about children and actual practices, it is useful to briefly examine the current practice of children receiving the Sacrament of Reconciliation. Despite debate about the developmental appropriateness of the Sacrament of Reconciliation for seven-year-olds during the 1960s–1970s, the Vatican and U.S. bishops have become increasingly insistent since the late 1970s that children receive the Sacrament of Reconciliation in second grade prior to receiving the Eucharist.[34] Such a uniform practice of insisting that all second graders receive the Sacrament of Reconciliation raises pastoral concerns, since it ignores the particular circumstances of each child and his or her readiness for the sacrament.[35] According to some religious educators and priests, insisting that children receive this particular sacrament without considering the child's perspective is especially problematic because a significant percentage of children at this age experience anxiety and fear during the process. Canon lawyer Monsignor Michael Smith Foster reflects on his experience of encountering a child in the confessional who was not ready to receive the Sacrament of Reconciliation:

> The child was forced to go; if he did not, there would be no First Eucharist. The child had to be placed in the chair by his father. He burst into tears as I greeted him, immediately wet himself and started to hyperventilate. He was quickly rushed out of the church and attended to by his father and teacher. The child was ready to celebrate First Eucharist, but not first penance. Since an exception to the policy was not allowed, the policy seriously harmed the child.[36]

This practice of making the Sacrament of Reconciliation a prerequisite for First Communion perpetuates the view of children as passive as it sanctions and condones the act of coercing some children to participate in an activity that feels uncomfortable to them. Since children are given no voice or influence about whether or when they desire this sacrament, this practice also does not foster children's own sense of agency and invite them to participate in making important religious decisions. Pastoral concerns raised by this one example of a religious practice involving children indicate a general need for Catholic leaders, educators, and parents to reflect more conscientiously about how they balance the value of transmitting their faith traditions and the value of respecting children's perspectives and agency.

Lastly, according to many Catholic clergy and educators, a third challenge facing the church is how to accord greater institutional priority to evangelizing its youth and focusing more explicitly on its Catholic social teachings. The 2002–2003 National Study of Youth and Religion (NYSR) found that Catholic teens consistently scored lower than other Christian teens on most measures of religiosity involving religious beliefs, practices, experiences, and commitments.[37] Part of the problem is that the U.S. Catholic Church invests fewer resources into youth ministry and education than do many other Christian denominations.[38] Analyzing this report, the National Federation for Catholic Youth Ministry (NFCYM) concluded that the American Catholic Church has not succeeded in "reaching the majority of young people or their families in any meaningful way."[39] NFCYM recommends that, despite the promising vision of youth ministry articulated by the bishops in their document *Renewing the Vision: A Framework for Catholic Youth Ministry*, the church must renew its commitment to pastoral ministry with young people, invite youth to participate more actively in the life of the faith community, and allocate the necessary financial and personnel resources to this ministry.[40]

Furthermore, my experience teaching as a Catholic theologian in a Jesuit university suggests that the Catholic Church needs to employ various research methodologies to evaluate how well Catholic parishes and educators are conveying the values of Catholic social teaching to youth. Although I do encounter several students every year in my classes who inspire me with their passion to work for greater social justice and peace, the majority of my Catholic students have deeply internalized the individualist, consumerist mentality. Some react with surprise when learning about Catholic social teaching for the first time as freshmen in college, which raises the question about the degree to which Catholic primary and secondary schools are prioritizing the need to educate youth about Catholic social teaching. The American bishops also recognize the need for greater improvement among Catholic educators and parishes to convey their tradition's social teaching effectively both to youth and adults: "It is clear that in some educational programs Catholic social teaching is not really shared or not sufficiently integral and explicit. As a result . . . many Catholics do not adequately understand that the social teaching of the church is an essential part of Catholic faith. This poses a serious challenge for all Catholics, since it weakens our capacity to be a Church that is true to the demands of the Gospel."[41] While Catholic clergy and educators undoubtedly face many challenges in this task, there are signs of hope that many clergy and teachers are beginning to reach out to youth and convey Catholic social teaching in new ways. Pope Benedict XVI has inherited from John Paul II a powerful means of reaching out to youth and inspiring their faith on annual World Youth Days—a powerful opportunity to communicate to youth their significance to the church and at the same time listen to their concerns. Moreover, recent publications about integrating Catholic social teaching into Catholic religious education indicate a growing enthusiasm among Catholic educators to teach children and youth about justice and peace in unprecedented, creative ways.[42] In 2000, the National Catholic Educational Association chose as its focus the challenge of integrating Catholic social teaching into Catholic schools. Research studies employing diverse methodologies, however, must be conducted to ascertain how well Catholic parishes and schools are equipping youth with resources to evaluate secular culture more critically and embrace the central values of the Gospel.

## Conclusion

According to John Paul II, the way a community treats children signifies the ultimate test of its values: "In the Christian view, our treatment of children becomes a measure of our fidelity to the Lord himself."[43] This chapter has sought to convey the Catholic tradition's rich theological vision of children's value and dignity within the family and larger society. As evidenced by enthusiastic crowds of Catholic youth who gather on annual World Youth Days, Catholicism's positive vision of youth as well as its powerful theological message of human fulfillment offer the church great potential for being a powerful advocate and guide for children and youth. To fulfill its great promise to communicate the good news of Christ, however, the church needs to examine critically its own practices involving children in order to ensure that church laws and policies are not only consistent with their teachings but also truly protect children, serve their best interests, and enhance their moral and spiritual development.

### NOTES

1.   Given the limited scope of the chapter, I will not be able to attend to the ethnic and cultural diversity of American Catholic practices involving children. I focus on official church documents and Catholic religious education materials to elucidate the Roman Catholic Church's views and assumptions of children.

2. Michael Smith Foster, "The Promotion of the Canonical Rights of Children," *CLSA Proceedings* 59 (1997): 165.

3. Ibid.

4. Hans Daigeler, "Responsible Parenting: Biblical and Theological Reflections," in *Responsible Parenting: CCCB Working Papers* (Ottawa: Canadian Conference of Catholic Bishops, 1983), 19.

5. Christine Gudorf, "Rights of Children," in *New Dictionary of Catholic Social Thought*, ed. Judith Dyer (Collegeville, MN: Liturgical Press, 1994), 144.

6. Foster, "The Promotion of the Canonical Rights of Children," 184.

7. "*Gaudium et Spes*," in *Vatican Council II : the Basic Sixteen Documents*, ed. Austin Flannery (Northport, NY: Costello, 1996), nos. 48, 50. See also *Catechism of the Catholic Church* (Liguori, MO: Liguori, 1994), para. 2227.

8. Leonard Rochon and Josephine McCarthy, "Building Christian Families," in *Responsible Parenting: CCCB Working Papers* (Ottawa: Canadian Conference of Catholic Bishops, 1983), 24.

9. U.S. Bishops, *Putting Children and Families First* (Washington, DC: USCCB, 1991), 7.

10. U.S. Bishops, *A Decade After Economic Justice for All: Continuing Principles, Changing Context, New Challenges* (Washington, DC: United States Catholic Conference, 1995), 5.

11. Ibid., 10.

12. John Paul II, *Sollicitudo Rei Socialis* (Washington, DC: Office of Publishing and Promotion Services, United States Catholic Conference, 1988), no. 28; U.S. Bishops, 1991, 6–7; Congregation for the Clergy, *General Directory for Catechesis* (Washington, D.C.: United States Catholic Conference, 1998).

13. U.S. Bishops, *Putting Children and Families First*, 3.

14. U.S. Bishops, *Renewing the Mind of the Media* (Washington, DC: United States Catholic Conference, 1998).

15. Gerald Grace, *Catholic Schools: Mission, Markets, and Morality* (London: Routledge, 2002), 20–21.

16. National Conference of Catholic Bishops, *Stewardship: A Disciple's Response* (Washington, DC: United States Catholic Conference, 1992), 34.

17. National Catholic Educational Association, *The First 100 Years* (Washington, DC: National Catholic Educational Association, 2004).

18. John Augenstein with Christopher J. Kauffman and Robert J. Wister, eds., *One Hundred Years of Catholic Education* (Washington, DC: National Catholic Educational Association, 2003), 17–18.

19. Terence McLaughlin, Joseph O'Keefe SJ, and Bernadette O'Keeffe, "Setting the Scene: Current Realities and Historical Perspectives," in *The Contemporary Catholic School*, ed. Terence McLaughlin, Joseph O'Keefe SJ, and Bernadette O'Keeffe (London: Falmer Press, 1996), 10.

20. http://cara.georgetown.edu/bulletin/index.htm.

21. Thomas H. Groome, "What Makes a School Catholic," in *The Contemporary Catholic School*, ed. Terence McLaughlin, Joseph O'Keefe SJ, and Bernadette O'Keeffe (London: Falmer Press, 1996), 121.

22. Leslie Scanlon, "How to Draw Kids into Mass," *U.S. Catholic*, August 2003, 12–17.

23. Sacred Congregation for the Clergy, *General Catechetical Directory* (London: Catholic Truth Society, 1971), 91–101.

24. National Conference of Catholic Bishops, *Redemptionis Sacramentum* (Washington, DC: United States Catholic Conference, 2004), no. 87.

25. http://www.catholiccharitiesusa.org/.

26. http://www.nccbuscc.org/cchd/. See also John P. Hogan, *Credible Signs of Christ Alive* (New York: Rowman and Littlefield, 2003).

27. Research Study Conducted by the John Jay College of Criminal Justice, *The Nature and Scope of the Problem of Sexual Abuse of Minors by Catholic Priests and Deacons in the United States* (Washington, DC: United States Conference of Catholic Bishops, 2004). Given that this number is based on self-reports of U.S. bishops, the number of priest perpetrators and victims is most likely higher than these figures. See Donald Cozzens, *Sacred Silence: Denial and the Crisis in the Church* (Collegeville, MN: Liturgical Press, 2004), 94; A. R. Sipe, *Bless Me Father for I Have Sinned* (Westport, CT: Praeger, 1999), 114–121.

28. Cozzens, *Sacred Silence;* Sipe, *Bless Me Father for I Have Sinned.*

29. U.S. Bishops, *Charter for the Protection of Children and Young People* (Washington, DC: Conference, 2002).

30. Canadian Conference of Catholic Bishops, *Breach of Trust, Breach of Faith* (Ottawa: Canadian Conference of Catholic Bishops, 1992), B-2.

31. Ibid.

32. Robert A. Orsi, "Crisis Highlights Catholicism's Troubled Theology of Children," *Boston College C21 Resources*, Winter 2004, reprinted with permission from the Spring 2002 issue of *Harvard Divinity Bulletin.*

33. Canadian Conference of Catholic Bishops, *Breach of Trust, Breach of Faith*, B-2.

34. National Conference of Catholic Bishops, *Redemptionis Sacramentum*, no. 87.

35. This practice is also theologically problematic because it subjects adults and children to different standards: whereas adults are only obligated by canon law to receive the sacrament annually if they have mortally sinned, children must receive the sacrament prior to Eucharist regardless if they have sinned venially or mortally.

36. Foster, "The Promotion of the Canonical Rights of Children," 192.

37. Christian Smith, *Soul Searching: The Religious and Spiritual Lives of American Teenagers* (Oxford: Oxford University Press, 2005), 194.

38. Ibid., 210.

39. Charlotte McCorquodale, Victoria Shepp, and Leigh Sterten, *National Study of Youth and Religion (NSYR): Analysis of the Population of Catholic Teenagers and Their Parents* (Washington, DC: National Federation for Catholic Youth Ministry, 2004), 62.

40. Ibid., 62–63.

41. U.S. Catholic Bishops, *Sharing Catholic Social Teaching: Challenges and Directions.* http://www.usccb.org/sdwp/projects/socialteaching/socialteaching.htm.

42. John T. Butler, Carlisle Burgoyne, William Davis, et al., *From the Ground Up: Teaching Catholic Social Principles in Elementary Schools* (Washington, DC: National Catholic Educational Association, 1999); Ronald Krietemeyer, *Leaven for the Modern World: Catholic Social Teaching and Catholic Education* (Washington, DC: National Catholic Educational Association, 2000)

43. Pope John Paul II, "Message to the World Summit on Children," September 22, 1990.

# 4

## Judaism and Children in the United States

ELLIOT N. DORFF

### Core Features of Judaism's Texts and Institutions

To understand Judaism's views of children and childhood within the context of American society and culture, one needs to know some basic things about the kind of religion Judaism is and at least the outlines of its diverse expressions. Like Christianity and Islam, Judaism is based on its holy scriptures, the Bible, but it has been significantly shaped by the ongoing tradition created by its leaders and adherents. It was the classical rabbis who decided which books became part of the Bible and which not. Judaism is then based on the rabbinic interpretation and application of the Bible (and especially the Torah, the first five of the Bible's books) to our own day. Major rabbinic works on Jewish law include the Mishnah (edited c. 200 C.E.), the Talmud (edited c. 500 C.E.), several codes of Jewish law (especially Maimonides' *Mishneh Torah* [1180] and Joseph ben Ephraim Karo's *Shulhan Arukh* [1565]), and rabbinic rulings on specific questions, including some very modern issues such as stem cell research. The Midrash consists of a variety of books exploring and developing Jewish theology and lore through homiletic interpretations of the Bible; medieval, modern, and contemporary Jewish literature and philosophy have continued that development, including theological interpretations of modern phenomena such as the Holocaust and the reborn state of Israel. In addition to these products of rabbis and thinkers, Judaism has been importantly influenced by how lay Jews have understood and practiced their faith over time.[1]

American Judaism includes four major movements and secular institutions. From the most traditional to the most liberal, the American Jewish movements include Orthodox (about 21 percent of synagogue members), Conservative (33 percent), Reconstructionist (3 percent), Reform (39 percent), and other types (Renewal, Traditional, nondenominational, and so on, for a total of 4 percent). Only 46 percent of American Jews, however, are affiliated with a synagogue.[2] The others may consider themselves to be religious but for financial or other reasons do not join a synagogue. A much larger percentage of the 54 percent who are unaffiliated with a synagogue are secular Jews, who may be actively involved in Jewish philanthropic and cultural activities but not religious ones. They can do this because Judaism is not just a religion (that is, a set of beliefs and rituals) but a civilization with an attachment to Israel and Hebrew and a vast store of moral values, laws, customs, literature, fine arts, and other cultural expressions—including even recipes and jokes. I am a Conservative rabbi, but throughout this chapter I shall try accurately to report how each of these groups of Jews interprets and applies the Jewish tradition on issues regarding children.

## Judaism's Theory about Children

I will first examine the ontological and moral status of children in Judaism. Exodus 21:22–25 in the original Hebrew (but mistranslated in the Septuagint, on which later Christian tradition bases its understanding of the status of the fetus) clearly asserts that if men fighting inadvertently hit a pregnant woman and cause a miscarriage, they must pay a fine that presumably must be based on how far along she was with the pregnancy. If they injure the woman, however, then it is "life for life, eye for eye, tooth for tooth," and so on.

Although the rabbis converted the penalty for personal injuries from retribution to monetary compensation, they continue the Torah's distinction between the status of the fetus and that of the woman. They rule that if a woman is having difficulty in childbirth such that doctors cannot save both the mother and the fetus, they must dismember the fetus in order to save the life of the woman, for she is a full human being and the fetus is not. (Safe Caesarian sections were not available until the 1950s.) The fetus becomes a full human being only when its head emerges from the vaginal cavity or, if it is a breech birth, when its shoulders emerge.[3] At that point, the usual rules of triage apply—namely, attend to the one we have the greater likelihood of saving.

This explains two things. First, although Jewish texts generally prohibit abortion—not as an act of murder (for the fetus is not a full human being who can be "murdered"), but rather as an act of self-injury—this prohibition is set aside when the mother's life or health is at stake.[4] Second, rabbis of all denominations of American and Israeli Judaism heartily endorse embryonic stem cell research, where embryos of five to eight days gestation that would otherwise be discarded are used for research to cure devastating diseases.

The fetus becomes a child, with the same legal protections against murder and assault enjoyed by all human beings, at the moment of birth. Still, if the baby dies within the first thirty days after birth, full mourning rites are not observed. This was based in part on the rabbis' doubt about whether the child was born full term ("a lasting being," a *bar kayyama*) or premature and in part on the fact that many children died soon after birth.[5] Orthodox Jews continue this practice. Because we now know much more about the gestational status of the fetus and can often intervene to save an infant at risk, the Conservative Movement's Committee on Jewish Law and Standards has ruled that nowadays the child should be construed to be a full human being in all respects immediately upon birth.[6]

From the age of a month (or from birth) to the age of twelve for girls or thirteen for boys, the child is classified as a minor (*katan* [male], *ketanah* [female]).[7] For the six months from the age of twelve years and one day to twelve and a half, a girl is called a "lass" (*na'arah*). The rabbis were interested in defining this middle period for women between childhood and adulthood because the Torah (Deut. 22) specifies a number of laws that apply specifically to a lass, and so the rabbis needed to define to whom such laws apply.[8] After that period, she becomes an adult (*bogeret*) for all purposes,[9] except that she becomes a woman (*ishah*) only when married.

During childhood, neither girls nor boys are legally responsible for their actions; they become so responsible only on attaining the age of majority. This leads the rabbis to a remarkable ruling. The Torah (Deut. 21:18–21) specifies that a stubborn and rebellious son is to be stoned to death by his parents. The rabbis, however, wanted to narrow the application of the death penalty. They therefore maintain that this law cannot apply to a minor of younger than thirteen, for minors are not legally responsible for their actions. The law, however, cannot apply to an adult son, because he is legally independent of his parents. So the rabbis made the law apply only to a boy from the age of thirteen and one day to three months thereafter, and then they added many further restrictions on this law, to the point that ultimately they maintain that "a stubborn and rebellious son never was and never will be"![10]

### Birth and Infertility

In the Hebrew scriptures, Sarah, Rebekah, Rachel, and Hannah all have difficulty having children, and Rachel dies in childbirth.[11] That these stories of infertility and difficulty in childbirth are so numerous in the Bible indicates that children are both hard to have and very precious, indeed a major bless-ing.[12] This requires a delicate balance between encouraging couples to have children and engendering sensitivity and compassion for those who would love to do so but cannot.

This balance is, if anything, harder to achieve in our day than in the past. That is because American Jews in far higher percentages than the general American population go to college and graduate school. Specifically, 55 percent of American Jews have a bachelor's degree, in comparison with 29 percent of Americans generally, and 25 percent of American Jews have a graduate degree, in comparison with 6 percent of Americans generally.[13] As a result, Jews commonly do not marry until their late twenties, and they do not try to have children until their thirties. Biologically, though, the optimal age for both men and women to procreate is twenty-two, and between ages twenty-seven and thirty-five a full 30 percent of couples are infertile.[14] Age is not the only factor in infertility, but it exacerbates all the other factors. As a result, Jews suffer from infertility more than other segments of the American population, and a significant percentage of American Jews in their thirties and forties are consulting infertility doctors and, if that does not work, adopting children.

At the same time, the Jewish community, which was never large, lost a third of its numbers in the Holocaust, with only 11 million left in 1945. Now there are between 13 and 14 million Jews in the entire world (13,155,000 as of 2007) with about 5.3 million in the United States. For comparison, of the more than 6 billion people in the world, Christians account for 33 percent; Muslims for 20 percent; and Jews for less than 1/4 of 1 percent (specifically, 2.19 Jews per 1,000 people).[15] Worse, at a reproductive rate of less than 1.9 children per couple (with 2.1 needed for replacement), the American Jewish community is not even reproducing itself.[16] Precisely when the Jewish com-munity in America and the world is facing a demographic crisis, American Jewish couples are postponing procreation until after graduate school and often finding themselves infertile when they do try to have children. More-over, 47 percent of Jews are marrying non-Jews, and two-thirds of children raised in homes of a Jew and a non-Jew are not raised as Jews.[17] Even those being raised as Jews are being exposed to less intense forms of Jewish life than are children of Jews married to Jews (either by birth or by conversion).[18] This adds further to the demographic crisis, making it excruciatingly difficult for rabbis and others to know how to encourage earlier marriage, endogamy (that is, Jews marrying Jews), and procreation without offending people.

### Childhood Dependence
Since Jewish law was created in antiquity and the Middle Ages, when virtu-ally all societies were patriarchal, it is not surprising that it is the father who

is obliged to support his children. Because daughters are more likely than sons to be accosted and raped, if the father is poor, his primary duty is to support his daughters, and he may have his sons of age six and above go begging to help sustain the family.[19]

Jewish law presumes that in a divorce, children younger than six years of age should remain with their mother; at ages six and above, boys should live with their father and girls with their mother so that each parent can model what it means to be an adult of the child's gender. However, ultimately it is the child's welfare that determines who should have custody. None of this applies to American Jews anymore, however, because American law has jurisdiction over issues of both support and custody.

### Responsibilities of Children and Parents

The two basic duties that children have to parents are honor (Exod. 20:12) and respect (Lev. 19:3). The rabbis, as usual, define these duties in terms of concrete actions: "Our Rabbis taught: What is reverence (mora) and what is honor (kavod)? Reverence means that the son must neither stand in his father's place, nor sit in his place, nor contradict his words, nor tip the scales against him [in an argument with others]. Honor means that he must give him food and drink, clothe and cover him, lead him in and out."[20] Note that although the obligations of respect apply primarily to young children vis-à-vis their parents, duties of honor focus primarily on what adult children must do for their elderly parents. In defining filial duties in this way, the Jewish tradition was also limiting them. Specifically, although one would hope that parents and children would love each other, children have no legal duty to love or even like their parents. Moreover, some rabbinic authorities maintain that children need not carry out the duties of honor or respect for parents who have abused them physically, sexually, or even, according to some, psychologically.[21]

At the same time, the Rabbis were fully aware that honor and respect involve attitudes as well as actions, and so the same action can fulfill or violate these commandments, depending on how it is done:

> A man can feed his father on fattened chickens and inherit Hell [as his reward], and another can put his father to work in a mill and inherit Paradise. How is it possible that a man might feed his father fattened chickens and inherit Hell? It once happened that a man used to feed his father fattened chickens. Once his father said to him: "My son, where did you get these?" He answered: "Old man, old man, eat and be silent, just as dogs eat and are silent." In such an instance, he feeds his father fattened chickens, but he inherits Hell.
>
> How is it possible that a man might put his father to work in a mill and inherit Paradise? It once happened that a man was working

in a mill. The king decreed that his aged father should be brought
to work for him. The son said to his father: "Father, go and work in
the mill in place of me [and I will go to work for the king]. For it
may be [that the king's workers will be] ill-treated, in which case
let me be ill-treated instead of you. And it may be [that the king's
workers will be] beaten, in which case let me be beaten instead of
you." In such an instance, he puts his father to work in a mill, but
he inherits Paradise.[22]

Parents, in turn, have responsibilities toward their children:

Our Rabbis taught that a man is responsible to circumcise his son,
to redeem him from (or for) Temple service if he is the first born
("*pidyon ha-ben*"), to teach him Torah, to marry him off to a woman,
and to teach him a trade. And there are those who say that he must
also teach him to swim. Rabbi Judah says: Anyone who fails to teach
his son a trade teaches him to steal.[23]

In modern America, the duties to teach children Torah and a trade have
become much more costly and long term than they were in the past, and
dating has replaced the matchmaker as the way to find a mate. These developments have led to considerable discussion within the Jewish community
as to the content and extent of these duties.[24]

If the father does not circumcise his son, the community has the
duty to see that it is done.[25] The community also has the duty to provide
schools to enable parents to fulfill their duty to teach their sons Torah, but
ultimately parents still retain the duty to ensure that the child is indeed
being educated by the school. Whether daughters should be taught Torah
was a major debate in rabbinic times and only became commonplace in
the twentieth century, when Jewish communities could afford that. Jewish
communities historically have seen it as their responsibility to find homes
for orphans and ultimately to provide them with money so they could
afford to marry.[26]

In modern America, Jewish communities still carry out these obligations.
Jewish male émigrés from the former Soviet Union in the 1970s through the
1990s were often uncircumcised, and Jewish communities arranged for them
to be circumcised in a hospital setting, often free of charge. Scholarship
funds to enable Jews to get a Jewish education are regularly distributed by
schools and informal Jewish educational institutions such as summer camps
and youth groups, although the money available for this purpose is not
nearly enough to meet the need. Finally, Jewish Family Service in most communities finds foster or adoptive homes for Jewish orphans and, in some,
operates an orphanage of its own.

To enable parents to carry out their responsibilities, they also have authority over their children. Thus parents were exempted from the usual penalties for assault vis-à-vis their children on the grounds that they had the right to discipline them.[27] Even so, the Conservative Movement's Committee on Jewish Law and Standards has recommended that parents refrain from hitting their children altogether and has insisted that if parents spank them at all, it must be done with an open hand (not a fist) and with no object used as a weapon.[28] Moreover, the focus in both the Jewish tradition and in contemporary Jewish life is not on discipline, but on teaching through modeling and warm, supportive interactions.

### The Sexuality of the Child

Jewish law presumes that a girl's vagina is not sufficiently developed for male penetration (and therefore for male legal culpability for rape or incest) until age three.[29] The Torah (Deut. 22:16) permits a girl's father to marry her off to a man when she is a minor (that is, from ages three to twelve), but the rabbis forbade that.[30] Still, in medieval times, rabbis worried that a father who could pay his daughter's dowry when she was young might not have the money to pay when she grew up; they therefore permitted child marriages to ensure that the daughter would not remain unmarried.[31]

A boy was presumed to be able to have an erection at the age of nine and one day.[32] From that day forward, his sexual penetration is assumed to have legal consequences for his partner, but he himself becomes liable for his sexual acts only at age thirteen.

Children were taught Jewish sexual morals along with the rest of the Jewish tradition. This included the ideal that sex be restricted to marriage. Male masturbation was prohibited. (The Rabbis did not say anything and may not have known about female masturbation.) These two features of Jewish sexual morals resulted in the expectation that men in their late teens would marry women a few years younger.[33]

Except for the Orthodox community, extended education has postponed the age of marriage for most Jews. Modern American rabbis have therefore had to address the realities of the long gap between the age of sexual maturity and marriage. Because the rationales for the ban against masturbation (that a man would lose his sanity, his hair, his potency, and so forth)[34] have proved to be medically false, the Conservative Movement's *Rabbinic Letter on Intimate Relations* prefers that unmarried people masturbate rather than engage in sexual intercourse, because masturbation is harmless while intercourse can transmit sexual diseases, may result in pregnancy, and often involves emotional miscues. The *Letter* also spells out the values that should inform intimate relations, whether the couple is married or not, including respect, modesty, fidelity, health and safety, and holiness.[35]

## The Stages of Growing Up

Aside from the transitional status of a lass between twelve and twelve and
a half, Jewish *law* knows only of children and adults; it has no separate legal
status for teenagers. Once one becomes an adult at age twelve and a half or
thirteen, all legal responsibilities and privileges apply. The only additional
legal marking points in a person's life are the minimal age for military service, which the Torah sets at twenty, and for levitical service in the Taber-
nacle and, later, the Temple, which the Torah sets at twenty-five or thirty.[36]
The Torah also determines that if a person makes a vow to the Temple for
purposes of its upkeep and instead of specifying an amount of money vows
his or her own worth or that of someone else, presumably on the slave
market, the vow's value varies by age, with people from twenty to sixty commanding the most money, people from five to twenty commanding less, and
people from one month to five years still less.[37]

Educationally and socially, though, the tradition has a clear set of expectations of people at various ages. As soon as children can talk, parents are
supposed to teach them two verses from the Torah, "Moses commanded us
[to learn and obey] the Torah, as the heritage of the congregation of Jacob"
(Deuteronomy 33:4) and "Hear O Israel, the Lord is our God, the Lord is one"
(Deuteronomy 6:4).[38] The Mishnah then spells out the curriculum by age:

> He [Judah ben Temah] used to say: At five years of age, the study of
> the Bible; at ten, the study of the Mishnah; at thirteen, responsibility
> for obeying the commandments; at fifteen, the study of Talmud; at
> eighteen, marriage; at twenty, pursuit of a livelihood; at thirty, the
> peak of one's powers; at forty, the age of understanding; at fifty, the
> age of counsel; at sixty, old age; at seventy, the hoary head; at eighty,
> the age of strength; at ninety, the bent back; at one hundred, as one
> dead and out of this world.[39]

In modern America, school curricula vary according to the movement.
Orthodox schools more or less follow the Mishnah's path, with the child's
studies progressing from the Bible to the Mishnah to the Talmud and with
general studies added on according to what state law and parents require.
Conservative schools also focus on biblical and rabbinic texts, but they
add modern Hebrew and some Jewish history and thought. Reform schools
emphasize the modern Jewish experience and values, with Jewish texts
excerpted and translated as examples for those purposes.

The rabbis recognized, though, that children teach adults too. Thus the
Talmud rules that only men who have children of their own are eligible to serve
on a court that is considering a death penalty case, for only such people know
the deep value of life.[40] Further, the Talmud asserts, "Much have I learned
from my teachers; more from my peers, but most from my students."[41]

## Judaism and the Child in Practice: Rituals and Institutions

Beginning with God's command to Abraham, Jewish boys through the generations have been circumcised on the eighth day of their life unless a boy's medical condition requires that it be postponed. As the Torah stipulates (Gen. 17) and as the liturgy accompanying the circumcision reaffirms, the circumcision is a sign of the Covenant between God and Abraham's descendants. Thus the Hebrew term for it is *brit milah*, the Covenant of circumcision. Just as a seal on a document changes the surface of the paper and thus makes its contents permanent, so too circumcision seals the Covenant into the boy's flesh, making it permanent as well. Furthermore, the fact that this seal is on the generative part of the male's body symbolizes that the Covenant lasts from generation to generation. The liturgy also ties the circumcision to Elijah and the hoped-for Messianic times that he will introduce.

Circumcisions usually take place in the family's home. The infant is brought in by family members, especially his grandmothers, and he is put on the lap of one of his grandfathers for the circumcision itself or symbolically before the circumcision, indicating the transferring of the Covenant through the generations. The father is responsible to circumcise his sons, but he typically appoints a specialist (a *mohel*) to do the surgery but says the blessing, acknowledging his duty to bring his son into the Covenant in this way. The boy is named as part of the circumcision ceremony, and parents often explain both the English and Hebrew names they have chosen for him. Ashkenazim (those of Northern and Eastern European ancestry) usually name their children after deceased relatives; Sephardim (descendants of Jews from the Mediterranean basin) customarily name their children after living relatives (especially grandparents, but not parents). Then the attendees say out loud, "Just as he has entered the Covenant, so may he enter the [world of] Torah, the wedding canopy, and good deeds." American Jews are increasingly adding to the traditional liturgy readings in English or Hebrew and songs so that family members and friends can actively participate. A festive meal follows.

Jews never used clitoridectomy to make the same statement about the women of the Covenant. In the role-differentiated society in which Jews lived until modern times, it was sufficient to tie the male head of the household to the Covenant to link his entire family to it as well.

The birth of a girl is instead celebrated with a special blessing recited during the Torah reading of the synagogue service, when her father (and, in Conservative and Reform synagogues, her mother as well) are called to the Torah to bless the baby and name her. In the past several decades, many families have additionally created new ceremonies to welcome the girl into the family and community.

Study of the Torah, the other parts of the Hebrew Bible, and rabbinic literature is a major focus of the Jewish tradition. It begins with teaching children, but in Judaism learning is lifelong. To symbolize that Jews view Jewish learning as sweet, schools often begin first grade by giving the children honey or some other sweet treat.

The Jewish rite of marking adulthood is bar mitzvah (for boys) or bat mitzvah (for girls)—literally, son (or daughter) of the commandments. It takes place at age twelve and a half for girls and thirteen for boys to mark and celebrate the fact that the child is now responsible for his or her own actions in Jewish law. The ceremony focuses on the Jewish texts the child has learned and the commandments she or he has fulfilled in preparation for taking on these adult responsibilities. The young adult chants in Hebrew, with the traditional melodies, some or all of the portions from the Torah and Prophets assigned in the liturgical calendar for the day; that typically includes several chapters of the Torah and a chapter from the Prophets. She or he also prepares a homily based on those readings and may lead all or part of the service. Many synagogues often require, in addition, that eleven- and twelve-year-olds consciously take on thirteen new commandments, including one or more social service projects, a study regimen, and some ritual commandments.

Orthodox synagogues do not allow females to lead the service, and that has meant that girls do not have an equivalent rite. In recent years, though, some Orthodox rabbis have created an alternative ceremony, allowed the young woman to give a homily after services, or permitted her to take part in services reserved for women only.

Far too many stop their Jewish education at bar or bat mitzvah, leaving them with the understanding of Judaism they had at that age. An increasing percentage of teenagers, however, continue their Jewish education in a Jewish day school or after public school hours and in summer camps and youth groups. Furthermore, more and more adult Jews are reclaiming their tradition through serious Jewish study in college and through the rest of life.

The Jewish calendar measures days from sunset to sunset. Thus the Sabbath, for example, begins on Friday at sunset and extends to sunset on Saturday. (Actually, so as not to violate the Sabbath, it begins eighteen minutes before sunset on Friday and ends about a half hour after sunset on Saturday.) On Friday night, it is traditional for parents to bless their children at the Sabbath table as part of the rituals before the meal. The parents put their hands on the head of each of their children in turn. Boys are blessed as Jacob determined, "May God make you like Efraim and Menashe" (Gen. 48:20), and girls are blessed with "May God make you like Sarah, Rebekah, Rachel, and Leah." Then both boys and girls are blessed with the priestly blessing (Num. 6:24–26). Because parents retain the responsibility of educating their children even if they send them to school, it is traditional for parents to discuss with their children during the Sabbath meals what they learned about the Jewish tradition that past week.

Children take special roles during the holidays as well. At the springtime Passover seder (a meal structured with an ordered ritual and much discussion of the Passover story) the youngest child who can asks the Four Questions that begin the conversation; and everyone, including the children, is supposed to be involved in the interpretation and expansion of the story. At the end of the meal the children hide a piece of unleavened bread that the adults have to find (or offer a gift to get back) in order to continue the seder. In early autumn, children often help to build or decorate the hut (*sukkah*) used during the Feast of Booths (Lev. 23:42–43) for meals and sometimes for sleeping. On Hanukkah (usually in December), children often get or give some kind of present each of the eight nights. On Purim (usually in March), children delight, even more than their parents, in dressing up in costume and in making noise each time the wicked Haman's name is mentioned while the book of Esther is chanted in the synagogue.

## Specific Institutions for Children

It is undoubtedly the home that plays the most important role in the Jewish and general formation of the child. Recognizing this, Judaism locates many rituals in the home (the Sabbath table, the seder, the sukkah, and so on). Further, parents are supposed to reinforce the Jewish education that their children receive in the school and synagogue through what they do and say in the home. Jewish art (including ritual objects such as a mezuzah on the doorpost, candlesticks for lighting the Sabbath candles, and special cups for the wine used to sanctify the Sabbath and other holy days) and Jewish music, newspapers, and books adorn a Jewishly committed home so that Judaism can pervade the life of the whole family.

God tells Abraham to teach his children (Gen. 18:19); and the commandment for each Jewish father to do likewise, which appears several times in the Torah, is enshrined in the sections chosen for the first two paragraphs of the Shema (Deut. 6:4–9; 11:13–21), a prayer that Jews recite twice daily. Many parents cannot fulfill this duty, however, because they themselves do not know much about the Jewish tradition, they do not know how to teach it, or they are too busy earning a living. Because of this, Jews created schools as early as the second century C.E.[42] In the United States, some children attend public schools and supplement that with Jewish religious instruction from elementary school through high school in "religious schools" or "Hebrew schools" during the late afternoons or evenings and on the weekends. This can range from two hours a week to as much as eight or ten hours a week. Others attend "day schools," private schools that include general and Jewish subjects during an extended daytime schedule from Monday through Friday. Most Orthodox children, about half of Conservative children, and some Reform and Reconstructionist children attend such day schools.

Each of the four American religious movements and a number of secular Jewish organizations run youth groups and summer camps for preteens and teenagers. In accord with their ideology, these groups engage the children in social, religious, social action, Zionist, athletic, and cultural activities.

## Teachers for the Jewish Present, Guarantors for the Jewish Future

The vital role that children play in both the Jewish present and the Jewish future is possibly best articulated by the following rabbinic story, a fitting ending to an article about the place and value of children in American Jewish life:

> Rabbi Meir taught the following: When the Israelites came to Mount Sinai to receive the Torah, the Holy Blessed One said to them: "By God! Should I give you the Torah? Give Me good guarantors that you will obey it, and [only then] will I give it to you." The people of Israel said: "Master of the universe: Our ancestors will be our guarantors." God answered: "They are not sufficient, for I have found fault with your ancestors, and they would therefore need guarantors for themselves! . . ." The Israelites again spoke: "Then let our Prophets vouch for us." But God answered: "I have found fault with your prophets as well [and they too would need their own guarantors]. . . ." The Israelites said "Our children will be our guarantors." And God said: "They are certainly good guarantors, and I will give you the Torah because of them. . . ."[43]

### NOTES

In the notes below, the following abbreviations are used:

M = Mishnah (edited c. 200 C.E.)

T = Tosefta (edited c. 200 C.E.)

J = Jerusalem (Palestinian) Talmud (edited c. 400 C.E.)

B = Babylonian Talmud (edited c. 500 C.E.)

MT = Maimonides' *Mishneh Torah* (1180);

SA = Joseph Karo's *Shulhan Arukh* (1565), with glosses by Moses Isserles.

1. For a description of this process, especially the legal aspects of the tradition, see Elliot N. Dorff and Arthur Rosett, *A Living Tree: The Roots and Growth of Jewish Law* (Albany: State University of New York Press, 1988).

2. *The National Jewish Population Survey 2000–01: Strength, Challenge, and Diversity in the American Jewish Population* (New York: United Jewish Communities, 2003), available at www.ujc.org (search for NJPS), 7.

3. M Ohalot 7:6. See David M. Feldman, *Birth Control and Abortion in Jewish Law* (New York: New York University Press, 1968), reprinted as *Marital Relations, Birth Control, and Abortion in Jewish Law* (New York: Schocken, 1973), esp. chaps. 14 and 15.

4. See Feldman, *Birth Control and Abortion in Jewish.*

5. B Shabbat 135b; *MT* Laws of Mourning 12:10. M Niddah 5:3, however, states that from the moment of birth, the child is to his or her parents and relatives "like a bridegroom [or bride]." That is, they presume that the child will live to be married, even if society is not certain until a month later.

6. Stephanie Dickstein, "Jewish Ritual Practice Following the Death of an Infant Who Lives Less Than Thirty-one Days," in *Responsa 1991–2000 of the Committee on Jewish Law and Standards of the Conservative Movement,* ed. Kassel Abelson and David J. Fine (New York: Rabbinical Assembly, 2002), 439–449.

7. *MT* Laws of Marriage 2:10.

8. *MT* Laws of the Virgin Lass *(na'arah betullah)* 3:2. There is an ambiguity here, though, in that Jewish law punishes a man who has sex with a girl from three years of age to twelve and a half: *MT* Laws of the Virgin Lass 1:8.

9. *MT* Laws of Marriage 2:1, 2.

10. B Sanhedrin 71a; *MT* Laws of Rebels 7:5–6.

11. Sarah: Genesis 15:2–4; 18:1–15. Rebekah: Genesis 25:21. Rachel: 30:1–8, 22–24. Hannah: 1 Samuel 1:1–20. Rachel dies in childbirth: Genesis 35:16–20.

12. So, for example, God's blessings for each of the Patriarchs is children, as it is for all who obey the commandments: Genesis 15:5, 17:4–21, 18:18, 22:15–18, 26:4–5, 28:13–15, 32:13, Leviticus 26:9; Deuteronomy 7:13–14; 28:4, 11; Psalms 128:6.

13. *The National Jewish Population Survey 2000–01,* 6.

14. For a popular version of the statistics on infertility, see Nancy Gibbs, "Making Time for a Baby," *Time,* April 15, 2002, 49–58.

15. Sergio DellaPergola, "World Jewish Population 2007," in *The American Jewish Yearbook 2007,* ed. David Singer and Lawrence Grossman (New York: American Jewish Committee, 2007), 551.

16. *National Jewish Population Survey 2000–2001*, 4.

17. Ibid., 16, 18.

18. Ibid., 19.

19. B Ketubbot 43a, 67a, 108b; B Bava Batra 139b, 140b.

20. B Kiddushin 31b. Cf. *MT* Laws of Rebels 6:3; *SA* Yoreh De'ah 240:2, 4; 228:11.

21. Specifically, Jacob ben Asher (1270?–1340, Germany, Spain) in Tur, Yoreh De'ah 240 and Moses Isserles (1525 or 1530–1572, Poland) in *SA* Yoreh De'ah 240:18, gloss, assert this. Moses Maimonides (1135–1204, Spain, Morocco, Israel, Egypt) in *MT* Laws of Rebels 6:11) and Joseph Karo (1488–1575, Spain, Portugal, Turkey, and Israel) in *SA* Yoreh De'ah 240:18, however, maintain that even abused children must carry out the duties of honor and respect for their parents. The psychological extensions of this are based on the stories of Dama, son of Netinah, and Rabbi Assi in B Kiddushin 31b; Dama's mother insulted him in public, and Rabbi Assi's made unreasonable demands of him (to find her a husband as handsome as he was!).

22. J Pe'ah 1:1 (15c); cf. B Kiddushin 31a-31b; *SA* Yoreh De'ah 240:4.

23. B Kiddushin 29a.

24. See Elliot N. Dorff, *Love Your Neighbor and Yourself: A Jewish Approach to Modern Personal Ethics* (Philadelphia: Jewish Publication Society, 2003), chap. 4.

25. B Kiddushin 29a.

26. B Ketubbot 50a; 67a-67b.

27. M Makkot 2:2; B Makkot 8a-8b. Nevertheless, some medieval and early modern rabbis opposed corporal punishment. See Gerald Blidstein, *Honor Thy Father and Thy Mother* (New York: Ktav, 1975), 123–126, 208–209.

28. Elliot N. Dorff, "Family Violence," in *Responsa 1991–2000 of the Committee on Jewish Law and Standards of the Conservative Movement*, ed. Kassel Abelson and David J. Fine (New York: Rabbinical Assembly, 2002), 773–816, esp. 782–785, 793–794, reprinted in Dorff, *Love Your Neighbor and Yourself*, 155–206, especially 166–171.

29. B Ketubbot 40b; Niddah 44b-45a; *MT* Laws of Marriage 3:11; Laws of the Virgin Lass 1:8.

30. *MT* Laws of Marriage 3:11, 19.

31. Tosafot, Kiddushin 41a; *SA* Even Ha-Ezer 37:8, gloss.

32. B Yevamot 96a–96b; Kiddushin 16b, 63b–64a; Sanhedrin 54b–55a; Niddah 32b, 45a, 47b.

33. B Kiddushin 29b-30a.

34. For example, *MT* Laws of Ethics (De'ot) 4:19. The *Boy Scout Handbook* continued to assert such beliefs into the 1950s!

35. Elliot N. Dorff, *"This Is My Beloved, This Is My Friend": A Rabbinic Letter on Intimate Relations* (New York: Rabbinical Assembly, 1996); reprinted in Dorff, *Love Your Neighbor and Yourself*, chap. 3.

36. For military service, see Numbers 1:3, 20, 22, 24, and others; for levitical service at age twenty-five, see Numbers 8:24; for this service at age thirty, see Numbers 4:3, 23, 30, and others.

37. Leviticus 27:1–7. See *MT* Laws of Valuations and Annulments 1:10.

38. B Sukkah 42a; *MT* Laws of Study (Talmud Torah) 1:6.

39. M Ethics of the Fathers (Avot) 5:23 (5:21 in some editions).

40. T Sanhedrin 7:3; B Sanhedrin 36b; *MT* Laws of Courts (Sanhedrin) 2:3.

41. B Ta'anit 7a; B Makkot 10a.

42. B Bava Batra 21a.

43. Song of Songs Rabbah 1:23 on Song of Songs 1:4.

# 5

# The Black Church and Children

CHERYL TOWNSEND GILKES

He shall feed His flock like a shepherd,
And carry the young lambs in His bosom.
–R. Nathaniel Detts, "Listen to the Lambs"

For the Lamb which is in the midst of the throne shall feed them, . . . and
God shall wipe away all tears from their eyes.
And God shall wipe away all tears from their eyes. . . . And . . . was there
the tree of life, . . . and the leaves of the tree were for the healing of the
nations.
–Revelation 7:17, 21:4a, 22:1–2

There is a vision living at the core of African American Christianity.[1] In that vision, articulated by John on the Isle of Patmos, there is a tree of life whose leaves are for "the healing of the nations" and a promise that God "shall wipe away all tears." Over the centuries, the preaching and music traditions have evoked and firmly implanted an image of God as loving parent through songs and prayers that celebrate God as mother to the motherless and father to the fatherless. That loving parent gathers his children, his little lambs, in his bosom—carrying, comforting, and caring for them.[2] Like a mother cleaning and kissing skinned knees, or, in the words of James Weldon Johnson, "like a Mammy bending over her baby," God offers a model of care that is personal and intimate.[3] At the same time God acts to bring freedom and liberation—"the healing of the nations." These two disparate activities, intimate personal care and social transformation, are endpoints on a continuum of religion and spirituality. This continuum is at the foundation of the Black Church and its approach to children, past and present, and emerged from the crisis of oppressive experience that is unique to black people in the United States.[4] One can argue that this crisis has always focused on the challenge of birthing and sustaining children first in slavery and then in the

85

context of every subsequent form of racial oppression with its specific manifestations of economic exploitation, social disadvantage, political exclusion, and cultural humiliations.

Children are perhaps the most important and enduring problem of practical theology for the Black Church in the United States. Every Children's Day, the second Sunday in June, black congregations remind themselves and their children that Jesus said, "Suffer the little children to come unto me and forbid them not, for of such is the kingdom of Heaven" and who warned that if we should "offend one of these little ones, that believe in me, it is better for him that a millstone were hanged about his neck, and that he were cast into the sea."[5] Throughout the biblical text, the prophets speak of "the widows and orphans" and remind the Black Church that God is a "father to the fatherless." Both historical circumstance and biblical mandate have made children the impetus for religious organization and spiritual practice within the Black Church. Although the executive secretary of a national black religious organization insisted that the Black Church needs a theology of children and childhood, the language of childhood, family, and kinship can be found at the core of African American religious practices and the construction of community.

Among African Americans, the sacred is the basis for imagining and operationalizing community. Whereas church and community among white people in America often involve specialized voluntary organizations, for African Americans church and community involve all the necessities of social life, the issues of survival in order to thrive and advance in hostile circumstances. In contradistinction to the racist dehumanization imposed by the dominating society, the starting point for membership in the black community is being simply and most profoundly "a child of God."[6]

Childhood and family are at the heart of African American Christian self-definition. Understanding the Black Church and its approaches to children involves understanding African American Christians' beliefs and practices surrounding children and their importance within the church and community. The practices of the Black Church have never been limited to the sphere of worship but also involve activism aimed at social transformation and social justice. This is particularly true with regard to public activism surrounding the problems facing children. As a result the prophetic practices of black Christians surrounding children have had discernible effects on public policy. An examination of the impact of black Christians and the Black Church on public policy allows us to draw inferences about the Black Church and its concerns for children. Ironically, the most visible and vigorous public advocacy surrounding children has been carried out through organizations outside the Black Church, organizations often created, shaped, or sustained by African American Christian women invoking the names and mission of the church.[7]

This chapter selectively reviews and describes the relationship of the Black Church and children. It argues that the Black Church has been one of the central engines of nurturance in the lives of most black children. In fact, when black family resources were limited, it was the Black Church that supplemented those resources. The Black Church is rooted in slave religion, and the problem of "stolen" and destroyed childhoods is a fundamental feature of this experience. In the face of AIDS, addiction, abuse, and gangs, the problem of stolen and destroyed childhoods persists. The persistence of inequality has perpetuated, destroyed, and disfigured childhoods among black Americans such that the life chances of black children remain among the worst in the nation and a powerful indicator of social policies inimical to all children, especially those who are poor. The Black Church is, and has been from its beginnings, an agency of socialization. Sociologists usually identify the family as an agency of primary socialization and all other aspects of social organization outside the family as agencies of secondary socialization. The Black Church, because it is an organization of families, is an agency of both primary and secondary socialization. The church, along with other aspects of community organization, also serves as a source of social and cultural capital for black children. Because of the pervasive problem of racial oppression and its destructiveness of black children, the church also participates in the constant struggle to establish the humanity of black children and to forge an inclusive future for them. Finally, the current reorganization of black communities, particularly the increased class segregation and the extensive geographic and social mobility of those who are well educated and credentialed, presents challenges to the contemporary church. Contemporary social problems, especially those related to impoverished youth, represent the most significant challenges to the contemporary black church that demand a practical theological response.

## Children: They Are the Church

Most African American children have an experience with church. If their parents do not bring them to church, they may send them to Sunday school with a neighbor's children or with relatives. Those children whom we would classify as "unchurched" sometimes come with their "churched" friends for special occasions such as Children's Day, Christmas, Easter, or the annual church picnic. Unchurched African American parents, sometimes through the promptings of the churched relatives, think that it is important for their infants to be dedicated, christened, or baptized. Black parents who are raised in or members of traditions practicing "believers' baptism" think that it is important for their children to be baptized, at the very least, by the age of twelve.[8] The folk belief that one needs to be "in the arc of safety" by the age of twelve is very strong. However, Baptist and other churches that do not baptize infants do practice baby "dedication." Baby dedications involve the public presentation of the child and the public pledge by "godparents" to care materially and spiritually for the child as if she or he were their own. If the parents are not members of the church, there are usually grandparents or other family members with enough clout to encourage the pastor to bless the child and to encourage the parents to bring the child to be blessed.[9] The theology undergirding baby dedication is the biblical mandate found in the stories of Samuel and Jesus. Samuel's mother, Hannah, offers Samuel to God in thanksgiving to God for her conceiving and bearing a son. Eventually Samuel, as a young child, hears and answers the call of God. The image presented in the story is of an eager little boy who, upon hearing his name called, persists in running to Eli the priest, who finally recognizes that it is God calling him and instructs the little boy to respond, "Speak, Lord; for thy servant heareth."[10] African American religious tradition underscored this story with the spiritual "Hush, Hush, Somebody's Calling My Name." That image is further strengthened by Joseph and Mary's presentation of Jesus in the Temple where Simeon and Anna both affirmed Jesus' redemptive and salvific role. Shortly after that Luke also tells the story of Jesus as a boy in the Temple.[11] Both stories are used as an argument for baby dedication and are often appealed to as an argument for the early inclusion of children in the life of the church if they are eager to participate.

Children are a taken-for-granted feature of black churches. Preaching to and with crying babies has, until recently, been a standard feature of the Sunday morning experience. One preacher joked to me that "you know when the service has gone too long because the babies start crying." Most parents with infants and toddlers discover that there is an eager group of adolescent girls who are happy to hold and care for the children during service. The parents who bring infants and toddlers to church are usually women. Ironically, black churches are divided over whether to have a separate children's church or even a nursery for children during the service. Many people feel that children should be treated as apprentice church members and that they should be in the service with their parents and the rest of the church family. Younger members sometimes argue for the importance of a religious experience adapted to the children's special capacities, while a significant constituency thinks that Sunday school should suffice for a specialized children's experience.

In the late nineteenth century and up until the 1960s that sense of apprenticeship ran so deep that a large number of churches had junior deacons, deaconesses, trustees, and junior usher boards. Junior usher boards and junior choirs are the most long-lasting contemporary survivors. Some black churches established a "cradle roll" as part of the Sunday school so that infants and toddlers had a place to be during Sunday school, and their names were publicly posted as part of the church body. However, when it is time for the worship service, everyone, including children, should be present.

In the Black Church, Sunday school is the most important activity involving children. During my own childhood (1950s and 1960s) some churches had a "report from the Sunday school" during the main worship service where the children (and sometimes the adult students as well) recited their memory verses for the congregation, answered questions from their pastor, and presented their offering. Nearly every black church celebrates Children's Day (the second Sunday in June); in some churches the children run the entire service and in others the children from the Sunday school are responsible for everything except the sermon. At Christmas and Easter, the Sunday school children provide a program to which the entire church is invited. Students from the oldest to the very youngest provide skits, songs, and recitations. Still today, the most popular aspects of these programs are the recitations by the youngest children. Very prominent African Americans, for instance, Oprah Winfrey and Henry Louis Gates Jr., identify these recitations at Easter or Christmas as their very first public speaking experiences. Most college-educated African Americans can point to their experiences of public speaking in church, and the thunderous adulation and affirmation that followed, as a significant aspect of their personal development. Even the child who has to be prompted through every word receives an enthusiastic and affirming response.

In spite of its centrality and importance, Sunday school in the Black Church is fraught with contradictions. Eric Lincoln and Lawrence Mamiya point out that the economic limitations of large segments of the community means that black churches often use Sunday school literature that ignores the black experience and fails to depict black people in any meaningful way:

> Although the majority of black clergy felt that it was important to have black figures portrayed in Sunday School literature, an informal survey of that literature used by the major black denominations revealed that only the black Methodist denominations (A.M.E., A.M.E. Zion, C.M.E.) were consistent in having black figures in their Sunday School literature. Many black Baptist and Pentecostal [congregations] continued to use educational materials put out by white denominations, especially Southern Baptists. In fact there is an increasing trend among black Baptists, especially in the South, of maintaining secondary affiliations with the Southern Baptists, entitling them to receive Sunday School materials and educational support from the white denomination.[12]

Although pastors are aware of the importance of black images for developing a healthy sense of racial identity, economic limitations and aggressive marketing practices limit the consistency with which black churches use Sunday school literature portraying the black experience. However, as one pastor told Lincoln and Mamiya, "'The Church has an obligation to teach about the contributions of our race. . . . If we don't do this, where are our kids going to get it.'"[13]

The other most significant experience of black children in their churches is the choir. Lincoln and Mamiya were amazed to discover that even the poorest and smallest churches had at least two choirs. The average number was at least three (2.89). Nearly 30 percent of black churches have four or more choirs. Singing is a central activity and it is something that children and teenagers are eager to do.[14] Because of the children's eagerness and the centrality of music to African American spiritual practice, the area of music is a significant opportunity for black children to acquire social and cultural capital.

Some church choirs involve children as young as two years old and perhaps younger.[15] I once watched a large junior choir of about sixty voices sing at an afternoon program. The larger children carried the smaller children to the front of the church and placed them on the choir stand. However, all of them knew how watch the director and wait for her signal. Very loudly and very clearly and very much in key, the children sang, "Jesus is a rock in a weary land . . . a shelter in the time of storm!" They were stunning. Some of the littlest children are some of the best church soloists. In my own congregation we have a little four-year-old who sings a knockout version of "Jesus Loves Me" while standing on her left leg and with her right leg bent behind her so she can hold on to her right ankle for security. A variety of black popular singers describe similar early childhood experiences where the affirmation of the congregation was the first indication that they had any talent. Children in black churches are also able to develop their talents on musical instruments. Church musicians will let little children use the instruments if they express an interest and these musicians sometimes develop an additional stream of income by providing lessons. Since the ability to play by ear is still highly appreciated, the church sanctuary and its instruments are also an important resource. Within the Church of God in Christ, choir directors, led by the ministry of Mattie Moss Clarke, have encouraged church musicians to attain classical training in addition to their ability to play by ear. Such double training has also placed black musicians at an advantage in high school and college music programs. In poor school districts where opportunities for ensemble singing and instrument training are limited or nonexistent in the public schools, these opportunities in the Black Church provide a significant opportunity that would otherwise not exist.

As children grow older, the opportunities for public participation in worship and the development of their talents expand. In addition to the youth and young adult choirs, there are organizations within black churches, particularly choirs and usher boards, that have developed organizational networks beyond the congregation. Sometimes called parachurch organizations, these also expand the opportunities that build black children's social and cultural capital.

One such organization is the National Association of Gospel Choirs and Choruses, an organization founded and developed by the "father" of gospel music, Thomas A. Dorsey.[16] During the final evening of the weeklong annual meeting of the National Convention of Gospel Choirs and Choruses, the youth concert takes place. Not only do all the "young people"—meaning everyone from children to very old young adults (early thirties)—participates in a choir that can be as large as six hundred voices. Young gospel music composers compete, first to have their music included in the concert repertoire—a repertoire that must be learned in a week—and then to see which song is chosen as "song of the year." It takes one of these concerts before one realizes that the popular musical artists who "make it" are only the tip of a very, very large iceberg of exceptionally talented black people. During the week, young people are able to get keyboard lessons and tutoring in workshops. Such realizations are repeated at organizations such as the Gospel Music Workshop and the Choir Directors' and Organists' Guild of Hampton University where musical talent is similarly nurtured. At Hampton, the guild also reinforces the importance of collegiate training in the musical arts for the service of the church. Other organizations, particularly of church ushers, also help children, adolescents, and young adults use their talents to compete for scholarships, providing another layer of reinforcement for academic achievement, particularly in the oratorical and musical arts.

Most black musical artists get their start in their churches. When they receive awards, for instance, the Grammy, the artists are sincere when they are thanking God, irrespective of how nasty and sacrilegious their music may be. Participation in church choirs is one of the most significant age-graded experiences for black children. It is also an experience in which expressions of talent are encouraged and where the truly gifted get a "head start." In his recent analysis of American congregations, Mark Chaves discussed the role of congregations in making the performing arts and artists available. When comparing black and white congregations, Chaves observed: "African American congregations apparently expose their constituents to more artistic activity than other congregations—a finding consistent with standard observations about the internally rich cultural life of organized black religion in the United States—but African American congregations do not facilitate contact with outside art worlds any more (or less) than white congregations."[17] Chaves failed to note, however, that instead of facilitating contact with outside art worlds, African American congregations are, in fact, sources of artists for these outside worlds and often are in conflict with the values and behaviors of these secular art worlds. What Chaves did not account for in observing this difference is the fact that black churches are the primary sources of popular and classical artists. Rather than paying artists to come in, black churches send artists out, artists whose principal creative growth occurred during their childhoods in the church.[18] The most prominent popular artists with church roots, among them Whitney Houston, Aretha Franklin, Billy Preston, Sam Cooke, and Toni Braxton, represent the blazingly prominent top of a mountain of black artists who serve as church-bred backup singers and instrumentalists in recording studios and on stage. Only recently, with the emergence of large churches with professionalized music ministries, have there been occupational avenues within the church for a large number of exceptionally talented black youngsters.[19]

Another important source of apprenticeship and service for children can be found in the junior usher boards. Usually connected to local, state, and regional networks of church ushers through the Interdenominational Association of Church Ushers, the children who participate as ushers not only serve in their local congregations but also are shepherded into a range of other activities that develop their musical talents and potential for leadership. Shaped through the biblical motto "I had rather be a doorkeeper in the house of my God than to dwell in the tents of wickedness," these children and teenagers are trained in the standardized practices of black church ushers—seating, crowd control, collecting offerings, emergency preparedness, and worshipful presence during Sunday service.[20] Not only do they participate in church worship as apprentices to the adults, but junior ushers often provide the primary service during monthly youth Sundays, when young people do everything except the sermon.

However, the integration of children in traditional church roles has meant that the level of reflection on precisely how and under what circumstances the Black Church serves children and on the theological foundations and consequences of that service has been low. However, children serve the church in a variety of ways and the folk reflections on their service are a significant core element in an emergent practical theology. The folk wisdom that says that "children are the church" means that their participation is assumed—taken for granted. Although there has been an old aphorism, "Children should be seen and not heard," it is neither true nor practiced in black churches. There are very well-established ritualized ways in which black children are encouraged to be seen and to insert their voices into the overall life of the church. If children express a wish to participate, the biblical models of Samuel and Jesus prompt adults to say yes to their assertiveness. If a child volunteers to read scripture and is too little to see over the pulpit, the response to the problem is "get a box" for her or him to stand on.

Over and over again, children are told that they are the future of the church, indeed they *are* the church, so that the assertive child is offered as many avenues of development as are available.

Practical theology in the Black Church, according to Dale Andrews, is the dynamic encounter between "a prophetic tradition . . . in a history of revelation and interpretation" and a "folk religion [that] reflects the cultural dimensions of beliefs, values, passions, worldview, and ways of knowing, all of which comprise a contextualized life of faith and meaning."[21] Children are the most important and least articulated problem in practical theology. In spite of the pervasive experiences of Sunday school, youth groups and departments, Children's Days, choirs, and "junior" organizations, there has been relatively little formal reflection on their importance. Yet the perpetual crisis of African American childhood has been central to African Americans' definitions of their situations in every historical period. The central emergency facing the church has been the reclamation and redemption of stolen and destroyed childhoods.

## Reclaiming Stolen and Destroyed Childhoods

The first children born of Africans in the New World created a religious crisis. Anthropologists Sidney Mintz and Richard Price have located the origins of African American culture in the "ritual assistance" provided by an individual from one African ethnic group to a member of another upon the birth of a child.[22] In all African cultures, the birth of children required some kind of ritual response. They argue that such interethnic ritual assistance represented "the birth" of African American culture. In the United States, the crisis of community organization occurred in conversation with Christians who eventually evangelized the slaves. The importance of children may be inferred from the activities of the Black Church as it organized and evolved from the churches formed during slavery to the institutions of freedom that reorganized during Reconstruction, confronted Jim Crow, facilitated reorganization during the Great Migration, and mobilized black people during the civil rights movement.

Historian Wilma King has extracted the experience of children during slavery from the larger discussion of slavery and the slave community. She points out that when emancipation occurred, the majority of freed people were under the age of twenty.[23] The United States was the first New World slave society to rely on natural increase, thus making the importation of African women a central strategy for exploitation. Two forces made women vital to the U.S. system of slavery: the exploitation of black women's fertility and the integration of women's roles into systems of African agriculture transplanted to the New World, for instance, rice growing.[24] Children's experiences were deeply embedded in the narratives about slavery and usually come to us through the voices of those who survived childhood and often lived lives of significance and distinction. The vast majority of enslaved children's experiences were enmeshed in the hardships of daily toil and survival that defined the black experience for more than 240 years. Since many children did not live to adulthood, survival was the most important childhood achievement.

Surviving childhood as slaves required that children learn not only what parents and other kin taught them, but also what their peer groups and the clandestine congregation, also known as the "invisible church," provided. Thomas Webber examined the education and socialization of children in the antebellum slave community. There were two primary interests at work, the master's and the slave community's. Webber described and analyzed the role of the slave quarters community as an agency of socialization and pointed to the clandestine congregation as a setting for learning that was almost as important as the children's family of blood and fictive kin and their peer group. Webber identified a number of themes that came through in slave narratives; several of those themes reflected the integrated roles of the family and congregation: the importance of community, the true religion of the slave community, the false religion of slaveholders, the primary importance of the spirit world, the primacy of learning to read and write, and the desire to be free. Slave children described the importance of hearing their mothers and aunts pray, especially for freedom, and they learned to protect and defend the clandestine congregation.[25]

Children, as they grew, became increasingly integrated into the world of work. The exploitation of all potential laborers was routine, so children's value was defined in terms of their ability to work and their growing potential as exploited labor. For some children, childhood involved apprenticeships with skilled workers such as blacksmiths and house servants. For others, their apprenticeship involved learning to work in the fields in order to grow as agricultural laborers. As children became more integrated as workers, they also experienced traumas and tragedies that robbed them of their childhoods. In addition to overwork, punitive violence and sexual assaults often brought suffering that terminated childhood as a protected space of learning and growth.

For the small proportion of slaves who learned to read, literacy was thoroughly integrated with spirituality.[26] While many historians estimate that 5 percent of the slave population could read on the eve of emancipation, Janet Cornelius argues that the numbers may have been higher.[27] One of the sources of literacy, perhaps the principal source, was the Bible. It was the most important primer for American culture at that time, and a few slave owners, before they were constrained by custom and the law, thought it their Christian duty to teach slaves to read. Literacy and spirituality were also linked among those Africans who were Muslim; their love for the Qur'an facilitated an attitude that favored learning to read what one freedman called "that blessed book." Historians, as a result, uniformly described an inseparable linkage between "the gospel and the primer."[28]

The crisis of destroyed and stolen childhoods continued after slavery with the debt peonage system. Large numbers of children were incarcerated and rented out to farmers and other employers. Not only did the children work alongside adults gathering crops, building roads, clearing forests, but they also endured death rates even higher than during slavery. The loss of their status as the property of the powerful placed their lives at greater risk than that endured during slavery.[29] Here the struggle over education was fierce, with black Reconstruction politicians, many of them ministers, leading the move to create public schools in the South. As would continue to be the case, all children benefited from the actions taken on behalf of black children. When Reconstruction ended, white supremacists kept the public school system, but as a segregated one.

To combat the resistance of the South to supporting black education, the Julius Rosenwald Foundation offered black communities matching funds to build schools. Black churches, often through their Sunday schools and Children's Day, raised tremendous amounts of money to meet the Rosenwald challenge. Both black and white denominations supported schools and sent educators to the South. The emerging leadership class of educators consisted of male preachers and women teachers; the women were often Christians seeking posts as missionaries or teaching school as an alternative to pastoring and preaching the gospel.

Because and in spite of the discrimination they faced, black women militantly and enthusiastically invested their talents in education. The vital and seemingly unbreakable connection between family and church was strengthened even more through the work of churchwomen who saw their mission as education and demanded an educated ministry. As the denominational organizations of black churches grew, black women controlled the missionary societies and supported, through those societies, the nurturance of children "in the Lord" both in the church and in the classroom.[30] The role of churches in the founding of black colleges was equally significant. Education was so embedded in the mission of black churches that the largest bodies, the Baptist Conventions, supported meetings focused on Christian education in addition to their annual meetings. Large numbers of children attended these conferences along with their parents and teachers. These Christian education conferences often introduced children to the religious world beyond their local communities and to the role models they needed to inspire them.

Urbanization and the Great Migration challenged churches in new ways that served to reinforce their importance as educational institutions. Some churches became "institutional" in their approach to serving their members, by providing a range of services, including adult education, employment, and cultural enrichment. Once again the provision of social and cultural capital was part of the sacred work of the church. Whereas the family has been characterized as a "haven in a heartless world," among African Americans the church became not only a haven but also a "rock in a weary land" by providing an alternative to instruction. Most important, the operations of the church continued to reinforce and concretize its beliefs about black people's full humanity while edifying the members not only with the formal doctrines of the faith but also with a tremendous amount of broader education and exhortations to become educated.

## Humanity, Family, Church, and Society: The Enduring Problem

During the 1960s, the Moynihan Report precipitated a debate over the historical role and functional efficacy of the African American family.[31] An important alternative assessment identified the religious orientation of black families as one of the central strengths that had enabled black people to withstand the destructive forces of slavery and subsequent forms of racial oppression.[32] Although wounded by their experiences, black people of all ages found in their churches an important "balm in Gilead" for the manifest and hidden injuries that came with life in racialized and racist America.

The civil rights movement produced a new black community. Those with education, talents, and credentials have been able to secure new locations within new neighborhoods and new social locations. This has led to the growth of new churches with transplanted populations who have been geographically, socially, or economically mobile. In a significant number of cases, people have experienced all forms of mobility at once. The black power movement and the challenge of Islam and other forms of nationalism have transformed the problems of cultural identity so that many of these new congregations have developed more Afrocentric approaches to biblical interpretation and to their historical role as educators and providers of social and cultural capital. The challenge of class mobility has generated a renewed concern with "prosperity" and the transformation of people's economic consciousness. Indeed, a tension has developed between churches whose ministries are viewed as progressive and prophetic and those whose ministries are viewed as centered primarily on prosperity. Those very large black churches classified as megachurches sometimes evince both orientations, celebrating the newly prosperous black middle class and gathering significant economic resources with which they are able to build schools, generate generous scholarship funds, hire youth ministers who can generate after-school programs, and build youth ministries that stretch beyond the walls of the church.

Sometimes when new churches are built, the congregation retains the old church edifice. Since it is often closer to the "hood," as the urban ghetto neighborhood is termed, the old church edifice can be dedicated to a full-time youth ministry that includes Sunday worship as well as community outreach. The Allen AME Church in Queens, New York, has developed precisely such a progressive approach to youth ministry alongside the economic education necessary to facilitate the stabilization of a new black middle class. The role of the Black Church as an agency of socialization and as cultivator of social and cultural capital remains as it addresses new problems and dynamic new social formations.

For African Americans who have lost ground and remain locked in disproportionately impoverished urban ghettoes, the church can be both a resource and a source of antagonism. Congregations exploding with newly middle-class and mobile members face choices that entail both outreach to and protection from the members of the community who have been left behind. As Omar McRoberts's research has shown us, impoverished urban ghettoes become the victims of newer congregations whose memberships enjoy cheaply rented worship spaces but, since the members are not geographic residents, fail to develop the community's infrastructure and advance the immediate neighborhood's social and economic stability.[33] These churches do not fulfill the historic role of the Black Church. These churches place their primary efforts with their own children, whose connections with the surrounding neighborhood may be antagonistic at best; they are admonished not to be like the church's immediate neighbors.

Megachurches in urban ghettoes find themselves hiring security forces to protect their property at the same time as they provide worship and social services for the neighborhood residents. These churches may also be required to protect the more affluent nonresident members from the criminal predations most often associated with poverty. By contrast, the professionalization that both the membership and leadership of these larger churches sometimes bring delivers resources to the surrounding community, creating new partnerships between commuter and resident church members. Increasingly, those megachurches that actively build relationships with their local communities, for example, Abyssinian Baptist Church in Harlem, in New York City; Bethel AME and Payne Memorial AME Churches in Baltimore; Trinity United Church of Christ in Chicago; Shiloh Baptist Church of Washington, DC; and First AME Church in Los Angeles use auxiliary charitable organizations, foundations, and community development corporations to carry out their missions to children among the membership and in the surrounding communities. Defending black childhood against the assaults of the popular culture is, for some of these churches, a full-time job, and they have the money and the staff to do so.

All these changes present new challenges at the same time they make demands for more of the traditional commitment to combat the theft and destruction of black childhood. The emergencies facing black children continue to present a crisis to the Black Church requiring it to confront the moral failures of prevailing social policy.

The language of family remains suffused throughout the Black Church. While family is affirming and uplifting, confirming the common humanity of the body of believers, it is also a close-knit primary group whose boundaries are difficult to penetrate. As new social boundaries arise and old ones are reconfigured, black churches are facing the demand for paradigm shifts that address new problems affecting the family. The shame associated with the problems of poverty often means that the church does not learn about family emergencies involving children until after the state—an institution often hostile to the intervention of the church, especially the Black Church—has irrevocably intervened. For those among whom Orlando Patterson has recently called "the disconnected fifth," the emergencies of stolen and destroyed childhoods persist.[34]

Children are the future, and those children who are present and assertively active in the church are the core of every generation of effective black leadership. Children continue to be the primary motivation for the most effective challenges that African Americans have mounted against the racial oppression they have faced in America. From the ritual assistance offered across ethnoreligious lines in the slave community; to the church-community collaborations for formal education; to Martin Luther King Jr.'s poignant description of the damage his children sustained when faced with the realities of segregation; to the effective faith-based organizations and their mobilizations around poverty, education, violence, and what the Children's Defense Fund calls the "cradle-to-prison pipeline"—the church and the child have been inextricably linked. In spite of the lack of an explicitly child-centered theology, the Black Church has been one of the central engines of nurturance and concerted cultivation in the lives of most black children.[35] Faithful to the biblical mandates that advise parents to present their children before the church and that rebuke those who would block children's access to Jesus, the church setting has been open to black children when all other avenues of human development have been closed. When black family resources were limited, it was the Black Church that supplemented those resources by supporting the community's efforts to provide education or by providing opportunities for the development of social and cultural capital within and beyond the congregation. When black family resources are overabundant, the church can also be a vehicle for teaching the importance of sharing and ministry to "the least of these."

American society has often operated as a vehicle of destruction in the lives of black children and the church has been significant in opposing that destructiveness. Within the continuum that comprises both intimate nurturance of the individual (carrying the lambs) and collective and organized opposition to institutions and social forces that destroy black people (healing nations), the Black Church has embraced children in a way that has consistently affirmed the full personhood of all people in their relationship to God. In a world of depersonalizing political economies and destructive public politics, that embrace sings constantly and consistently, "If anybody asks you who you are, tell them you're a child of God." That song, along with the persistent biblically based assertion that "God is no respecter of persons," has been the most significant starting point of a practical theology that redeems and re-creates childhood. Early in the twentieth century, W.E.B. Du Bois prayed a prayer that still defines the mission of the Black Church with and for us all: "Mighty causes are calling us—the freeing of women, the training of children, the putting down of hate and murder and poverty—all these and more. But they call us with voices that mean work and sacrifice and death."[36] These mighty causes persist in serving as the most vital foundation for a constructive theology of children in the Black Church. As history near and distant has shown, when the Black Church succeeds in its advocacy for children, the lambs can be carried and the nation healed.

## NOTES

1. Throughout this chapter I will use the phrases *the Black Church* and *African American Christianity* to denote the totality of predominantly black congregations and denominations in the United States. There is no one volume that analyzes the history and complexity of the hundreds of religious networks that constitute "the Black Church." For an understanding of how diverse, numerous, and complexly organized black religious organizations can be, see Wardell Payne, ed., *Directory of African American Religious Bodies: A Compendium by the Howard University School of Divinity* (Washington, DC: Howard University Press, 1991).

2. See also Alice Walker, "The Welcome Table," in *In Love and In Trouble: Stories of Black Women* (New York: Harcourt Brace Jovanovich, 1973), 81–87.

3. James Weldon Johnson, *God's Trombones: Seven Negro Sermons in Verse* (New York: Viking Penguin, 1927), 20.

4. In spite of the recent emphases on the African Diaspora and the Black Atlantic, I focus on the people, organizations, and institutions in the United States. At times, for stylistic purposes, I may refer to *the United States* and *America* interchangeably.

5. Mark 10:14b, 9:42 KJV (King James Version).

6. Like the term *the Black Church*, the term *the black community* may carry a totalizing implication that masks tremendous varieties of geographic and social locations.

My use of the term *black community* is grounded in James Blackwell's *The Black Community: Diversity and Unity* (1974; New York: HarperCollins, 1991).

7. See especially http://www.childrensdefense.org/site/PageServer, the Web site for the Children's Defense Fund, an organization devoted to child advocacy founded and led by civil rights activist and lawyer Marian Wright Edelman. See also Marian Wright Edelman, *Guide My Feet: Prayers and Meditations on Loving and Working for Children* (Boston: Beacon Press, 1995). Beginning in 1896, the National Association of Colored Women sought the primary, elementary, and secondary education of children; housing for unwed mothers and their children; and the education of black women who were the principals of schools funded by Baptist and Methodist Churches.

8. The largest denominational traditions among African Americans are the Baptist groups and the Church of God in Christ. These traditions require that one be capable of making a coherent profession of faith in order to be baptized, assessed by deacons and deaconesses. The Methodist traditions (AME, AMEZ, and CME) baptize infants and often insist on enforcing the "one baptism" rule when faced with adults and children who wish rebaptism by immersion.

9. Black churches struggle with how to deal with unwed mothers and their babies, sometimes dedicating the babies and including the grandparents along with the mother and the godparents, sometimes insisting that the mother publicly apologize for her bad behavior and rejoin the church, and more rarely disfellowshipping both the unwed mother and father until such time as he offers to marry the mother of the child.

10. See, in particular, 1 Samuel, chap. 1–3, 1 Samuel 3:9 KJV (King James Version).

11. Luke 2:21–38, 41–52.

12. C. Eric Lincoln and Lawrence H. Mamiya, *The Black Church in the African American Experience* (Durham: Duke University Press, 1990), 317.

13. Ibid., 318.

14. Ibid., 377–378.

15. My assessment of the age of the children came from both size and the telltale bulge that indicated some of them were still in diapers.

16. For an extended discussion of Thomas A. Dorsey's role in the development of gospel music and the National Association of Gospel Choirs and Choruses, see Michael W. Harris, *The Rise of Gospel Blues: The Music of Thomas Andrew Dorsey in the Urban Church* (New York: Oxford University Press, 1992).

17. Mark Chaves, *Congregations in America* (Cambridge: Harvard University Press, 2004), 178.

18. The painful and conflicted relationship between the sacred and the secular has been a permanent crisis in the experience of black performing artists in popular culture. Black churches send a contradictory message that encourages achievement but often does not prepare young people to confront the secular world of entertainment.

19. Lincoln and Mamiya, *The Black Church*, 377–381.

20. Psalms 84:10b, KJV (King James Version).

21. Dale Andrews, *Practical Theology for Black Churches: Bridging Black Theology and African American Folk Religion* (Louisville: Westminster John Knox Pres, 2002).

22. Sidney W. Mintz and Richard Price, *The Birth of African American Culture: An Anthropological Perspective* (1976; Boston: Beacon Press, 1992).

23. Wilma King, *Stolen Childhood: Slave Youth in Nineteenth-Century America* (Bloomington: Indiana University Press, 1995).

24. Deborah Gray White, *Ar'n't I a Woman: Female Slaves in the Plantation South* (New York: Norton, 1985); Judith A. Carney, *Black Rice: The African Origins of Rice Cultivation in the Americas* (Cambridge: Harvard University Press, 2001).

25. Thomas L. Webber, *Deep Like the Rivers: Education in the Slave Quarter Community, 1831–1865* (New York: Norton, 1978).

26. See Wilma King's chapter linking church and literacy, in King, *Stolen Childhood*, 67–90; Leon F. Litwack, *Been in the Storm So Long: The Aftermath of Slavery* (New York: Vintage Books, 1979).

27. Janet Duitsman Cornelius, *When I Can Read My Title Clear: Literacy, Slavery, and Religion in the Antebellum South* (Columbia: University of South Carolina Press, 1991).

28. Litwack, *Been in the Storm So Long.*

29. Richard Wormser, *The Rise and Fall of Jim Crow* (New York: St. Martin's Press, 2003). See also the PBS series of the same name; part 2 graphically depicts the exploitation of child labor through the criminal justice system.

30. See Marcia Y. Riggs, "African American Children, 'The Hope of the Race': Mary Church Terrell, the Social Gospel, and the Work of the Black Women's Club Movement," in *The Child in Christian Thought*, ed. Marcia J. Bunge (Grand Rapids, MI: Eerdmans, 2001), 365–385.

31. For the complete text of Daniel Moynihan's report on "the Negro family," a discussion of the public conflict, and the critical commentary on the report, see Lee Rainwater and William L. Yancey, *The Moynihan Report and the Politics of Controversy* (Cambridge: MIT Press, 1976).

32. For a discussion of this and the four other core strengths see Robert Hill, *The Strengths of Black Families* (New York: Emerson Hall, 1972).

33. See Omar McRoberts, *Streets of Glory: Church and Community in a Black Urban Neighborhood* (Chicago: University of Chicago Press, 2003).

34. Orlando Patterson, "A Poverty of Mind," *New York Times*, 26 March 2006, http://www.nytimes.com/2006/03/26/opinion/26patterson.html.

35. Annette Lareau, *Unequal Childhoods: Class, Race, and Family* (Berkeley and Los Angeles: University of California Press, 2003).

36. W.E.B. Du Bois, *Prayers for Dark People* (Amherst: University of Massachusetts Press, 1980), 21.

# 6

# Latter-day Saint Children and Youth in America

DAVID C. DOLLAHITE

Some of the concepts of the view of childhood held by the Latter-day Saints can be found in stories told about the early life of their founder and first prophet, Joseph Smith. Brother Joseph, as he was known to the Saints, often took time to play games with children and youth. Some Mormons, with their early American sense of propriety about religious leaders, were troubled by Joseph's playful nature. One day a Brother Wakefield came to the Prophet's home to discuss church business. He was told that Brother Joseph was translating the word of God. Brother Wakefield waited some time and when the Prophet appeared he immediately began playing with a group of children. Brother Wakefield considered this action so inconsistent with the calling of a prophet that he left Mormonism.

Joseph's special concern for the spiritual and social well-being of children and youth perhaps derived from his own experiences as a youth. He was very young when he began his earnest search for religious truth and received heavenly manifestations. Religious controversy swelled in the area where he grew up as leaders and members of various churches vied for converts and contended hotly with those of other faiths. As a fourteen-year-old youth, he prayed for answers and received a vision in which he saw God the Father and Jesus, who told him not to join any of these churches. As Joseph told others of his vision, intense persecution from those in his village of Palmyra, New York, followed. But he continued to affirm that he had seen God. He said:

Having been forbidden [by God] to join any of the religious sects of the day, and being of very tender years, and persecuted by those who ought to have been my friends and to have treated me kindly, and if they supposed me to be deluded to have endeavored in a proper and affectionate manner to have reclaimed me—I was left to all kinds of temptations; and, mingling with all kinds of society, I frequently fell into many foolish errors, and displayed the weakness of youth, and the foibles of human nature.[1]

Joseph's love and appreciation for children and youth also derived from his experience growing up in a large and close family. When he married, he and his wife, Emma, created a home that welcomed natural and adopted children. Like many others of that era, they lost several infant children to fatal illnesses. During that time the Lord revealed to Joseph that children who die in infancy are saved in God's kingdom. In addition, he was given revelations concerning the potential for marital and parent-child bonds to last beyond the grave.

Given Joseph Smith's early spiritual and social experiences, his devoted attention to children, and the revelations he received about the divine nature and potential of children and about eternal families, it should not be surprising that Mormonism highly values spiritual development in children and youth—particularly in the context of home and family life.[2] Indeed, its doctrines, covenants, and practices focus on the value of each individual child and helping each to come to know, love, and serve God and His children on earth.

This chapter discusses how children and youth are understood in the Church of Jesus Christ of Latter-day Saints (LDS, Mormon, the Church of Jesus Christ). It focuses on how Mormonism supports and guides children in light of the threats of contemporary American life. In so doing, I address core theological beliefs pertaining to LDS children and youth, major religious practices and institutions involving children and youth, and common challenges faced by American LDS children and youth.

In my discussion here I will address the doctrines that all human beings are spirit children of heavenly parents with whom they lived before birth; that children have eternal potential to become like their heavenly parents; that children are born innocent; that children have moral agency that allows them to make moral choices; that beginning at age eight, children are held accountable for moral decisions; that children who die before they become spiritually accountable are saved; and that gender is part of one's eternal identity.

The beliefs and practice I discuss pertaining to youth comprise the following: youth have obligations to God and to their religious community, all youth are expected to abide by standards of sexual purity, male youth are expected to prepare themselves for future full-time missionary service, and young men and young women are taught to prepare themselves for marriage and family life as the most important religious duties on earth. Further, I will address these religious practices: the naming and blessing of infants; baptism and confirmation of eight-year-old children; ordination to the priesthood of twelve-year-old young men; and temple baptisms, endowments, and sealings of youth and young adults. Before addressing these issues, I identify myself in relation to Mormonism and provide a brief historical and demographic profile of the church.

The reader should know that this chapter is written from the perspective of an active and devoted Latter-day Saint. I was raised an Episcopalian and was an acolyte in that faith as a child. I converted to Mormonism at age nineteen. After serving an LDS mission in New England, I met and married my wife in the Salt Lake Temple and we are raising our seven children in the faith. I have served in various capacities in the church, including as the bishop of a congregation of Brigham Young University (BYU) students. Both my teaching and scholarship at BYU focus on religion and family, including working with other BYU scholars to edit two volumes on LDS marriage and family life.[3] Therefore, I provide a believing insider's perspective on Latter-day Saint children, youth, and family life.

## Historical and Demographic Profile

The Church of Jesus Christ of Latter-day Saints was established in 1830 in upstate New York. The church is considered a restoration of the church and gospel founded by Jesus Christ, which Latter-day Saints believe fell away after the apostles were martyred. From the beginning the Saints were persecuted for their beliefs and practices and were forced from one place to another, finally being led to the Rocky Mountains by Joseph Smith's successor Brigham Young.[4]

As of April 2008, the church had more than 13 million members in 170 nations.[5] More than half of current church members live outside the United States, speak a language other than English, and are converts to the church.[6] Now the fourth-largest and the fastest-growing major religious denomination in the United States, it has about 5.5 million American members.[7] In addition to being the dominant faith in Utah (70 percent) Mormons constitute a significant minority of religious adherents in parts of several states in the intermountain West.[8]

On the basis of growth patterns and its unique doctrine and practice, sociologist Rodney Stark declared Mormonism a "new world faith" and projected a worldwide LDS church membership of more than 50 million by the year 2040.[9] Religious scholar Harold Bloom correctly stated that Mormonism is as distinct from traditional Christianity as Christianity is from Judaism, or as Islam is from Christianity.[10] Latter-day Saints are Christian (their first article of faith enjoins "faith in the Lord Jesus Christ"), but because their beliefs differ from those of traditional Christian theology (for example, they believe that Christ and God the Father are distinct beings), they are considered non-Christian by some other faiths.

## Core Theological Beliefs Pertaining to Children

Core LDS beliefs pertaining to children concern the doctrines of God the Eternal Father, the Lord Jesus Christ, the nature of the human soul, and issues of parental responsibility for the child. A sacred thread running through all LDS beliefs and practices is that the purpose of life is for children and youth to prepare themselves to form eternal marriages and families.

Latter-day Saints believe that God is literally the eternal father of all human beings, who are considered "spirit sons and daughters of heavenly parents."[11] God the Father is a glorified, perfected, omniscient, and perfectly loving and merciful being who has a glorified body of flesh and bones. Young LDS children are taught to pray to "Our Father in Heaven" or "Our Heavenly Father." They are taught to sing the song "I Am a Child of God."

What Latter-day Saints refer to as "Heavenly Father's Plan of Happiness" is the doctrine that guides all church programs, teachings, ordinances (sacraments), and policies. The church provides doctrine, covenants, and ordinances that help children and youth understand and live this plan. The divine plan centers on God's spirit sons and daughters coming to earth through birth so that they can experience mortal life and death; learn to distinguish good from evil and choose good; learn to keep God's commandments and serve Him; and make sacred covenants with God, especially the covenants of baptism and eternal marriage.

Latter-day Saints believe that all human beings are spirit children of heavenly parents (Heavenly Father and Heavenly Mother) and are therefore of infinite and eternal worth and believe that every human being has potential to become like their heavenly parents through the atonement of Jesus Christ and by obedience to the gospel of Jesus Christ. Latter-day Saints hold that the atonement of Jesus Christ is the means by which all people may be forgiven of their sins, become spiritually clean, and return to the presence of God. Because of the atonement of Jesus Christ, "little children," who have not yet arrived at the "age of accountability" (typically age eight) and those who, because of mental or emotional limitations, never become accountable before God for their own sins, are saved in the kingdom of God. Because of the atoning sacrifice of Jesus Christ, children are born innocent. If an infant or child dies before reaching the age of accountability (typically age eight), she or he is saved in the celestial kingdom—the highest of three "degrees of glory" or heavens. LDS scripture states that "every spirit was innocent in the beginning; and God having redeemed man from the fall, men became again, in their infant state, innocent before God."[12]

Latter-day Saints believe that God has granted moral agency or free will to every human being. Thus each child is taught that she or he may choose to believe in God and may "choose the right" through obedience. LDS beliefs and practices strongly emphasize the eternal importance of individual agency, so there are strong prohibitions against coercion in religious upbringing. Parents, leaders, and teachers are expected to exercise kindness, patience, long-suffering, love, and gentleness in all their dealings with their own children and with others of Heavenly Father's children (D&C 121:33–46).

Latter-day Saints believe that gender is part of a person's premortal, mortal, and eternal identity, and there are some gender-specific aspects of being an LDS child or youth. Many things are the same for both genders: boys and girls both are offspring of divine parentage, both have eternal potential to become like their heavenly parents, both are baptized and confirmed and take the Sacrament of the Lord's Supper each week, and both make sacred covenants in holy temples (more will be said about temples later).

The main gendered differences in LDS life involve priesthood and motherhood. Priesthood is conferred only on LDS boys and men. Priesthood's most important responsibilities involve marriage, fatherhood, and service to God's children. LDS boys and men are taught that the most important priesthood service they will ever do will be within their homes. Indeed, priesthood, marriage, and fatherhood are nearly inseparable in LDS doctrine and practice. Motherhood is considered coequal with priesthood and a holy responsibility and opportunity for daughters of God. LDS girls and young women are taught the eternal importance of the divine work they perform in nurturing and providing life to God's children as wives and mothers.

## Parental Responsibility for the Child

Parents have the primary responsibility to nurture children. Children are considered to be God's children, and earthly parents have only a custodial relationship with their children unless and until parents and children are sealed in the temple and remain true to temple covenants throughout this life. Those covenants involve kindness, gentleness, and love toward children and youth. Parents are obligated to teach children and prepare them for baptism (D&C 68:25, 27–28). A well-known passage from the Book of Mormon states: "And ye will not suffer your children that they go hungry, or naked; neither will ye suffer that they transgress the laws of God, and fight and quarrel one with another, and serve the devil . . . but ye will teach them to walk in the ways of truth and soberness; ye will teach them to love one another, and to serve one another."

In an oft-quoted passage from the Doctrine and Covenants, the Lord rebukes an early member of the church by saying, "But I have commanded you to bring up your children in light and truth. . . . You have not taught your children light and truth, according to the commandments; and that wicked one hath power, as yet, over you, and this is the cause of your affliction" (D&C 93:40, 42).

Children are considered a parent's greatest "stewardship" or sacred responsibility, and Latter-day Saints believe that they will have to make an account before God about how they have treated their child (D&C 72:3) and that only if they have been righteous on earth can they expect to have eternal association with their children, who will, like themselves, be mature adults in heaven (what Latter-day Saints call the celestial kingdom).

In addition, the First Presidency and Council of the Twelve Apostles, considered living prophets and apostles, have responsibility to teach and inspire all church members, including children. This is done through semi-annual worldwide General Conference broadcasts from Salt Lake City to homes and church buildings throughout the world and through articles in three monthly magazines that many members subscribe to (the *Ensign* for adults, the *New Era* for youth, and the *Friend* for children).

## Major Practices and Institutions Involving Children and Youth

Religious practices and institutions involving children and youth have been developed on the basis of these foundational doctrines. In this section I will address the following: core religious practices involving children, family religious practices, church institutions for children and youth, changes in childhood traditions, the role of the church at various stages in children's development, the ideal voice of children in the religious community, and changes in programs for children and youth over time.

There are several central religious practices pertaining to children, among them naming and blessing of children, baptism, confirmation, ordaining to the priesthood, missionary service, and temple endowments and sealings. In the Doctrine and Covenants it states, "Every member of the church of Christ having children is to bring them unto the elders before the church, who are to lay their hands upon them in the name of Jesus Christ, and bless them in his name" (D&C 20:70). Typically the "naming and blessing" of a child is done by the father, who stands before the congregation together with other elders (often including the child's other adult male relatives). They encircle the infant while cradling her or him in their hands and the father names and blesses the child by the power of the priesthood he holds.

LDS children are baptized by immersion, typically at the age of eight. Most children raised in an LDS home are baptized by their father. However, the child may also be baptized by a grandfather, uncle, older brother who has the authority, or any other person who holds the priesthood. Following baptism the child is confirmed as a member of the church and is given the Gift of Holy Ghost by the laying on of the hands of one who holds the priesthood—again, typically this is performed by the child's father.

For LDS boys who have been baptized, the following four years are a time of preparation to be ordained as a Deacon in the Aaronic priesthood at age twelve. Boys are ideally ordained by their fathers. Fathers who hold the priesthood (nearly all LDS fathers) will ordain their sons to various offices of the priesthood beginning when the boys are age twelve and continuing until the father ordains the son as an Elder in the Melchizedek priesthood when the latter is age eighteen or nineteen. Ordinations can create a powerful intergenerational bond between fathers and sons.

LDS temples are where the most sacred covenants and ordinances take place—those that "seal" or eternally bind husband to wife and child to parent. All programs and curricula in the LDS church are intended to help prepare children and youth to be willing and able to make and keep these covenants. Temple sealings are the crowning ordinance in LDS life and foster a profound sense of closeness among family members.

Latter-day Saints believe that when Jesus said to the apostle Peter that "whatsoever ye shall bind on earth would be bound in heaven" (Matt. 18:18), he was referring to the sealing powers of the priesthood that Peter received from Jesus. Joseph Smith received these same sealing powers through angelic ministration (D&C 110:12–16). Joseph taught that the "sealing powers" manifest in LDS temples exist in order to forge eternal family bonds that allow family members to be bound to each other on earth and in heaven. If a child's parents had made the covenant of marriage by being sealed in the LDS temple "for time and all eternity" before the child was born, then the child is considered to be "born in the covenant" and is born already sealed to faithful parents. Beyond salvation the most important spiritual blessing desired by most of those who convert to the LDS church is to go to the temple to be eternally sealed as a couple and family.

## Religious Practices in the Home

By far the most important institution for the religious upbringing of LDS children and youth is the home. The home-based religious practices pertaining to children that will be addressed here involve family prayer, family scripture study, family home evening, father's blessings, family service, family work, and family history and genealogy. Of course, not all LDS parents perform their religious responsibilities and not all LDS families observe the practices mentioned below. But active LDS parents and families believe that they should observe these principles and practices. LDS children and youth are taught to pray to their Heavenly Father at least daily and preferably twice a day (morning and evening). LDS families are also strongly encouraged to hold family prayer daily. Personal and family study of scriptures is strongly encouraged. Most LDS families attempt to maintain this practice but many find it difficult, especially with increasing family activities that characterize many families with several children of varying ages.

LDS families are strongly encouraged to hold a weekly family night (typically on Monday evening) called Family Home Evening, involving gospel instruction, prayer, singing of hymns, family recreational activity, and refreshments (treats of some kind). LDS fathers are encouraged to give father's blessings to their children at regular times (birthdays, beginning of the school year) and trying times (a child's illness or discouragement). A father's blessing involves the father laying his hands on his child's head and pronouncing words of love, inspiration, comfort, counsel, and encouragement. These blessings tend to promote increased bonds between fathers and their children.[13]

Individuals and families are encouraged to provide meaningful service. Many LDS families try to involve their children and youth in establishing patterns of service for their fellow Mormons, neighbors and friends, or both. Mormons are taught the importance of work. Many families try to involve their children and youth in meaningful work to develop their character and teach them to set goals and work toward achieving them.

Latter-day Saints emphasize family history, genealogy, and temple work. This involves searching out one's ancestors, writing up their history, and then going to the temple to do vicarious baptisms and temple sealings for these ancestors so that deceased individuals may be saved, couples may be married eternally, and generations may be sealed together eternally.

## LDS Institutions for Children and Youth

Although it would be difficult to overstate how important family example and home instruction is, the church maintains a number of important efforts to complement and supplement family efforts. Much of LDS religious life is focused on children's development. There is clear and orderly progression for children and youth with clear rites of passage. Parents are often called to teach and lead their children in the Primary and youth programs of the church.

This section covers LDS institutional programs for children and youth. Of course, not all LDS kids are actively involved in church programs, and the degree of influence on children and youth depends both on the quality of adults leading the programs and on the personal traits and choices of the child. I will discuss the following programs: Children's Primary, Young Men and Young Women, and Seminary.

The Primary is an organization that provides religious instruction for children aged three to twelve. Primary classes are held for two hours each Sunday. Each quarter a Saturday activity is held. The curriculum has been developed with consultation from child development experts and is developmentally appropriate. At age eighteen months, children enter the Nursery, where they engage in supervised play and religious songs, stories, and activities. Children enter the Primary organization at age three and advance into new classes each year.

The first major rite of passage for a child is baptism and confirmation at age eight. Parents feel an obligation to prepare their children well for this important event and most children are excited to be baptized. The Primary curriculum for children before age eight is oriented toward helping the child learn the basic doctrines and covenants they need to know and accept to be baptized and then to make righteous choices. In the same way that other Christian children and youth wear jewelry carrying the abbreviation WWJD (What Would Jesus Do) many LDS children and youth wear a ring showing the abbreviation CTR (Choose the Right) to help them remember to exercise their moral agency righteously.

From age eight to twelve, children focus on an increasingly sophisticated and deepened understanding of gospel principles and practices. As they approach the age of twelve, they become more excited to graduate from Primary and become a Young Woman or a Young Man. The Young Men and Young Women programs provide Sunday instruction and weekly weeknight activities for youths aged twelve to eighteen. The Young Women use the church's Personal Progress program and the Young Men use the church's Duty to God program.

At age twelve girls enter a class for young women called Beehives and boys are ordained Deacons in the Aaronic priesthood. At age fourteen young women become Mia Maids and young men are ordained Teachers. At age sixteen young women become Laurels and young men are ordained Priests. Another major milestone that occurs at age sixteen is that young women and young men now are allowed to date—although they are encouraged to date in groups to avoid "pairing off." They are taught to not engage in any sexual relations until marriage.

Seminary is a program involving daily religious instruction for high school–aged youth. In Utah and some parts of other states with a large concentration of LDS youth, schools offer "released-time" Seminary where students take a religion class during regular school hours. In most places however,

LDS high school students attend Seminary before the school day begins. During their four years of Seminary, with fifty minutes of class each weekday, a four-year Seminary graduate will have spent more than five hundred hours in focused study of the Old Testament; the New Testament; the Book of Mormon; and LDS Church History, including the Doctrine and Covenants.

## The Voice of Children and Youth in the Faith Community

Rather than having a pastor who delivers a sermon each week, LDS Sunday gospel instruction is conducted by members of the ward. In addition, each month a "Fast and Testimony Meeting" is held where anyone—of any age—who desires to stand and share their religious beliefs and experiences with the congregation may do so. LDS children begin giving "talks" (short prepared sermons) in Primary at age three. Most LDS families involve their children in giving lessons in Family Home Evenings and so children learn to prepare and deliver messages, talks, ideas, and activities—often using some type of visual aid to assist them.

After children become Young Women and Young Men at age twelve they typically give one or two talks each year before the entire congregation. Thus, the average LDS person will have given dozens of talks by the time she or he becomes an adult. Each of the three age groups of Young Women and Young Men (twelve and thirteen, fourteen and fifteen, and sixteen and seventeen) has a president that leads and directs activities (there are a total of six presidents). This responsibility changes about every six months so that by the time individuals leave the youth program of the church they have likely served as a president (or counselor to a president) more than once. The presidents conduct weekly meetings on Sunday and on a weeknight. Each month these six presidents meet with the bishopric of the ward (a bishop and his two counselors) to plan activities, discuss the needs and desires of those they are responsible for, and receive guidance from the bishop and other youth leaders.

Thus most LDS children and youth become fairly competent and confident at public speaking. They learn how to speak, share strongly held beliefs, conduct meetings, advocate for their fellow youth with adult leaders, speak with those not of their faith, and in other ways raise their voice and lead groups.

## Changes in Childhood Education

Over time there has been great stability and consistency in core doctrines and practices. However, given dramatic societal changes, the LDS church has also increased emphasis in some things and shifted its focus in some ways. The church's programs and instruction for children and youth have increased attention, beginning from an early age, on the importance of marriage and family life. Plural marriage was practiced in the early church but was discontinued in 1890.[14] There also has been increased emphasis on preparing LDS children and youth to attend the temple to perform vicarious baptisms for deceased ancestors. Youth begin attending the temple at age twelve and typically attend at least once a year with their youth group and are encouraged to attend with their parents. Finally, every LDS young man is expected to prepare himself to serve a two-year full-time mission when he turns nineteen. However, while a mission was once considered a kind of rite of passage for LDS young men, in recent years church leaders "raised the bar" on qualifying for full-time missionary service so that those who have significant physical, mental, emotional, or spiritual limitations are now "honorably excused" from full-time missionary service. Because missionary service is considered a priesthood responsibility, young women are not expected to serve but may do so if they choose (for eighteen months beginning at age twenty-one).

There also have been recent innovations in the use of media for children and in education. In the past few decades the church has increased the degree and sophistication of media products oriented toward children and youth. Many videos, magazines, pamphlets, films, and Web sites (for example, www.lds.org and www.mormon.org) have been produced to teach young people the gospel and prepare them for the strong opposition to some of their basic religious beliefs and practices that they will experience from contemporary American culture. Furthermore, LDS scripture states that "the glory of God is intelligence" (D&C 93:36). Thus, like the Jewish community (see Dorff, this volume), Latter-day Saints have always valued education for children and youth. But recently there also has been increased emphasis on getting as much education as possible to enable LDS youth to be well prepared for the increasingly competitive and dynamic labor market.

## Common Challenges Faced by American LDS Children and Youth

Common challenges faced by LDS children and youth include the child's obligations to parents and community, sexual chastity in contemporary culture, and perceptions of the threats and opportunities of American society for children and youth.

Children are taught that the gospel of Jesus Christ is about serving and even sacrificing for others. Contemporary American parents are surrounded by a popular culture that encourages them to provide their children with a continual supply of amusement and material possessions. Parents are expected to make sacrifices for their children but are not encouraged to ask their children to make meaningful sacrifices in turn. Therefore, requests from parents and church leaders for children and youth to give up valued personal time, activities, possessions, and status for religious reasons is not easy; sacrifice is a form of "countercultural" activity.

Latter-day Saint parents teach their children that God has asked them to sacrifice personal time, money, energy, comforts, and "things of the world." Children are expected to "honor thy father and thy mother" (Exod. 20:12). Children are asked to keep the commandments and prepare themselves to make and keep sacred covenants. At age eight, children make the covenant of baptism, which involves covenanting to take upon oneself the name of Christ, keep His commandments, always remember Him, and comfort those who need comfort. Practically, this involves attending church, saying personal prayers, being honest, paying tithing (10 percent of income), keeping the Sabbath day holy (refraining from work or shopping on Sunday), and obeying parents.

Young Women often perform service for their communities, for example, engaging in disaster relief in LDS efforts to get aid to people stricken by natural calamities, visiting elderly and shut-in members, working in homeless shelters, and performing many other types of service. Young Men have additional significant priesthood responsibilities, among them preparing and administering the Sacrament (of the Lord's Supper) to the congregation each week, going to the homes of members each month to receive fast offerings (free will offerings to aid the poor given by those who fast for two meals or twenty-four hours), making monthly "home teaching" visits to the homes of two to four families to inquire about their well-being and deliver a message from church leaders, and performing various types of service in their communities. Most Mormon children and youth attend public schools, although there are some who homeschool or attend private schools. LDS youth tend to be very involved in extracurricular activities. One of the challenges is that many LDS youth are extremely busy and some are quite stressed from their efforts to fulfill various personal, family, educational, and church obligations.[15]

In contemporary American popular culture, sexual experience is regarded by many as a natural, normal, and desirable part of growing up. However, LDS children and youth are taught to obey the "law of chastity," which prohibits all sexual activity (including masturbation) before (and outside) marriage. Obviously, as children reach adolescence this issue becomes more challenging for them. Many counsel with their bishops (lay congregational leaders) about how to "keep morally clean" and resist sexual temptations, which come from many directions. This focus on chastity is a significant part of the church experience of most LDS youth, as they will hear and read many talks and lessons and articles from church magazines on this topic during their teens. Those who transgress the law of chastity are encouraged to repent of sexual sin by confessing to God and to their bishop, who will help them overcome their guilt and strive to avoid repeating the sin. While contemporary America is more religious than other modern Western industrialized nations, popular culture is aggressively secular. Like many other religious people, Latter-day Saints are deeply concerned about the general decline of standards and values upholding religion, marriage, and family. They are particularly concerned about the increase in violence, sexuality, and brutality in contemporary media directed toward children and youth.[16]

Latter-day Saints believe that children and youth face several threats from American society, including excessive materialism, radical individualism, unbridled hedonism, use of harmful substances, and negative influences from popular culture. American culture preaches a gospel of material success, which requires working long and hard in order to be able to afford the newest and best products and services. In contrast, the LDS church teaches members to pay tithing (as noted earlier, 10 percent of income) for the building up of the church, to fast and make generous "fast offerings" each month to help the poor in their congregation and throughout the world, and to contribute to the missionary and humanitarian aid programs of the church. LDS youth are strongly encouraged to work and save to pay for as much of their full-time mission expenses as possible (about ten thousand dollars for a two-year mission). Children are taught to pay tithing from an early age. Many tithe on their allowance, babysitting income, and income from part-time jobs in high school.

American society is highly individualistic and encourages children and youth to reject authority and do whatever they want to do. In contrast, the LDS Church emphasizes obedience to God and focus on social groups, such as the family and the "ward family" (fellow congregants). Much time and energy is spent serving others and denying the self in order to please God and build His church and kingdom. Although many LDS children and youth have an admirable orientation to others and to causes beyond themselves, the siren song of radical individualism calls to them on a daily basis and not all are able to resist its allure. Latter-day Saints see American society as strongly oriented toward physical and emotional pleasure. Commercials portray personal pampering that everyone is entitled to. Latter-day Saint life is intended to be joyous and positive and to include wholesome recreational activities. Joseph Smith taught that fun, dancing, playing instruments, and recreation are part of the joyful religious life. There is no ascetic tradition in LDS life and Mormon children and youth are likely to participate in many of the same recreational and artistic activities that other American kids do. However, LDS children and youth are taught about the serious problems that attend the use of illicit substances and sexual activity outside marriage. They are also taught to avoid certain kinds of entertainment, such as X- or R-rated films, sexually explicit or violent music and video games, and pornographic content on the Internet and in other media.

Many American youth experiment with and become addicted to various substances as part of growing up. LDS children and youth are taught to obey the "Word of Wisdom," which requires abstaining from alcohol, tobacco products, drugs, coffee, tea, and any other addictive or harmful substance. Like the laws of Kashrut that distinguish Jewish children and youth from their non-Jewish and nonobservant peers, adherence to the Word of Wisdom distinguishes LDS children and youth from their non-LDS peers and raises many opportunities for LDS to explain their faith and stand up for their beliefs. Of course some LDS youth are teased or shunned by their peers, but most find a group of friends who respect their beliefs and practices and support them in their lifestyle.

American media places a never-ending series of pop celebrities in front of children and youth. These celebrities (musicians, sports figures, actors, and so on) often target children and youth to entice a type of "worship" through various forms of "devotion" such as watching and listening to them; copying their clothing, hairstyle, language, and mannerisms; paying for their products; posting their image on the walls of bedrooms or on computer desktops; and adopting their philosophies. In contrast, LDS parents, leaders, teachers, and written materials encourage youth to chose heroes from the Scriptures, the history of the church, the child's ancestors, or contemporary sports and entertainment figures who uphold standards of virtue.

## How Are LDS Kids Doing Spiritually?

Despite these challenges, American LDS children and youth have many opportunities to live their faith and grow spiritually and in other ways. I conclude by presenting data addressing how LDS kids are doing in contemporary America. Recently, a national study of the spiritual and religious lives of American teens from numerous faith communities was reported in the book *Soul Searching*.[17] This study of 3,370 teens, by University of North Carolina at Chapel Hill sociologists Christian Smith and Melinda Denton (neither of them LDS), found that LDS youth were highly involved with and committed to their faith. The study compared youth from various faiths on a variety of spiritual and religious variables. Below is a summary of the findings (with page numbers) from *Soul Searching*:

Mormon teens are the most likely among all U.S. teens to hold religious beliefs similar to those of their parents (35).
Seventy-one percent of Mormon teens attend church at least weekly (38).

Mormon teens are highest in the importance of their faith shaping daily life
and major life decisions (40).

Mormon and black conservative Protestant teens are the most likely to hold
traditional, biblical religious beliefs (44).

Mormon teens were highest in having a very moving or powerful spiritual
experience and highest in reporting they had "ever experienced a definite answer to prayer or specific guidance from God" (45).

Mormon teens were the most likely to report that they denied themselves
something as a "spiritual discipline" (46).

Mormon teens appear to pray the most often (47).

Mormon teens reported being the most involved in religious youth groups and
were the most likely to claim to be leaders in their youth groups (53).

Families of Mormon teens appear to talk about religious and spiritual matters the most (55).

Mormon, black Protestant, and conservative Protestant teens are most likely
to pray with their parents (55).

Mormon teens (23 percent) are most likely to frequently express their faith
at school (59).

Mormon and Jewish youth reported noticeably higher levels of pressure and
teasing from peers than did Christian teens (59).

The number of nonparent adults who played a meaningful role in a teenag-
er's life was noticeably higher for Mormons (61).

Mormon youth were the highest percentage (83 percent) reporting that they
anticipated attending the same type of faith community when they were
twenty-five years old and the lowest percentage (2 percent) to say they
anticipated attending "a different kind of congregation" (66).

I believe that Kenda Dean, a Methodist scholar of youth ministry at Princeton Theological Seminary, correctly interpreted these data by proposing that
Mormonism provides LDS teens with "a consequential faith" characterized
by (1) a substantive doctrine of God, or "a creed to believe"; (2) a community
of consequence, or "a place to belong," which for Mormons is "family"; (3) a
morally significant universe, or "a call to live out"; and (4) the opportunity
of being asked to contribute to God's ultimate transformation of the world,
or "a hope to hold on to."[18]

## Conclusion

Latter-day Saints believe that their doctrine and practice were revealed by
a loving Father in Heaven to ancient and modern prophets in order to help
His children return to Him as families to live with Him and become like
Him. Latter-day Saint children and youth are taught by parents and living

prophets and apostles that they are on earth to learn to prepare for eternal life. Eternal life centers on marriage and family life.

Contemporary American LDS children and youth find themselves surrounded by a popular culture that actively opposes many of the basic beliefs and practices they hold dear. Latter-day Saints believe that God has restored ancient truths and reveals additional truths to guide parents and religious leaders in teaching children and youth. In their homes, churches, and temples LDS children and youth seek to worship and serve God and fulfill their Heavenly Father's plan of happiness for His children.

## ACKNOWLEDGMENTS

I am grateful to Jenet Jacob, Raymond Bucko, Mary Dollahite, Loren Marks, and Jeff Hill for helpful questions and suggestions on a previous draft.

## NOTES

1.  *Pearl of Great Price, Joseph Smith History* (Salt Lake City, UT: Church of Jesus Christ of Latter-day Saints), 1:28.

2.  For information on Joseph Smith's family life, see David C. Dollahite and E. Jeffrey Hill, "Shared Leadership in the Home: Principles from the Lives of Joseph and Hyrum Smith," in *Joseph and Hyrum Smith: Lessons in Shared Leadership*, ed. Mark E. Mendenhall, Hal B. Gregersen, Jeffrey S. O'Driscoll, Heidi S. Swinton, and Breck England (Provo, UT: BYU Religious Studies Center, forthcoming).

3.  See Craig H. Hart, Lloyd D. Newell, Elaine F. Walton, and David C. Dollahite, eds., *Helping and Healing Our Families: Principles and Practices Inspired by "The Family: A Proclamation to the World"* (Salt Lake City, UT: Deseret Book, 2005). See also David C. Dollahite, ed., *Strengthening Our Families: An In-depth Look at the Proclamation on the Family* (Salt Lake City, UT: Bookcraft, 2000).

4.  For an excellent history written by an award-winning non-LDS historian see, Jan Shipps, *Mormonism: The Story of a New Religious Tradition* (Urbana: University of Illinois Press, 1987). See also Richard L. Bushman, *Joseph Smith: Rough Stone Rolling* (New York: Knopf, 2005).

5.  *Ensign* 38, no. 5 (2008): 25. *Ensign* is the official magazine of the LDS Church.

6.  Elder Henry B. Eyring, "Hearts Bound Together" (address given at 175th annual conference of the Church of Jesus Christ of Latter-day Saints, Salt Lake City, UT, April 3, 2005), http://lds.org/conference/talk/display/0,5232,49–1–520–26,00.html.

7.  Eileen W. Lindner, ed., *Yearbook of American and Canadian Churches* (Nashville, TN: Abingdon Press, 2005).

8.  Dale E. Jones, Sherri Doty, Clifford Grammich, James E. Horsch, Richard Houseal, Mac Lynn, John P. Marcum, Kenneth M. Sanchagrin, and Richard H. Taylor, *Religious Congregations and Membership in the United States, 2000* (Nashville, TN: Glenmary Research Center, 2002). See especially maps at 547, 562.

9.  For a sociological analysis of Mormon growth, see Rodney Stark, *The Rise of Mormonism* (New York: Columbia University Press, 2005).

10.  Harold Bloom, *The American Religion: The Emergence of the Post-Christian Nation* (New York: Simon and Schuster, 1992).

11.  First Presidency and Council of the Twelve Apostles of the Church of Jesus Christ of Latter-day Saints, "The Family: A Proclamation to the World," *Ensign* 25, no. 11 (1995): 102.

12.  Doctine and Covenants 93:38. The Standard Works (accepted canon of scripture), include the Holy Bible, the Book of Mormon, the Doctrine and Covenants (hereafter cited as D&C), and the Pearl of Great Price.

13.  David C. Dollahite, "Fathering for Eternity: Generative Spirituality in Latter-Day Saint Fathers of Children with Special Needs," *Review of Religious Research* 44 (2003): 237–251.

14.  As part of the prophesied restoration of all things (Acts 3:21; Eph. 1:10; Rev. 11:3) to be accomplished in the last days and as an Abraham-like test (D&C 132:28–37), Joseph Smith was commanded to practice plural marriage (polygyny). Polygyny was practiced by most Old Testament patriarchs (Abraham, Jacob, Moses, David).

15.  David C. Dollahite and Loren D. Marks, "Teaching Correct Principles: Promoting Spiritual Strength in Latter-Day Saint Young People," in *Nurturing Childhood and Adolescent Spirituality: Perspectives from the World's Religious Traditions*, ed. Karen M. Yust, Aostre N. Johnson, Sandy Eisenberg Sasso, and Eugene C. Roehlkepartain (Lanham, MD: Rowman and Littlefield, 2006), 394–408.

16.  David C. Dollahite, "Latter-day Saint Marriage and Family Life in Modern America," in *American Religions and the Family: How Faith Traditions Cope with Modernization*, ed. Don S. Browning and David A. Clairmont (New York: Columbia University Press, 2006), 124–150.

17.  Christian Smith with Melinda L. Denton, *Soul Searching: The Religious and Spiritual Lives of American Teenagers* (Oxford: Oxford University Press, 2005).

18.  Kenda Dean, "Numb and Numb-Er: Youth and the Church of "Benign Whateverism" (paper presented at the International Association for the Study of Youth Ministry, London, January 3–7, 2005).

# 7

# Native American Children and Religion

ROGER IRON CLOUD AND RAYMOND BUCKO

The place of children within the Native American religions presents a unique situation historically and culturally. There was and is no single Native American religion just as there is no single Native American culture, or a single way in which Native children are considered across a wide span of religious practices. Today there are 561 federally recognized tribes, while other groups continue to seek recognition.[1] At the time of European contact, according to estimates, the number of Natives in North America was between 1.3 million and 10 million people.[2] The 2000 census places the number of Native people who self-identify as solely Native American at 2.4 million (1 percent of the total population), with 4.3 million more who self-identify as "Native American and other" (1.5 percent of the population).[3] A third of the Native population is under eighteen years of age.[4] More than half of all Native Americans live away from reservations.[5]

Despite the wide variety of Native American cultures, languages, political structures, and belief systems, Native North Americans share a set of post-European-contact ordeals that bind them together:

> The common theme that all Native American cultures share is the post-contact decimation of peoples, the destruction of native life-styles and languages, and the subordination of aboriginal peoples in what has been called a "civilizing" process toward a superimposed "superior" mode of life. The subjection to a dominant, White, racist society is the common experience for Native Americans in the present day.[6]

Government and churches both used schools in their efforts to assimilate Natives into the mainstream culture, and this policy placed Native children at the center of a concerted institutional effort to "civilize" the Indians. In the nineteenth-century paradigm of cultural evolutionism, Indians as a group were placed at the lowest (or "savage") rung of culture. They were seen more as children than as adults and therefore needed guardians to make proper decisions for them. As Commissioner of Indian Affairs Thomas J. Morgan said in 1891, education would accelerate the cultural evolutionary process: "A good school may thus bridge over for them the dreary chasm of a thousand years of tedious evolution."[7] In accordance with these notions, the American school system was used to separate Native children from their cultural and religious practices in order to inculcate "civilized" habits of thought and behavior.

Any attempt at a broad overview of the position of children in all American Indian religious traditions would result in either gigantism or banality, so we focus on the Oglala Lakota of western South Dakota. Roger Iron Cloud is himself an Oglala; his work is informed by his own childhood experiences and by professional expertise in early childhood development. He has worked with the Oglala Sioux Tribe and in Washington, DC, Raymond Bucko is Roger's Hunka (brother by Lakota adoption); he is a Jesuit priest and anthropologist who has worked with the Lakota people since 1976.

In this chapter, we have sought to honor a variety of voices among the Oglala, past and present, on the topic of the position of children in Lakota religion. Roger has had many conversations with his own relatives and friends. While they have graciously allowed their voices to be heard for this work, we choose to protect their anonymity and are grateful for their generosity.

## The Lakota People

The Oglala Lakota are one of seven bands of the western or Teton division of the Sioux. They refer to themselves as the Lakota, while Sioux is the name used today to encompass both the western Lakota and eastern Dakota peoples. The Pine Ridge Reservation is the National territory of the Oglala Lakota. The 2000 census estimates the reservation population of Native people at about fourteen thousand, although some claim that it is as high as twenty-four thousand. Significant populations of Oglalas and other Lakota are found in towns neighboring the reservation as well as in major American cities and throughout the world.

## Lakota Belief/Metaphysics

A contemporary voice explains the core of Lakota belief in this way:

The Lakota believe there is a strong bond between Wakan Tanka or God, with the natural world consisting of the land, the animals and nature in general and the Lakota. The Lakota also maintain a close connection with the spirit world and have a reliance on generations past to provide safekeeping and safe welfare for those in this lifetime. Through prayers and reverence for the spirit world, the Lakota maintain a link with not only the physical realm, but the realm beyond life on earth. The Lakota have an extremely close connection to their spiritual roots and there is a resurgence of traditional religious practices and beliefs. For some, there is still the Christian path and while this belief system is not to be denied its influence and impact, be they Catholic or Episcopalian or Presbyterian or so many others which sprang up over the years, Christian churches are experiencing dwindling attendance. This due to what many perceive to dogma and acculturation practices of the Federal Government imposed upon the Lakota.

The other unifying factor of these varying degrees of beliefs is the fact that the Lakota believe that no matter how one believes, we are all praying to a Greater Being. Nothing is forced; there is no doctrine, no extremism, no proselytizing, nothing compulsory about religion. It is all regarded as an individual and very personal matter to be respected. . . . The members of the various churches who attend regularly tend to be older and to cling to base teachings from their childhood, when practicing the Lakota religion was banned.

Thus, while there is a unifying set of ritual practices and belief in a single divinity worshiped in many ways, there is no Lakota dogma. The focus of Lakota religion is orthopraxis, not orthodoxy.

## Kinship

Since kinship is the defining element in Lakota culture, it's crucial to maintain kin unity despite the variety of religions held by relatives who may be Mormons or members of other Christian denominations or the Native American Church, which holds that peyote is a divine substance that can bring enlightenment and healing to participants when partaken in a proper ritual context.

In Lakota society community and kinship are one. The name Lakota itself means "allies" and Lakota are related to each other through birth, marriage, or adoption. Dakota anthropologist Ella Deloria notes the importance of kinship for Dakota and Lakota, past and present:

Kinship was the all-important matter. Its demands and dictates for all phases of social life were relentless and exact; but on the other hand, its privileges and honorings and rewarding prestige were not only tolerable but downright pleasant and desirable for all who conformed. By kinship all Dakota people were held together in great relationship that was theoretically all-inclusive and co-extensive with the Dakota domain. Everyone who was born a Dakota belonged to it; nobody need be left outside.[8]

Both by tradition and in contemporary society today Lakota do not distinguish themselves primarily as a nuclear family or even as a Nation (although this is important politically) but as a *tiyospaye*: an extended family. These units lived in a balance between communal dependency and individual autonomy.[9] The Oglala people are made up of a series of *tiyospaye,* which remain viable social units today, although there are cross-cutting allegiances to district, town, reservation, and Nation.

Within families, individuals may adhere to the theological beliefs and practices of those religions while integrating Lakota values; others, in more fundamentalist groups, discourage traditional Lakota ritual practice. Mainline Christian bodies are far more ecumenical and adaptive. For example, Catholic grade schools and the high school on Pine Ridge today teach Lakota religion as well as Catholicism.

## Values

In addition to metaphysical beliefs, the Lakota focus on teaching and *living* key virtues as examples to children. One early Lakota teacher stated that the four Lakota virtues are bravery, generosity, truthfulness, and begetting children.[10] Another formulation states the four values as bravery, fortitude, generosity, and wisdom.[11] Values specific to women are industry; hospitality; kindness; chastity, for the unmarried; and fecundity, for the married.[12] One contemporary teacher expressed the importance of values in Lakota life in this way: "I have tried to raise my child by encouraging her to learn all she could, to learn the positive teachings of the Lakota. Supporting the positive is all pervasive and permeates everyday life and this too is spirituality. We try to live by the Seven Values of Lakota Life: Praying, Respect, Caring & Compassion, Honesty & Truth, Generosity and Helping, Humility and Wisdom. This is how we live."

## Stories

Lakota have a wide variety of sacred and secular stories, often used to teach children. Many of these stories also feature children with mystical powers who save the people from disasters. Iktomi, a humorous trickster

character, teaches by negative example. Joking and teasing are also important in educating children, and a sense of humor is inculcated early in
Lakota children. Family members, particularly grandparents, are the key
teachers for Lakota children:

> I learned that everything that we pray for is for all, or "the whole"
> of everything and not for the self. We pray and learn to respect our
> elders and children, for those less fortunate. We pray for balance, to
> respect our Mother Earth. We pray for our self for emotional, mental,
> and spiritual balance. The core teaching of the Lakota religion is that
> of respect. Respect is always reinforced by all; it's reinforced by our
> Aunts, our Uncles, our Grandparents, our Parents. That is the core
> principal of the Lakota religion. We are taught gender roles, as we are
> now teaching our own children. I was taught by my grandmother that
> I was to help with food, to use nature for plants for medicine, foods,
> shampoos, or soaps. My grandmother taught me that a mother never
> leaves her children and to always takes care of them, as they are very
> important, very special. My grandmother taught me that we must
> have generosity, to give to those less fortunate. She was always giving
> things away. My grandmother said the Lakota are poor because they
> always give everything away. My grandmother also taught me to never
> ask for anything in return for giving.

The Sacred White Buffalo Calf Woman gave religious rituals to the Lakota.
She appeared mysteriously, presented the Lakota with the sacred pipe, and
taught them to be moral and upstanding.[13] In one version of the story, the
Sacred Woman specifically addresses children:

> Then turning to the children: "My little brothers and sisters: Your par-
> ents were once little children like you, but in the course of time they
> became men and women. All living creatures were once small, but if no
> one took care of them they would never grow up. Your parents love you
> and have made many sacrifices for your sake in order that Wakantanka
> may listen to them, and that nothing but good may come to you as you
> grow up. I have brought this pipe for them, and you shall reap some
> benefit from it. Learn to respect and reverence the pipe, and above all
> lead pure lives. Wakantanka is your great grandfather [sic].[14]

## Ritual

Children attend most Lakota rituals, and several are specifically for children.
One ancient tradition was to have an upright relative of the same gender
breathe into an infant's mouth to impart that person's goodness to the

child.[15] Children, by tradition, also had their ears pierced, and the practice is being taken up in a religious way today. An Oglala at the turn of the twentieth century explains this ritual: "Piercing the ears is a custom that the Oglalas and Lakotas have practiced from ancient times. This is done to show that they are Lakota. Anyone may have his [sic] ears pierced, a man, a woman, or a child. This is a sign that the one having his ears pierced will live according to the Lakota customs and obey their laws."[16] The making of relatives (Hunka) honors individuals through prayer and ritual gift- and name-giving and incorporates them into a kinship structure. Another Oglala at the turn of the twentieth century described the reasons for the ceremony: "If a man's heart is good towards a child because he likes the child, or because he likes the father, or the mother, then that man may adopt that child as his own. In old times this was done by initiating the child as a Hunka. The man then became like her father. The man must be like her father at all times."[17] Today this ceremony is used for adoptions and as a rite of passage into adulthood for both boys and girls.[18] Children are also given Indian names at this time, with prayers said for their well-being. In the vision quest (Hanblecheyapi) ritual, one seeks a guiding vision for a successful life. This ritual was and is undertaken by young men, and sometimes women, from postpuberty onward. While visions are sometimes consciously sought, they may come unexpectedly to anyone of any age. The classic example is Black Elk, who received his first vision during an illness when he was nine.[19]

The most important communal ritual for the Lakota is the Sun Dance. Today many families and groups sponsor this ritual. The majority of participants are adults, but children are permitted to dance and young girls play an important role as the four maidens who begin chopping down the sacred cottonwood tree. Black Elk states that the cottonwood is sacred because its leaves are a template for the tipi, the discovery of which he attributes to children who used cottonwood leaves to make toy houses: "This too is a good example of how much grown men may learn from very little children, for the hearts of little children are pure, and, therefore, the Great Spirit may show to them many things which older people miss."[20]

The vision quest is the main rite of passage to adulthood for males, but females have two rituals that mark this transition. The Buffalo Sing ceremony (tatanka lowanpi; also called isna ta awi cha lowan) is a religious ritual in which a young girl is set apart at her first menses and symbolically taught the virtues and skills of womanhood. Prayers are said for the girl, and there is a feast and giveaway at the end.[21] The Tossing of the Ball (tapa wakan yap) ritual has seen some revival recently; it requires a young girl to toss a ball made of buffalo hair and hide in four sacred directions, west, north, east, and south, and then straight up in the air, representing the all-pervasiveness of the divine in the universe. Guests scramble to catch the ball each time it is thrown, and they pray that future generations might have wisdom and strength.[22]

In addition to such traditional rituals, children of parents who participate in Christian churches are baptized; additionally, certain of the Christian churches and Mormonism include First Communion, first confession, and confirmation rituals for children (see chapters in this volume on those religions). The Native American Church's children's rituals include birthday meetings, as well as children's versions of the sunset-to-sunrise prayer sessions characteristic of this group's central worship. One of our contemporary teachers enumerates other rituals for children: "The Native American Church and Lakota religion almost parallel each other but in the Native American Church we have a baptism and first communion. The Native American Church and Lakota religion both have coming of age ceremonies for a man and a woman only more so in the Native American Church."

## Nurture and Protection of Children

Families, communities, and the tribe, as well as state and federal agencies, are all concerned with the nurture and protection of children. Whereas schools were once used to remove Lakota children from their culture, contemporary schools are an important locus for training young people in Lakota values, Native language skills, and cultural knowledge. The federal government sponsors the Head Start program on the reservation, and the Indian Child Welfare Act is federal legislation designed to protect the cultural rights of children by supervising adoptions so that children remain within their cultural group. The Oglala Sioux tribe has an office for early childhood development and employs young adults through YO! a youth opportunity program. The tribe also sponsors Court Appointed Special Advocacy (CASA), which focuses on child advocacy and has offices in the main communities on the reservation. Another program, Wankayeja Pawicapiya (Children First), employs the skills of traditional ritual leaders in working with abused children.

Schools sponsor traditional dances and drum groups for youth. A private foundation created the Sue Ann Big Crow Center in Pine Ridge for youth activities. The tribe also maintains a foster grandparents program to allow children valuable time with elders. Churches offer youth groups and youth opportunity. Sports are also important on the reservation, with basketball sustaining the highest interest. Young people also form groups for Native games, including a variety of "hand games."

Recently, there's been a resurgence of some old societies that were highly structured organizations in pre-reservation times, principally Tokala (Kit Fox) and the Cante Ohitika (Brave Heart) societies. Each of these trains young men for specific duties and responsibilities in relationship to Oglala society and culture. Children are dependent on the web of kinship relations into which they are born, but they're also trained to be independent and their autonomy is respected. One contemporary teacher expressed the relationship this way:

> When a child is in the womb, we welcome the spirit of the child. When the child is born, we keep the belly-button of the child in a small leather beaded turtle. The turtle represents long life so that the child will have a long life and we keep that turtle with us so the child will always stay close to us. The significance of a child's given name and their Hunka name receive a lot of thought as to what they will be called in this world. As the child grows older we have the *wacihi* ceremony for girls and the *wiyaka* ceremony for the boys. These are puberty rites of passage.

Lakota in the past and present honor children as sacred.[23] A nineteenth-century teacher stated: "Little children are *wakan* [sacred] because they do not speak,"[24] and a contemporary teacher agreed: "As a child, I was taught that the child is sacred. My grandmother always did special and little things for me." Another teacher explains:

> Children are Wankanyeja, Sacred Beings, and how you treat them is how you live their lives. We are here to take care of them because they do not belong to us, they are gifts to be taken care of. Wakan Tanka can take them if we do not treat them correctly. At birth, the midwives and elders will sing welcoming songs, clean the mouth out so the baby can breathe. Children are dependent for food, care, and love. When they are young, we teach them not to cry. When we are pregnant we are taught to take care of ourselves, not to go around in a bad manner, to think good thoughts and to sing to the child.

In addition to the honoring of individual children there is another important concept in Lakota culture, the seven generations. This term expresses both the interconnectedness of generations and the important responsibility the Lakota have to future generations.[25]

## Social Roles

What is notable about the Lakota and indeed about many Native groups is the recognition of a child's personal autonomy. Traditionally, children were never hit, and this is largely the case today. Oglalas generally prefer to talk to the children as adults when they need correction. Decisions that don't present immediate personal danger were and are respected.[26] One of our teachers states: "The ultimate authority over a child is that of Tunkasila [God] but children have a choice to stay on this earth or leave and go back to Tunkasila. Children do not belong to us, we are only caretakers, and ultimately children belong to Tunkasila." One of our teachers sums up the relationship between parent and child today:

> Children depend on us for security, for nurturing and to provide a safe environment for them. We learn just as much from children as they learn from us. We let the child simply learn to be itself. Parents, the *tiospaye*, and the community at large have daily authority over the child and parents teach at home, they teach respect, generosity, prayer, and the responsibility to carry oneself in a respectful manner in society. The child's obligation is to respect itself and parents in the community and if that is taught in the home, the child will not embarrass or bring shame upon the family. These are all things my Grandmother taught me. We are taught that each gender has a specific role and to conduct ourselves in a respectful manner. We learn that we each have different roles such as being a Water Woman or a Road Man [ritual roles in the Native American Church]. We are taught how to conduct ourselves according to each of the specific protocols set out for us.

In addition to males and females, the Lakota recognize a man who fulfills a woman's role as a *winkte*. Such individuals traditionally received their calling in a dream, and afterward they were obliged to fulfill their role in order to live a full life. A *winkte* might be called upon to give a secret name to a child, which was believed to be powerful protection against illness for the child. The *winkte* might also be able to cure certain illnesses.[27] Ethnographic literature makes clear that while a *winkte* had an ambivalent position culturally, the person was socially respected. One of our contemporary teachers bears this out:

> Lakota Religion has a place for all children; they are *wakan*, or holy; both male and female children have their roles and responsibilities in our society. Even what we call a *winkte*, or a child who would be called a homosexual by the outside society, that child is special. They are close to being on par with Medicine Men, they once were chosen to name children. They had a special place in the arts, in chores; they are in tune with both the male and female worlds. Today the greater society has changed our perceptions and attitudes towards *winktes*.
>
> The sexuality of a child has no bearing in the Lakota religion, as all children are sacred. That's why we say children are *wakanyeja*, which literally means "sacred child," and we put our children first in all things.

## Life Stages

In Lakota, children, the first stage of life, are referred to collectively as *wakanyeja*.[28] Lakota language and culture mark a further four stages in the life of females and males: *wincincala—hoksila* (girlhood—boyhood), *wikoskalaka—koskalaka* (female—male adolescence), *wiyan—wicasa* (womanhood—manhood) and *winunhcala—wicahcala* (female—male old age).[29] The early stages of life were marked by little gender distinction. Boys and girls played together. As children matured, they came under the tutelage of the same-sex parent. Life passages were marked through rituals as mentioned above. Today rites of passage also include graduation from grade school, high school, college, and professional school; entrance into the military and completion of military terms; the first time one dances at a powwow; and birthdays.

## Social Roles

Because children's personal autonomy is respected among the Lakota, much attention is given to the raising of children and to their education. Children have a voice in where they will attend school, what kinds of activities they will participate in, and even how and when they will worship. Young children are active in assisting their extended families in religious observances by helping with cooking, firewood gathering, and participation in prayer. High school students are encouraged to develop leadership skills and to become involved in community affairs. They arrange debates between tribal council candidates and test them with their own questions. Students are also active in participation and organizing prayer walks, taking aim at issues such as drug and alcohol abuse.

Two contemporary voices express well the Lakota understanding of the role of children in these vital areas:

> Children have a huge unspoken voice and a lot of power in the religion because they are sacred. Lakota religion looks toward the future through children, as they are the future; teaching children well will ensure that the religion will be ongoing.

> My grandparents were Episcopalian and also practiced the Lakota religion and went to ceremonies but they never pushed anything on me as a child. There were no preachings, just practice. I was never pushed in any one direction. They never pushed a doctrine. I think it was in my late teens that the Ecumenical movement made the Catholic Church more tolerant of other religions but other religions were more inviting and more tolerant than those of us who were Catholic. The Indian religion ignored admonishment of the church of not practicing

other religions [Lakota religion allows participation in other religious rituals]. It allowed us to make up our own minds in how we prayed and believed. Today I do not need a formal structure to pray. I can have a relationship with the Creator anywhere. Because of this relationship, I never tried to push one religion on my kids. My kids are now more open to other faiths. Each has chosen his or her own path and way to pray. One daughter goes to Mass sometimes because she wants to, whenever she wants, especially on special days like Christmas, Easter, Lent, things like that. She will also go to other churches, like the Pentecostal Church. I say my own prayers in my home and I go to sweats and ceremonies. A couple of my kids pray with the Sacred Pipe, go to sweats. I have a son who is married to a Buddhist and practices the Lakota religion but is still respectful of his wife's way and partakes in some of her practices. I have one daughter who wants to learn more about Christianity. We have less of a structure for religion and have more of a belief in broader religious knowledge. I try to be a good role model and not doctrinaire about which direction they should go. You perpetuate by modeling. Respect is fundamental in teaching from parents. I teach my children to be respectful, to care for the elders, do for them, wait on them, to clean the house, to do chores. Understanding the young and respecting them is fundamental, as they have peers and don't want to be preached at or simply talked at. You have to understand their own thinking and talking. Being respectful of them and modeling.

Telling stories is a traditional and important way to maintain a distinctive Lakota identity. Yes, there is widespread concern about the impact of the external influences the media can have on the youth through controversial lyrics, violence in films and movies, and posturing of public figures who portray the image of that of a gangster or extol gang activity. There is fear that such influences erode family cohesion, foster lack of respect, and are all contrary to Lakota values. The youth listen to today's music or watch things such as MTV and see outside world influences such as fashions or witness negative attitudes toward authority, and this erodes cultural values, principally respect. Suicide, drugs, sexually transmitted diseases, and violence have an impact on reservation youth. One of our contemporary teachers expressed concern over specific threats that bear on their children: "There are many good things and there are bad influences affecting our children and society. Alcohol and drugs are extremely dangerous and bad influences and certain types of music. Our children hear this music from the outside world and they have a lot of peer pressure, the gangster rap music is a bad influence. The Internet is an influence that is both good and bad and one has to be careful in using and monitoring that."

## Conclusion

Lakota religion, like all dynamic spiritual systems, continues to adapt to the changing conditions of the Lakota people. Since the 1970s there has been an increasing consciousness and revival of Native traditions throughout the United States, but the Lakota are known for the retention and continuity of their religious traditions, despite pressure in the past to assimilate and encroaching secularism and materialism today. Two of our contemporary teachers give voice to the dynamics of Lakota tradition:

> The religion always changes and we adapt as society changes accord-
> ing to external influences. We were once based on the buffalo and
> were a nomadic, warrior society and prepared our children for war
> and to protect the family. Honor was attached to specific deeds and
> actions. Now honor is brought on by things like education. Children
> are extremely important in the cultural and generational continuity
> of the Lakota by ensuring that children are brought up in the ways
> in which we believe and practice the religion. Today what is central
> is maintaining the importance of family, praying with the pipe, puri-
> fying ourselves and our houses with sage, conducting family sweat
> lodge ceremonies. Respecting our ways is the best way to continue
> our Lakota way of life. We live the religion; there is no separation of
> church and state like there is in the outside world. We have no written
> rules like many religions. Many religions have too many protocols and
> are fear based as opposed to being faith based. We pray for guidance,
> we pray so children remember who they are, who we are as Lakota.
> Our religion gave our grandparents strength to continue on living and
> being Lakota. The opportunities of America are getting an education,
> to gain an understanding of American society and how it operates.

A contemporary voice speaks of how vital Lakota children are to the continuity of this sacred way of life:

> I feel because of our religion and our *tiospaye*, that we as Lakota
> through our children will always survive, we will always remain to be
> Lakota. Despite the dire living conditions and poverty, we have relied
> upon our elders for guidance, our children and the unborn for contin-
> uation of our religion, and Wakan Tanka for protection. This despite
> the many obstacles we have faced in years past and the challenges
> which confront us now. We are constantly confronted with the threat
> of losing our homelands, of losing rights guaranteed under the 1868
> Fort Laramie Treaty and guaranteed under the Second Amendment of
> the U.S. Constitution. Today, with the ways in which the schools have
> adapted to a pluralistic teaching approach of affirming our culture

and their usage of parent and advisory groups in adopting community decisions in teaching our children, there have been significant changes for the positive in our communities. Children are proud of who they are, proud to be Lakota, proud of their religion and culture. They will continue the teachings of our elders and continue to fight for our rights and the rights that allow us to remain to be Lakota.

Contemporary Lakota stress that their own sacred beliefs and practices have a positive life-giving impact on every aspect of their lives, particularly in the care of their children, the true hope of the future. Lakota today rely on the internal resources of their own spiritual traditions, their enduring culture, their kinship system, and the talent of their own people to both heal the past and create a better present and future. Lakota also share a second Nationality and cultural interest in larger American society, a society that has brought tragedy and loss and, less frequently, benefit and gain. Lakota people continue to sort out what is beneficial and what will ultimately harm them and their children, as do all members of American society. Lakota look to their children, as they have in the past, to continue their unique way of life, a life which is at root religious.

## NOTES

1. Bureau of Indian Affairs, "Department of the Interior: Indian Entities Recognized and Eligible to Receive Services from the United States Bureau of Indian Affairs; Notice," *Federal Register* 70, no. 226 (2005).

2. David P. Henige, *Numbers from Nowhere: The American Indian Contact Population Debate* (Norman: University of Oklahoma Press, 1998).

3. Stella U. Ogunwole, *We the People: American Indians and Alaskan Natives in the United States: Census 2000 Special Reports* (Washington, DC: United States Department of Commerce, 2006), 1.

4. Ibid., 5.

5. Donald L. Fixico, *The Urban Indian Experience in America* (AlbuquerqueL University of New Mexico Press, 2000).

6. Beatrice Medicine, "Child Socialization among Native Americans: The Lakota (Sioux) in Cultural Context," *Wicazo Sa Review* 1, no. 2 (1985): 23.

7. David Wallace Adams, *Education for Extinction: American Indians and the Boarding School Experience, 1875–1928* (Lawrence: University Press of Kansas, 1995), 19.

8. Ella C. Deloria, *Speaking of Indians* (Lincoln: University of Nebraska Press, 1998), 24–25.

9. Ibid., 40.

10. James Walker, "The Sun Dance and Other Ceremonies of the Oglala Division of the Teton Sioux," *Anthropological Papers of the American Museum of Natural History* 16, no. 2 (1917): 160.

11. Royal Hassrick, *The Sioux: Life and Customs of a Warrior Society* (Norman: University of Oklahoma Press, 1964), 32.

12. Medicine, "Child Socialization among Native Americans," 24.

13. William K. Powers, *Oglala Religion* (Lincoln: University of Nebraska Press, 1975); Marla N. Powers, *Oglala Women* (Chicago: University of Chicago Press, 1986).

14. Frances Densmore, *Teton Sioux Music*, Bulletin of the Bureau of American Ethnology 61 (Washington, DC: Government Printing Office, 1918), 65–66.

15. Raymond J. DeMallie, "Teton," in *Handbook of North American Indians*, ed. Raymond J. DeMallie (Washington, DC: Smithsonian Institution, 2001), 808.

16. James Walker, *Lakota Belief and Ritual*, ed. Raymond DeMallie and Elaine Jahner (Lincoln: University of Nebraska Press, 1980), 191–192.

17. Ibid., 211.

18. Powers, *Oglala Women*; Marla N. Powers, *Lakota Naming: A Modern-Day Hunka Ceremony* (Kendall Park, NJ: Lakota Books, 1991).

19. Raymond J. DeMallie Jr., *The Sixth Grandfather: Black Elk's Teachings Given to John G. Neihardt* (Lincoln: University of Nebraska Press, 1984).

20. Joseph Epes Brown, *The Sacred Pipe: Black Elk's Account of the Seven Rites of the Oglala Sioux* (New York: Penguin Books, 1987), 74–75.

21. Ibid., 116–126.

22. Ibid., 127–138.

23. Powers, *Oglala Women*, 53.

24. Walker, *Lakota Belief and Ritual*, 69.

25. Vine Deloria Jr., "American Indians and the Moral Community," in *For This Land: Writings on Religion in America*, ed. James Treat (New York: Routledge and Kegan Paul, 1999), 179.

26. DeMallie, "Teton," 809.

27. Hassrick, *The Sioux*, 133–135, William K. Powers, "The North American Berdache: Reply to Callender and Kochems," *Current Anthropology* 24, no. 4 (1983): 467–462.

28. Albert White Hat, *Reading and Writing the Lakota Language: Lakota Iyapi Un Wowapi Nahan Yawapi*, ed. Jael Kampfe (Salt Lake City: University of Utah Press, 1999), 88–89.

29. Ibid.

# 8

# Children in American Islam

JANE I. SMITH

To better understand the views of childhood in Islam, it is important to understand the diversity of this world religion, even in the United States. As the religion of Islam, and thereby Muslims, come increasingly into the American public eye, people want to know who "they" are, what "they" believe, and why "they" do certain things in the name of their faith. It is very difficult to explain that there really is no "they," that American Muslims represent the most heterogeneous Islamic community in the history of the world. This diversity is expressed in racial-ethnic identity, cultural expectation, religious practice, and the degree to which they choose to participate in American society and political life. Therefore the first thing to be said about American Muslim children is that there is no norm and little if any common identity other than a generalized Islam. A Muslim family may be American born, African American, recently emigrated, or on a brief sojourn.

Even the term *Muslim* has its complications. Some who come from Muslim cultural backgrounds may choose to identify themselves in just that way—that is, not as participating in any religious practices or wanting to be seen as part of Islamic movements in America. Others are trying to practice the requirements of the faith as observantly as possible, whether they are Sunnis, Shi'ites, or members of the many Islamic sectarian movements in this country. As Muslims differ, so will their children, in cultural grounding, in religious practice, and in what they expect as budding citizens of the United States.

## Foundations of the Qur'an and Tradition

The starting point for all observant Muslims is the Qur'an, which they believe to be the inerrant revelation of God's word for humanity. As always in this text, passages dealing with children stipulate clearly that God is in charge. Children are God's blessings and gifts, whom he may choose to withhold from would-be parents or bestow in either male or female form (vv. 7:49, 198). Because the Qur'an affirms that all humanity accepted Islam while nascent in the loins of Adam (vv. 7:172), a child is considered to be born in a condition of natural affinity to Islam, turning to God in submission.

Contrary to some popular assumptions, the Qur'an does not favor one gender over the other, although for clearly specified reasons male children are to receive an inheritance equivalent to that of two female children (vv. 4:11–12). It is the responsibility of the mother to suckle and give sustenance to the child and of the father to provide for his family from his means. A number of verses make it clear that as the child is the product of the marriage bed, his or her first and natural guardian is the father (vv. 7:32, 34:2–3).[1] Therefore in cases of divorce, children have traditionally been taken care of by the mother when the child is young, and then given to the father at age nine, twelve, or fifteen, depending on the school of law adhered to. Orphans are given special attention in the Qur'an, and they and their property are to be cared for responsibly by their appointed guardians. Because of this system of protection for children, adoption is not generally an option in Islam. The Qur'an also specifies that children have the obligation to be good to their parents and to take care of them.

Many of the traditions in Islam deal with children. In one often-quoted passage, for example, paradise is said to lie at the feet of mothers. The traditions are replete with instructions for the care of the child, and parents are urged to cherish their children and treat them in such a way as to inculcate self-respect.[2] Children who die before attaining "the age of discretion" are considered to be in the natural state of Islam or right submission to God, and therefore go directly to paradise. Therefore, the prayers in a funeral service for a child are not for forgiveness but for his or her well-being in the presence of God. A young person who has died early may, however, serve as a means for the recompense and reward of the parents.[3]

American Muslims, while acknowledging the divine nature of the Qur'an, nevertheless differ in the extent to which they understand its stipulations to be normative for them, particularly in matters of male authority over the family, custody of children, and inheritance.

## Growing Up in the Family

When a Muslim child is born, it is generally expected that the father or another male relative will whisper a verse of the Qur'an into the ear of the baby as soon as possible, with special means provided if the baby is in an incubator. The first of the traditional life cycle rituals observed in most Islamic countries, and by some American Muslims, is called 'Aqiqa, an initiation ceremony to welcome the baby some seven days after it is born. The prescribed elements of the ritual include selecting a name, perhaps shaving the child's head, and assuring the child that she or he is under the sovereignty of God. The traditional custom of sacrificing an animal and distributing the meat to the needy is usually replaced in America by a charitable gift.[4]

Another of the rites prescribed by Islam, one that is specifically applied to boys, is circumcision. In many cultures this is done after the child reaches boyhood as a kind of rite of passage, often providing the occasion for community celebration with the sacrifice of an animal and much feasting. In America most Muslim baby boys are circumcised in the hospital shortly after birth without the accompanying rites, sometimes in conjunction with the 'Aqiqa ritual. Nowhere in the Qur'an or the reliable traditions is there any requirement that girls must be circumcised. Because female circumcision is still a popular practice in certain areas of Africa, however, in rare circumstances immigrant families from those countries may want to continue the practice in the United States, which can be the cause of considerable controversy. Most Muslim families are quick to affirm that female circumcision is not legitimate according to orthodox Islam.

Whether or not birthdays are observed is often the subject of disagreement, some parents feeling that such practices do not conform with Muslim custom. Muslim children note the excitement their friends feel at the coming of their birthday celebrations and may feel that they are missing out on important occasions. In fact, parents often do allow birthday parties, and the occasion of the first birthday is celebrated with special fanfare. Islamic holidays, or 'Eids, are the times when Muslim children receive special gifts.

Socialization of children in all Islamic countries takes place primarily in the context of the home, and Muslim families in American are eager to continue that process here. The traditional nuclear family, in which grandparents, cousins, aunts, and uncles form an immediate context for raising a child, however, is often hard to replicate in the United States. If family members are not available, often close friends or certain communities within the local mosque can serve as a support group for a child and can help with child care if a mother is employed. If older relatives such as grandparents do live in the home or neighborhood, the situation may turn out to be contentious as well as supportive. Generally grandparents understand their responsibility to be teaching their grandchildren the elements of their particular cultural heritage and way of practicing the faith.[5] But this stress on ethnic affiliation may be at odds with the intention of parents that their children find their primary identity as American Muslims who happen to have a certain cultural heritage.

Many Muslim families find that while their children are sliding effortlessly from their familial cultural identities as they have grown up with them in the home into complete ease with American culture, the older generations (which may include parents as well as grandparents) are much more comfortable with the old cultural ways. Teenagers can find it irritating if their grandparents fail to learn English or to adapt to American culture, especially if the older generation insists on strict modes of behavior that the teens find restrictive and outdated. Muslim girls also may find themselves very frustrated if their families, following traditional customs, allow boys more freedom to interact socially with their peers than their sisters are permitted.

American Muslims view the family as the context in which right values can be inculcated into their children, particularly in the face of what they see as the disintegration of morality in American culture as a whole. Wanting both to educate their children in the virtues extolled by Islam and to protect them from the dangers of American society, they use a great many means of fostering what they see as an "Islamic environment" in the home. Islamic rituals for children, such as naming ceremonies and coming-of-age rituals are celebrated in many homes, along with reading stories from the Qur'an, the life of the Prophet, and early Islamic history. Often Muslims will have Islamic art and symbols prominent in every room, including children's bedrooms, to ensure that their child feels surrounded by the elements of the family's faith. Children are taught the elements of the ritual prayer as soon as possible and are encouraged to join family members in performing the prayer in the home at the prescribed times. Ritual observances, such as breaking the fast at the end of Ramadan, both in the home and at the mosque, always include special activities for children.

How to raise your child in a proper Muslim home has become a very popular topic recently, and with a tap of a few computer keys one can find online articles as well as references to a plethora of books and other print literature treating everything from positive parenting skills to children's eating habits. Some of these works are written abroad and translated into English for American consumption, and others are composed by American-born Muslims who better understand the complexities of American culture. Muslims in America have been among the first to take as full advantage as possible of the recent development of Internet communication to express their opinions and publicize their writings. Many opinion pieces and electronic articles are available on the general topic of raising children in America.[6]

Just as books, articles, and online discussions help parents in structuring the good Islamic family, so a great variety of instructional materials are available to help children learn and have fun at the same time. Children can look at videos about Islam and its heroes, play Islamic games online, and have instruction in Arabic from beginning to advanced. Parents who want their children to learn Qur'an recitation or the stages of the prayer can turn to Sound Vision Foundation's program, which, as the foundation puts it, is "helping tomorrow's Muslims today!"[7] Islamic stores offer a huge variety of Islamic toys and games, puppets, music, and ways for children to interact with video and internet presentations. Children can do Islamic puzzles or construct models of the Ka'ba in Mecca or the Dome of the Rock in Jerusalem. Parents and children can quiz each other about facts of the faith or play Islamic card games. Mission: Survival, for example, is an educational adventure game designed to help children understand their Islamic identity, cope with societal challenges, and reinforce Islamic values.[8] Children's Islamic books and magazines are easily available at bookstores, groceries, and from the Internet. Many of these products, such as Islamic cartoons or films with Muslim heroes and heroines, serve both as instructional tools and as entertainment.

Little girls who want to play with a Barbie doll can be introduced to her Muslim counterpart, Razanne, billed by Online-Islamic-Store.com as "the perfect gift for all Muslim girls." She comes with a choice of blonde, brown, or black hair and a fair, olive, or black complexion. Razanne, who is twelve inches tall, is assured to build Muslim identity and self-esteem and to provide an Islamic role model. A doll can be purchased dressed as a Muslim Girl Scout, a teacher, or just a playmate, and an African American Razanne is ready to demonstrate the positions of prayer. The dolls have changeable headdresses, so that a little girl can choose Razanne's dress to match that of her mother.

Muslim families generally do not use babysitters for their children, although this is changing. If members of the extended family are not available to be with children when parents need to go out, the parents simply take their children with them. Muslim children have the reputation of being well-behaved in such circumstances, although clearly there are exceptions, sometimes linked to differences in cultural backgrounds. Children are usually brought to Muslim gatherings such as mosque programs, local and national meetings of Islamic organizations, and women's circles for instruction in the Qur'an or for social encounter. Because such gatherings are almost always multiethnic, often including African Americans as well as those from immigrant backgrounds, children learn early the diversity of the Muslim community in America and the support of being connected to a variety of groups. They also learn a lot about Islam, and family takes on a wider definition than simply mother and father.

## Education

How to provide an adequate education for their children is one of the most important issues on the agenda of most American Muslims. They ponder the alternatives of public school, a private Islamic school, or homeschooling. Most parents who decide on a public school education are also eager that their children begin to learn some of the essentials of Islam, which they can do in weekend or Sunday schools or sometimes in after-school sessions held at the local mosque or even in a private home. Debates rage over which context provides the best overall education for the child. One hotly contested issue is whether it is better to try to isolate children from the dangers of society at large that they will probably experience in public school—unfortunately all too often including sex, drugs, alcohol, and violence—or whether such isolation will keep them from learning the coping skills that they will need once they get out into the world.

The reality is that in America there are only a little more than two hundred Muslim schools, of which most offer kindergarten through sixth or eighth grade, with only around a dozen being high schools. Estimates indicate that not more than 3 percent of Muslim children have much formal training in Islam outside of what they receive in the home, and often that comes in the form of a kind of a packaged curriculum used at the mosque and developed in countries such as Saudi Arabia and Iran; this is not designed with the needs of American children in mind.[9] It is only quite recently that efforts at Islamic education have been more focused, helped by the foundation in 1998 of the nonprofit Islamic Schools League of America, incorporated in Virginia. The purpose of the foundation is to partner with Muslim educators and Islamic organizations to help develop quality education for Muslim children in a specifically Islamic environment. Among the first Islamic educational institutions in America were the Clara Muhammad Primary Schools. Begun by the wife of Elijah Muhammad, head of the Nation of Islam until his death in 1975, these schools, originally designed for African American children, now have students from all ethnic backgrounds.

A number of problems make the task of Islamic educators difficult. Among them is that of determining an appropriate curriculum. Often schools opt for curricula used in local district schools, including the same textbooks, so that students who move from an Islamic school to a private high school will not find themselves unprepared for the new environment. Certain expendable subjects, such as art, music, and physical education, may have to be eliminated to make room for teaching more specifically Islamic subjects such as Arabic, the Qur'an, and Islamic history. A major problem for parents contemplating sending a child to an Islamic school is cost. Usually these schools, if they are good, are quite expensive, and parents who want their children to begin with such education at an early age are looking at a large cumulative bill. While there is general agreement that "Muslim schools give students a sense of self-worth, pride and cultural identity they could never get in a public schools," unfortunately the liabilities often make the choice difficult for parents.[10] Many such institutions are said to be disorganized; staff turnover is endemic because of poor wages for teachers and culture clashes between administrators; and schools are frequently simply not up to the academic standards of public institutions, let alone other private institutions.

Despite the difficulties, most children appear to enjoy their Islamic school education very much. Most reports indicate that they feel protected from the prejudices of American society, are proud of being Muslim instead of humiliated by the anti-Muslim rhetoric their parents cannot protect them from hearing, and seem to accept readily the requirements of dress and behavior codes. The Pledge of Allegiance takes a slightly different shape at some of these institutions; this pledge recited by students at the New Horizons School in Pasadena, California, is one alternate version:

> As an American Muslim, I pledge allegiance to God and His prophet. I respect and love my family and my community, and I dedicate my life to serving the cause of truth and justice.
>
> As an American citizen, with rights and responsibilities, I pledge allegiance to the flag of the United States of America, and to the Republic for which it stands, one nation, under God, indivisible, with liberty and justice for all.

Many of the Muslim children who attend public schools find that their problems are the usual ones faced by young people and cannot be attributed to the fact that they are Muslim. In other cases, however, it is simply difficult for a child to be Muslim when her or his classmates are not. The majority of Muslim girls do not cover their hair or wear Islamic dress in school, even when they reach puberty. Those who do may find it difficult to make friends, and if they are not jeered at they usually find themselves on the outside of social groupings.[11] Often parents object to their daughters participating in physical education activities that force them to wear compromising dress, especially when classes are mixed gender, and some schools have allowed for accommodating clothing such as modest uniforms that cover the whole body as an alternative to more revealing bathing suits or gym suits. Even boys often choose to cover to the knees.

While some of the Islamic schools in America are mixed gender, others respect the wishes of more conservative members of the community to keep girls and boys separate. Considerable attention has been given recently to the way that sexual education is carried out in the public schools. Conservative Muslim parents object if such classes are mixed gender or include detailed descriptions of anatomy, methods of contraception, or support for alternatives to male-female sexual relationships.

While a number of efforts have been undertaken recently by Muslim and non-Muslim groups to make sure that unflattering and false images of Muslims found in children's public school textbooks are changed, unpleasant stereotypes still abound, and the distinct cultural identities of the many Muslim communities in America are not recognized or valued. Muslim parents and others are working with public school teachers and administrators to help them better understand Islam so as to be able to instruct their students. Summer training for social studies and high school teachers is available in many areas, often supported by U.S. government funding. A 2003 study of Muslim children in urban communities, particularly in New York City, found that they had difficulty when they had to counter negative stereotypes about Islam and Muslim values, that Muslim girls felt particular pressure to "fit in" at school while trying to meet the expectations of their parents, and that these students wished that more attention would be paid by the school to Islamic holidays.[12]

A very small number of Muslim parents are sufficiently concerned about the problems of both public and Islamic schools that they opt for homeschooling. Studies done by the Department of Education just before the events of September 11, 2001 (9/11), estimated that around 2 percent of Muslim children were taught at home, a number that has probably risen over the last few years. While parents who send their children to public school may worry about too much socialization with non-Muslims, homeschooling parents have the opposite concern, that their children may be too isolated from other children and not well prepared for the difficulties of real life. Homeschooling recently has received support through the establishment of a wide range of Muslim-specific homeschool networks and e-mail and print resources. Organizations such as the Muslim Home School Educators Network have been established in Massachusetts and Texas to share Internet-based information on curriculum, instructional resources, and legal issues for Muslim homeschool families.

## Religious Practices

The general expectation is that children will begin participating in the rites and obligations of Islam when they reach the age of majority. This is understood to be the age of puberty, though some scholars are more specific. Grand Shi'ite Ayatollah Saanei, for example, reports on his Web site that at the completion of fifteen lunar years for boys and thirteen lunar years for girls, majority has been attained and children are expected to perform those religious duties that are considered obligatory. Youth may be expected to take part in observations such as prayer with the family; attendance at the mosque; fasting during the month of Ramadan; or going with their families on the pilgrimage to Mecca, which is required of Muslims once in a lifetime. The age at which children are expected to fast differs, although most agree that boys and girls should not jeopardize their health by going without food during the day until at least the age of puberty. Children are encouraged to study Arabic, and a few who are particularly talented may be rewarded with a party or celebration for having read the entire Qur'an in Arabic. Families that are not religiously observant may find that their children want to carry out the duties of Islam on their own, or with other young people at the mosque.

When are girls expected to make a decision about whether to wear Islamic dress? Most families, even if they are practicing and the mother wears the hijab, encourage girls not to consider veiling until they are at least at puberty.[13] In some instances, little girls of age six and beyond are encouraged to dress in long skirts and veils. The choice of whether to wear any form of Islamic dress, however, is generally expected to be that of the child, and often she puts off this decision until she reaches the age of eighteen or so or enters college or university, where she can find groups of young women similarly dressed. Girls in their teens are especially attracted to new contemporary styles of Islamic dress, such as elaborate denim outfits currently being designed by African American women, or the athletically oriented gear that will allow them to be modest and yet able to participate in sports.

One of the problems many Muslim families face is whether to allow their children to participate in Christian holiday observances. Muslim children may be perplexed and disappointed if their families choose not to celebrate Christmas by having a tree and buying presents for each other. While some families see no problem with a secular Christmas tree, or believe that Christmas should be a time for Muslims to celebrate the birth of their beloved prophet Jesus, others are telling their children that as Muslims it is important to remember and observe their own holidays, such as the two major 'Eids, or celebrations, at the end of Ramadan and the pilgrimage, as well as the observance of the birthday of Prophet Muhammad. On 'Eid days families may hang balloons and lights around the house and help children to enjoy celebrations connected with their life as Muslims. Many promotional materials are available to help children not feel excluded at Christmas and Easter, but included in their own special holidays.

In Shi'ite mosques special efforts are often made to reenact the drama of the battle of Kerbala, at which the beloved grandson of the Prophet Muhammad, Imam Husain, was killed. Children watch in fascination as the battle lines are drawn and the audience participates with shouts and groans. The mosque is used to instruct the children, to help them feel part of their ethnic and religious heritage, and to make it clear to them how Shi'ite Islam differs in some respects from Sunni Islam. These rituals, which traditionally have been carried out in Urdu or some other language representative of an area of the world in which Twelver Islam is observed, are often now translated into English specifically so that the children can understand and identify their content.[14]

It seems clear that many second- and third-generation Muslim youth have become increasingly interested in Islam, not simply as a part of the culture of their families, but as a religion of which they are visibly proud. Muslim organizations, both local and national, are doing as much as possible to foster and nurture the participation of youth in various group activities. The Islamic Society of North America sponsors the Muslim Youth of North America (MYNA), while the Islamic Circle has begun a regular group for youth called Muslim Children of North America. These two largest of the Muslim religious organizations are trying hard to provide ways for youth to socialize in an Islamic atmosphere, learn more about their religion, and have fun together in supportive contexts such as summer camps and conferences.

Increasing numbers of young people are getting involved in learning circles in which they dedicate themselves to reading, memorizing, and even reciting the Qur'an. They study traditional commentary on the holy text and contribute to conversations about the necessity of new kinds of individual interpretation of text and tradition. Many young American-born Muslims, including African Americans, have gone much further than their parents in learning Arabic, Islamic law, and memorization of the Qur'an.[15] For girls, especially, learning circles in which they can participate with older women provide support and solidarity as they contemplate their own roles in the understanding of their religion. Some teens take the occasion of Ramadan to go to retirement homes and other communal settings to talk about Islam and practice Da'wa (calling), not as proselytizing but as inviting others to understand the true meaning of Islam.

## Prejudice and Identity Issues

There is little doubt that the climate of the United States in relation to Islam has changed significantly since 9/11. Polls show that despite Muslim efforts to explain Islam and defend it against charges of violence, public opinion has become less tolerant of Islam. Muslim children from the earliest age pick up these feelings, and they suffer greatly when they are teased by schoolmates for being "bomb throwers" or "ragheads." The Internet is full of advice to parents about how to help children understand what is happening when they see frightening images of destruction apparently caused by Muslims or find Arabs and Muslims in America being arrested and blamed for the terrible tragedy of 9/11. Many efforts have been made to help parents create a safe atmosphere in the home, to talk openly about who is responsible for what, and to let children act out their feelings when they are hurt and anxious. Teenagers, especially, may hide their emotions, and parents are encouraged to anticipate anger and depression by providing continuing support and expressing their own appropriate anger and pain.

Often these experiences of public prejudice connect with other feelings that Muslim children may have about being "different." Those who are of immigrant heritage, even if racial-ethnic connections are distant, may have darker skins, names that raise suspicion, and families who speak a language or observe customs that differ from those of other children. Young Muslims may be embarrassed to bring their friends home. African American children often experience the double prejudice of being black and being Muslim. These prejudices have long been reinforced by the entertainment media. Children are exposed to programs ranging from those featuring Porky Pig to *Law and Order* in which Muslims are never the heroes and the villains are often portrayed as dirty, lying, evil Arabs. Studies have shown what a deleterious effect such programming has on how Muslim children view themselves and their families, as well as the ways in which non-Muslim children view Arabs and Muslims.

A great deal of literature is available to parents to help Muslim children and youth understand their own identity, or identities, in the face of these difficult circumstances. Teens are given special attention, with much advice offered in texts and online.[16] Teens themselves are contributing to this literature, with works such as Sumaiya Beshir's *Everyday Struggles: The Stories of Muslim Teens*, a collection of short stories written by Muslim girls for their peers.[17] One enterprising fourteen-year-old has even founded *MG Magazine*, written by and for Muslim girls. Native Californian Yasmine El-Safy says that she started *MG*, with the assistance of her parents, because she found other teenage journals to be too concerned with fashion and makeup and not enough with values. She invites contributions not only from Americans but from young people around the world to help teens figure out together how to find their identity and live ethically and morally.

A fascinating area that some youth, most notably but not exclusively African American, are beginning to explore is rap music. While some interpreters insist that music is an inappropriate pastime for Muslims, others are open to new ways in which music can express Islamic identity. Rap music has become representative of a kind of identity politics, in which a style of music rarely associated with any kind of religion can be used to express pride in being Muslim. Particularly popular are the rappers called Native Deen,[18] whose lyrics from "M-U-S-L-I-M" (on the album *For the Cause of Allah*, 2002) contain these lines: "Don't know about you, I know about me, / I'm proud because I'm rolling Islamically. . . . / Don't ever frown, or your head looking down, / If you read the Qur'an you're the best in the town." Another song, called "Busy Bees," talks specifically about an MYNA conference, rapping out praise for young women who have the courage to put on Islamic dress.[19] One observer of young Muslims in America and Western Europe sees issues such as dress and music as part of "cool Islam." Turning consumerism to their own ends, these young people develop and buy Islamic products (such as halal or permissible McDonald's hamburgers), write and perform Islamic music, and in general find ways in which to express their identity as modern Muslims while using, rather than rejecting, the capitalism of the modern West. The Prophet, they observe, was a great merchant.[20]

On college and university campuses, Muslim youth movements have become very popular since 9/11, as has the wearing of Islamic dress.[21] For many girls this means wearing a headscarf along with jeans and sweaters, keeping the arms and legs covered. African American women, particularly those associated with the Ministry of Warith Deen Mohammed, tend to choose Islamic dress that reflects an African heritage, including head wraps that may leave the ears and upper neck exposed. Young men often wear small round caps, some with African designs. The choice of dress, while affirming a general affiliation with Islam, thus often also reflects another dimension of the search for identity. Many youth report that they are happy to find solidarity in numbers and that association with other young Muslims has given them courage to publicly affirm their faith with whatever symbolism that might involve.

## Concerns to Be Addressed

Many problems remain to be dealt with among Muslim youth in America, and often parents are extremely reluctant to even admit that they exist. Only recently have articles begun to appear in Muslim journals about drug use even by young children, described by one worried parent as "a creeping enemy" that includes everything from inhaling household products to shooting heroin. The first thing we need to do, she argues, is take the subject of drugs, along with premarital sex and other taboo topics, out of the box in the back of the closet into which we have thrown them, talk about them, and seek help.[22] Another subject to which attention is only beginning to be given is the problem of abuse of children, along with women, in the family. Recent research has revealed the persistence of this problem, exacerbated by the extreme reluctance of many Muslim women, particularly from immigrant families, to report their abusive husbands to the authorities.

Custody of children after divorce remains a problem for many American Muslims. While mothers who try to retain custody until their children are adults are often successful in American courts, many lack the support of their families when they try to abrogate traditional Islamic family law. More Muslim women today are insisting on agreements specifying their marital rights—including those concerning custody—before marriage. In many Muslim cultures marriage is contracted early for girls, often well before the age of eighteen. Early marriages for children in the United States are relatively unusual now, although there are some occurrences. So-called arranged marriages, interestingly, are slightly on the increase as some young people think that their parents may be helpful in bringing about a union based on strong family commonalities. Still, girls who enter wedlock at a young age, especially if they are married to older men, often suffer a great deal and may find it very difficult to find help.

Loyola University professor Marcia Hermansen argues that one of the taboo topics now beginning to be discussed in Muslim circles is the attraction for some Muslim youth, especially boys, to global movements of Islamic militancy.[23] She feels that a number of young people, often encouraged by mainstream Islamic organizations in America, are choosing to find their identity in a narrow, rigidly conservative brand of Islam that condemns both the ethnicity often stressed by their families and the more liberal climate of contemporary America. There is little question that the conservative and sometimes radical preaching of such groups as the Saudi-influenced Wahhabis in a small number of mosques in America is appealing to some Muslim youth, particularly those who are disturbed by elements of American foreign policy or, as is often the case with African Americans, are struggling with poverty and joblessness. To the extent to which it is true, this attraction to radical Islam may prove to be a growing problem for the American Muslim community.

For most observant American Muslim families, however, perhaps the greatest challenge is that faced by virtually all religious communities in the West today: How do they keep their young people involved in the faith when they hit adolescence, are beguiled by the consumerism and materialism of American culture, and question what may suddenly seem like unnecessary strictures and particularities of their family's faith? As one twelve-year-old boy asked his parents, "I'm old enough now to think for myself. Why do I have to follow all the rules set by old guys centuries ago. I can be a good person without all that."[24]

Today's Muslim children are growing up in what are both the most comfortable and the most difficult of times. Islam in many ways is a religion that is finally accepted on the American scene, yet at the same time prejudice against Islam rises as acts of perceived terrorism increase. American-born Muslims, for the most part, do not face the hard problems of economic survival suffered by their forebears, yet affluent Muslims are regularly excluded from the social circles of their financial peers. Young Muslims are extremely active in politics, education, social services, and the arts, and yet they often run into the walls of discrimination. It is this generation's children who soon will carry the responsibility of helping determine what it means to be Muslim in America, and in many ways boys and girls well short of the voting age are already busy at that task.

## NOTES

1. Saleem Qureshi, "The Muslim Family: The Scriptural Framework," in *Muslim Families in North America*, ed. Earle Waugh et al. (Alberta: University of Alberta Press, 1991), 55.

2. See Katherine Ewing, "Childhood: Premodern and Modern; The United States," in *The Encyclopedia of Women in Islamic Cultures*, vol. 3 (Leiden: Brill, 2006), 87–89.

3. Maulana Muhammad Ali, *The Religion of Islam* (Cairo, United Arab Republic: National Publication and Printing House, n.d.), 448–449.

4. Talsim Madhani, "Coming-of-Age Rituals: North America," in *The Encyclopedia of Woman and Islamic Cultures*, vol. 3 (Leiden: Brill, 2006), 71–72.

5. R. Ross-Sheriff and A. Nanji, "Islamic Identity, Family, and Community: The Case of the Nizari Ismaili Muslims," in *Muslim Families in North America*, ed. Earle Waugh et al. (University of Alberta Press, 1991), 113.

6. See, for example, Robert King, *Muslim Family Values*, Indystar.Com, September 10, 2005.

7. See Sound Vision Foundation's Web site, http://www.sound.vision.com.

8. See the Fine Media Group's Web site, http://finemediagroup.com.

9. Abdul Malik Mujahid, "Muslims in America: Profile 2001; Islamic Education," http://www.soundvision.com/info/yearinreview/2001/profile.asp.

10. Sharifa Alkhateeb, late president of the Muslim Education council in Virginia, cited in Samana Siddiqui, "Muslim schools vs. Public schools," http://www.soundvision.com/Info/education/pubschool/edu.muspubl.asp.

11. See, for example, Richard Wormser, *American Islam: Growing Up Muslim in America* (New York: Walker, 1994), chap. 4, "High School: The Good and the Bad," 45–54.

12. Iftikhar Ahmad and Michelle Y. Szpara, "Muslim Children in Urban America: The New York City Schools Experience," *Journal of Muslim Minority Affairs*, 23, no. 2 (2003): 295–301.

13. The term *hijab* refers specifically to a scarf or headdress, but can be used more generally for long or concealing clothing, including the scarf or veil.

14. See Vernon Schubel, "Muharram Majlis: The Role of a Ritual in the Preservation of Shi'a Identity," in *Muslim Families in North America*, ed. Earle Waugh et al. (University of Alberta Press, 1991), 128–129.

15. Jamillah Karim, "Between Immigrant Islam and Black Liberation: Young Muslims Inherit Global Muslim and African American Legacies," *Muslim World* 95 (2005): 502.

16. See, for example, Ekram Rida and Mohamed Rida, *Muslim Teens*, www.kvision-books.com.

17. Sumaiya Beshir, *Everyday Struggles: The Stories of Muslim Teens* (Beltsville, MD: Amana, 2004).

18. *Deen* is the Arabic word for religion.

19. Yvonne Haddad, Jane Smith, and Kathleen Moore, *Muslim Women in America: The Challenge of Islamic Identity Today* (New York: Oxford University Press, 2006), 37.

20. Amel Boubekeur, "Cool and Competitive: Muslim Culture in the West," *ISIM Review* 16 (2002): 12.

21. Nadine Naber in "Muslim First, Arab Second: A Strategic Politics of Race and Gender," *Muslim World* 95 (2005): 480, says that at the University of California, Berkeley, a girl has to wear the hijab to be considered "cool" in her Muslim Student Association.

22. Lobna Mulla, "Muslim Youth and Drugs: The Reality," *American Muslim Online* 4, no. 4 (2003): 14.

23. Marcia Hermansen, "How to Put the Genie Back in the Bottle: 'Identity' Islam and Muslim Youth Culture in America" *Progressive Muslims* (Oxford: Oneworld, 2003): 306–339.

24. Cited by Mahan Mirza at "Conversations with Our Neighbors of Other Religions" (public interfaith event, Connecticut Council for Interreligious Understanding, Hartford, CT, December 4, 2005.

# 9

# Hindu Children in the United States

RAYMOND BRADY WILLIAMS

Hindu children were absent from American neighborhoods and schools prior to 1965 because of restrictive immigration laws. Then doors to America reopened to welcome immigrants from every country, a welcome extended to those in two preference categories: first, professionals in medicine, science, and other fields needed to fuel the American economy in the second half of the twentieth century and, second, family members to be reunited with immigrants who had obtained a green card for legal residence or U.S. citizenship. Most Hindus came as students or young professionals as part of the brain drain and then returned to India for marriage or, after five years of residence, to bring spouses and children. The great majority of Hindu children are in families with roots and relatives in India, even though a few families may have emigrated after a generation or more in East Africa, England, Fiji, or Canada. The official designation is "Asian Indian." Their experience of socialization is different from immigrants from China and Japan who joined settled communities or from Vietnamese or Cambodians who came as refugees.

Hindu children are a growing segment of American social and religious life. Asian Indians number more than 2 million, up from the 1.7 million counted in the 2000 census.[1] Asian Indians identified as under the age of eighteen numbered 416,428, and those listing Asian Indian in combination with another designation were 494,468, which suggests a significant number of intermarriages by Asian Indians.[2] Hindus constitute more than 80 percent of the Indian population, so even if a larger percentage of members of minority groups emigrate, American Hindus number well more than a million, with more than four hundred thousand children.

The number of immigrants admitted from India numbered seventy-nine thousand in 2005, double the average of those arriving in the 1990s, and approximately ten thousand were under the age of eighteen.[3] Asian Indians and other Asians rank better than other groups in key indicators of child well-being, such as infant mortality rate, child death rate, teen death rate, teen birthrate, teen school drop-out rate, and percentage of children in single-parent homes.[4]

Because Hindu immigration developed recently and because it continues apace, each Hindu child has a specific location in an age group and in an immigrant generation. It is difficult to identify the generations in a Hindu gathering. Anthropologists refer to "the living present," which includes three generations generally in close contact. Studies of immigrants conceive generations differently. It is common to refer to children as being "first and a half generation," those who come as small children with their parents; as "second generation," those born in the United States; and, now increasing in numbers, "third generation," born of newly married couples reared and educated in American culture. The Asian Indian grandparent generation is just now emerging, as families bring grandparents from India to live with them and as the second generation has children. The levels of socialization, relative familiarity with Hindu practices and Indian culture, and comfort with living in American society are complicated and diverse. The differences in age, status, and life experiences in immigrant families create challenges for parents and religious institutions.

The Hinduism of immigrants is a constellation of diverse elements. Gujaratis, Tamils, Telegus, Bengalis, and those from other states and regions of India create subethnic linguistic groups. Vasudha Narayanan notes the diversity of Hinduism in India: "There are no generic Hindus: everyone comes with a regional, language, and caste identity, and would frequently identify herself/himself as belonging to a particular community which venerates a historical teacher and which worships a particular god or goddess."[5] Religious leaders and teachers from diverse groups travel regularly to the United States to help parents socialize their children and shape American Hinduism. So if a classmate says, "I am a Methodist; what are you?" a knowledgeable Hindu playmate might respond, "I am a second-generation Gujarati Vishnava worshipper of Krishna affiliated with the Gita Mandal at the Rama-Sita Temple and a member of the shakha youth wing of the Hindu Swayamsevak Sangh that is the American affiliate of the Rashtriya Swayamsevak Sangh in India," but she or he will probably reply simply, "I am Hindu."

The early immigrants established Hindu organizations and temples in order to socialize their children. A reason for the power of religion among immigrants, and, in fact, in this nation of immigrants, is that religion provides a transcendent basis for personal and group identity for new groups of immigrants as they make their way and socialize their children into American society. Parents turn to religion and religious practices as a significant way to maintain their identity and create an Indian consciousness among their children. Religious identity and organizations are not preserved and constructed in order to maintain separation from American society, but to provide a stronger foundation from which to negotiate a new group's place in American society. Contemporary mobility creates the opportunity and necessity to redefine religious traditions in order to affirm identity, which leads to freedom and malleability. It also leads to intentionality in shaping traditions that promise to be effective for new generations. Such freedom, malleability, and intentionality are core attributes of modernity.

A circular pattern of modernity develops whereby the needs of the children of immigrants lead to development of revised religious practices and institutions, which mold the identity of a new generation of American Hindus, thereby shaping American Hinduism as a new religious form. Three strategies of adaptation to American society are common in American Hindu organizations.

1. An ethnic strategy of adaptation emphasizes the regional-linguistic forms of Hinduism and values customs, arts, literature, and performances and religious leaders who are Gujarati, Bengali, Keralite, Hindi, or associated with a specific region or language of India. Religious rituals and programs are generally in the ethnic language.
2. A hieratic strategy emphasizes allegiance to a guru or other religious leaders affiliated with a particular *sampradaya* (religious tradition/ group). The primary rituals and sacred texts are those that recount the deeds and teachings of the founders and teachers, some of whom are elevated to divine status.
3. An ecumenical strategy reconstructs a *sanatana dharma* (eternal law) form of Hinduism that values traditional texts, an array of deities, and a way of life that preserves an essential Hinduism that most Hindus recognize and value and that is adapted to the demands of American society.

Most Hindu individuals and institutions adopt strategies that involve a mixture of all three and, like individuals, emphasize one of the other components as circumstances dictate and as it is advantageous in relation to the settled society.

The Bochasanwasi Akshar Purushottam Sanstha (BAPS) Swaminarayan group is a very successful Hindu group in America. It follows a hieratic strategy of devotion to a living guru, Pramukh Swami, an ethnic strategy of attracting primarily a regional linguistic following of Gujaratis, and an ecumenical strategy of reaching out to other regional linguistic groups with a message of *sanatana dharma*. It has six hundred temples, nine thousand centers, and seven hundred sadhus in India and abroad. Fifty-eight of the temples are in the United States, and a number of sadhus reside in the major temples and travel regularly to visit families and centers across the country. Several of the sadhus grew up in America and Britain and are part of the new breed of Hindu religious leaders.

Amid all these types of diversity, a question arises: How do children learn to be Hindus in America? Any attempt to answer involves both process and content. The *process* by which children become Hindus is participation in Hindu activities in their homes, temples, and *satsang* (religious meetings). The *content* are the texts, rituals, beliefs, and worldview that they, their parents, their primary social groups, and even their neighbors and associates identify as Hindu.

## The Process of Transmission of Traditional Homes

The home is the primary school of Hinduism, and the home shrine is the first temple for children. A Hindu marriage ritual establishes the wife and husband as religious specialists for the home shrines. Parents are the first priests and gurus. It is possible for a family to be fully Hindu and observant and only rarely go to a Hindu temple. Home shrines contain images and photographs of deities, gurus, and deceased parents. Food is offered to the deities before it is eaten by the family, so small shrines are often kept in the kitchen. Children observe devout parents performing morning and evening rituals (*puja*) that are as elaborate as rituals in some temples or as simple as a brief prayer and reading or reciting a sacred text. Pictures and statuary that adorn many homes convey messages about Hindu identity and commitment. Entering some homes, especially into the more private areas, is like entering homes in India.

Pramukh Swami instructed BAPS Swaminarayan Hindus to give special attention to families, children, and youth. His statement "Children are society's true wealth" is a motto for followers. The sadhu in charge of children's activities in the United States has commented, "To prevent [the children] from burning in the materialistic melting pot of America, [Pramukh Swami] constantly nurtures the children and parents with guidance, inspiration and knowledge." Pramukh Swami instructs every family to have a regular evening gathering in which to communicate openly about their daily challenges and their progress in spiritual development. It is common for family and friends to gather for a special ritual (*satyanarayana puja*) on auspicious occasions, such as housewarmings, anniversaries, or graduations. Worship at the home shrines and discussions at family gatherings supplement rituals and classes in the temples and centers.

Family behaviors are governed by complex systems of purity and pollution, as seen in such factors as proscribed foods, appropriate tasks of the mother or older girls during their monthly period, days of fasting and feasting, and behaviors deemed to be insulting. Birth rituals cleanse from ritual pollution, but such pollution is not considered "original sin." Children are not inherently sinful or polluted. The mother is the primary teacher and disciplinarian, but in theory, the eldest male is the head of the family, the final decision maker, the person who is responsible for the behavior and honor of the family, and the representative of the family to the community. Because in most families the mother is the teacher and religious specialist for the family, observing religious duties and taboos, she is "the primary mason of ethnic identity"—and of religious identity as well.[6]

A child is the subject of life cycle rituals, some of which are conducted by Brahman priests (*pujaris*), that are prescribed in Hindu texts. The four traditional stages of life are student, householder, semiretired person, and renunciant or religious seeker. Until the student stage, the small child is considered as innocent and lacking sin or effects of personal karma. A child is welcomed at birth by the act of putting a small amount of honey in the mouth and whispering the name of god in the ear of the child. The naming ritual a few days after birth is often transformed into a baby shower in America. The hair-cutting ritual is omitted or abbreviated. Hindu parents normally keep their children with them at temples and social gatherings, girls with their mothers and boys with their fathers. A majority of Hindu children in America now live in homes in which both parents work outside the home, and it is a relatively new development that children are sent to child-care facilities. Some families bring grandparents from India so they can help with child care. The sacred thread ceremony for Brahman boys at around seven years of age marks entry into the student stage of life, an age that Piaget considers a major cognitive turning point toward increased memory and a shift from preoperational to operational activities.[7] That marks the age of accountability for Hindu children, a time when boys assume duties outlined in the sacred texts that are appropriate to students. The traditional pattern was that boys would leave home to live with a teacher (guru) to learn sacred texts and rituals and the duties of the next stages of life. Puberty rituals for girls function in a similar manner, but girls remained at home to learn the duties of wives and mothers. That changed long ago in India, and the universal public education system produced the physicians, scientists, and engineers of the brain drain, some of them women, who came to the United States.

Modern education also delayed marriage for most Hindus, both in India and abroad, into the middle or late twenties. Previously, early entry into family occupations and early marriage meant that a stage of adolescence was not part of the Hindu construction of childhood. Indeed, adolescence acquired the status of a unique developmental period in the West only in the late nineteenth century. Contemporary Hindu families and organizations respond to the changes with a concept of "youth" that extends until around twenty-five years of age, when it is devoutly hoped by most parents that their children will be married. Indeed, Hindu youth organizations and meetings are viewed as relatively safe places where youth and their parents can scout out suitable marriage partners. The older unmarried youth often assist with the teaching and training of the children in Hindu organizations and temples.

Many Hindu parents discourage interaction with children and youth of the opposite sex, strictly prohibit dating, and hope for an arranged marriage within the Hindu community. Youth, especially females, who gain a reputation of dating may find it difficult to find a spouse from a respectable family. A gender difference is evident in that parents are generally stricter with daughters than with sons.

American Hindus often quote a Upanishad, "The whole world is one family," and say that family values are a major contribution of Hinduism to America. One important social goal of Hindu teaching in America is to strengthen family ties for children and householders.[8] Respect for parents and elders and the honor of the extended family are corporate values that are in tension with the contemporary American emphasis on individual rights and prerogatives. Sudhir Karkar, following Erik Erikson, calls these internalized norms the "communal conscience."[9] Vasudha Narayanan says simply, "The language of 'rights' is alien to this [Hindu] milieu."[10] The Hindu self and family are integral rather than separate concepts, and individuals are expected to make sacrifices on behalf of the group.[11] The nuclear family of immigrants in America is very different from the extended family in the Indian joint family system, in which the parents, the father's parents, the married sons and wives of their children, unmarried sons, and unmarried daughters live in the same household, with a common kitchen and joint property. The system is breaking down in India under the pressures of modernization, but remnants are preserved in America in titles used for each individual according to their family relationship, rather than personal names.[12] Knowing the appropriate respect, service, and assistance to be expected from and given to each is a significant part of socialization in the family. It is not uncommon to see children reach down to touch their parents' feet, or even to prostrate themselves before their parents, as a mark of respect. Indeed, the Vedic text encourages children to respect their mother and father as gods.[13]

## Temples

Hindu temples are constructed and other religious institutions form at the time children of immigrants reach the age to be socialized outside the home and can be viewed as substitutes for absent extended families. Many of the services provided by Hindu institutions are informal, performed on a case-by-case basis to meet economic, psychological, or cultural needs, similar to what would occur within a family whose members help each other. Immigrant parents search for "people like us" who can help them raise children to be "like us." Hindus go to the temple to see the deity and to be seen by the deity (*darshan*).[14] Families or individuals view the deities in each shrine, offer gifts of food and money, circumambulate the shrines, and receive a blessing from the deity that is administered by the temple priest (*pujari*). Although temple priests perform the cycle of daily and annual rituals, the Hindu calendar is abbreviated for immigrant families, who celebrate most of the major festivals on weekends.

Parents take children to temples for occasional Hindu rituals. It is difficult, however, for children to appreciate the meaning of the rituals, because they are conducted in Sanskrit, a sacred language twice removed from the English with which the children are comfortable. Temple priests, although well trained by ritual specialists in India, are generally not fluent in English or familiar with the needs of children of immigrant families. Hence, temple leadership is generally in the hands of lay Hindus.

## Organizations and Institutions

The search for other Hindus to help rear children leads to group meetings (*satsang*) for study of sacred texts, singing of sacred songs (*bhajans*), and formal classes for the children. Prema Kurien notes that group religious activity does not occur widely in traditional Hinduism, although adherents of what is termed "neo-Hinduism"—some of whom are active in the United States—do organize such activities.[15] Parents enroll their children in these classes to learn the fundamentals of Hinduism and about Indian culture.

Swaminarayan temples and centers developed elaborate, graded classes and programs for children and youth from eight to twenty-two years of age, separated by gender. Men teach boys, and women teach girls, thereby conforming to the special discipline of this group. English is the language of instruction. Bal/Balika Mandal in three grades that match public schools are for children from first through eight grades. Kishore/Kishori Mandal in

three grades is for high school students and college-age youth. Young professionals from ages twenty-three to thirty-five join the Yuvak/Yuvati Mandal,
some of these young adults volunteering to teach the children and youth.
Larger centers have Shishu groups for kindergarten and younger children.
Sadhus travel regularly to train volunteer teachers, to interact with children
and youth, and to oversee local activities. One sadhu explained, "When you
speak in mass meetings, the ears are listening, but when you meet personally, the heart listens."

This sadhu indicated that the primary aim of programs for children is
"character building" focused on three important things: to develop virtues
such as humility, tolerance, and service and to organize children's lives
through training programs in time management, cleanliness, personal
health care, and diligence; to instill pride in and dignity toward Indian
culture through traditions, history, and heritage; and to foster Hindu faith
through daily prayers, *satsang* meetings, rituals, spiritual readings, and
devotional singing. Children's meetings follow agendas of moral stories,
skits, dramas, motivational talks, sports, competitions, and other activities
through which children learn moral and religious values.[16]

All the centers follow the same curriculum, precisely prescribed from
the main Swaminarayan temple in Amdavad, Gujarat. The publication center in Amdavad prepares the lesson plans and instructional material that
is used everywhere. Volunteer leaders have access to a restricted Web site
that provides guidance for all the lessons and activities. Hence, all children
and youth in centers throughout the world have the same lessons and programs each week.

Children and adults voluntarily take extensive Swaminarayan examinations that supplement the classes and cover grade-level books printed in
Amdavad.[17] The Satsang Examination Program consists of a nine-year course
that includes two for children; four for youth; and three advanced courses
of six examinations, referred to as postgraduate work. The examinations are
prepared by Swaminarayan sadhus at the Sadhu Training Center in Sarangpur, Gujarat, and are printed in Gujarati, Hindi, and English at Amdavad
and administered annually at the centers in the United States on the third
Sunday of February. Volunteers in Amdavad, primarily schoolteachers and
principals, grade the examinations.

At twenty-four years of age, youth move into the regular *satsang* meetings, conducted in Gujarati. This marks a significant change in status that
normally involves marriage and a move into the householder stage of life.
The educational program is significant for the socialization of children growing up in America, and it is also important for the development of adult
leadership. A common statement is that if you want to know something
well, you should teach it. Adults who serve as volunteers in the educational

program participate in a significant educational and leadership program as well. Some of the youth raised in America request permission from Pramukh Swami to become sadhus and go to India for training at the Sadhu Training Center in Sarangpur. After initiation as sadhus, they become religious specialists for peers and their children as assigned by Pramukh Swami. They engage in a special relationship between world renouncers and householders that is significant in Hinduism both in India and in the United States.[18]

Religious arts transmit tradition. Young Hindu girls attend classes and lessons in classical Bharata Natyam dance. The dance involves intricate hand gestures, facial expressions, costume, and body movement that enact events from the Hindu tradition. Developing out of the temples of South India, Bharata Natyam is a form of religious expression, even though some Indian girls approach it as a more secular art form. A dance teacher in an ashram expressed the religious significance: "The . . . power comes from a dual focus on dance and the religious dimension that enfold and empower it. . . . We are able to tell them about our culture, and through the dance we are able to influence them about our *Sanatana Dharma*. . . . Classes are in Sanskrit. Memorizing *sloka* [verses] of the root dance scripture, *Natya Shastras* is mandatory."[19] Vasudha Narayanan indicates that Bharata Natyam dance classes are a primary means of introducing young girls to Hindu culture.[20] Major holidays and festivals include dance performances. Some boys and girls learn to play traditional Indian musical instruments and to sing sacred songs (*bhajan*). Children and youths also learn and perform dramas that enact events from the sacred texts. Stories—told, read, pictured, and enacted—transmit knowledge of Hinduism and messages so that the images in the temples, home shrines, and children's books come alive in performances.

Many temples, organizations, and study groups sponsor summer camps for children and youth, and some sponsor retreats for youth. Like other religious summer camps, the focus is on socializing children and youth in the beliefs, practices, and duties associated with specific traditions of the sponsoring organization, on assisting parents in nurturing respectable behavior, and on creating peer support groups for young adults who will become leaders in American Hinduism. Some Hindu camps are held in India, especially those sponsored by hieratic groups.

Trips to India for devout families are both secular holidays and religious pilgrimages. Visits to grandparents and other relatives are occasions for some of the life cycle rituals that permit the extended family to participate. Pilgrimage to famous temples and monuments introduce children to contemporary expressions of Hinduism. Visits to gurus and other religious specialists are common to show respect and to obtain guidance about family problems and prospects. Such trips can be disorienting for parents, who return to an India very different from that of their childhood memories, and also for children, who have difficulty communicating with relatives, absorbing omnipresent Hinduism, or fitting in with cousins and peers. They are often objects of admiration, envy, and dismay. They are American Hindus, even though they are sometimes said to have more detailed knowledge of aspects of Hindu thought and practice than that of their Indian cousins.

In the early days of community formation, parents decried the lack of Hindu materials in English for the instruction of children. Parents purchased materials written in Indian English that presupposed an Indian cultural setting, but both parents and children were dissatisfied. They imported picture books for children (*Amar Chitra Katha*), similar to American comic books, presenting the stories of Hindu deities, saints, and heroes in simple form. Vasudha Narayanan notes the change from first-person transmission of tradition: "The voice of the grandmother has now been replaced by the illustrated page of the *Amar Chitra Katha*."[21] A major religious and cultural event in India was the showing on national television serialized versions of the ancient Hindu epics of the *Ramayana* and *Mahabharata* in the early 1990s. Parents and religious groups purchased videotapes of these programs, which became popular in the United States as well. One sadhu charged with teaching children in America noted that there is still a lack of books in English on Hindu thought that will hold the attention of the second and subsequent generations of Hindu children.[22] Some groups maintain publishing houses in India to prepare materials in English for British and American Hindus. New computer technological capabilities fueled the development and distribution of a wide array of materials on CD-ROMs, DVDs, and the Internet to guide Hindu children and youth.

Virtual Hinduism is developing rapidly in the twenty-first century. Just as early institutions and organizations came into existence to assist in the socialization of children, a great deal of Hindu material on the Internet is directed at children and youth. In light of the prominence of scientists and computer specialists among early immigrants and the growth of the information technology industry in India, it is no surprise that the Web sites of national organizations, for example, the Vishwa Hindu Parishad and the Hindu Swayamsevak Sangh; of sectarian organizations, such as the Chinmaya Mission and the Bochasanwasi Akshar Purushottam Hindu Mission; and of local temples, among them the Hindu Temple of Kentucky and Hindu Temple of Atlanta, are sophisticated and point children and youth to appropriate materials.[23] The Swaminarayan home shrine is supplemented by the home virtual classroom through computer access to information and interactive learning programs on the *satsang* Web site. A special section for children reinforces many of the lessons that children learn at home and in the temples.[24]

Formats for teaching material change as rapidly as the technology. They include stories in written, animated, and audio forms; graded curricula and examinations; language instruction in Sanskrit and regional languages; and interactive learning lessons such as quizzes, games of matching symbols, painting, and crossword and other puzzles. Web sites host discussion forums and chat rooms for children and youth. They also provide chat rooms for parents where they can discuss issues related to raising children in America. If the home shrine is the first temple of Hinduism and the home the first school, the computer desk is another potential religious center in the home. Virtual pilgrimage and *darshan* are now available to anyone who has access to the Internet.[25]

Internet access creates a virtual connection for a new transnational Hinduism that parallels kinship and economic networks along which travel cultural and religious messages and artifacts. The Web sites connect children who are proficient in English and live in India, East Africa, Britain, Canada, the United States, and other countries where Hindus reside, as a visit to a Web site guest book shows.[26] Primary mediation of religious material moves into the hands of technologically skilled editors of Web pages and those who gain their allegiance and service. Technological modernization and free access to new modes of communication mean that religious knowledge is no longer mediated or controlled for children by parents, teachers, or priests. The process will shape the beliefs and practices of American Hinduism in the future and the formation of Hinduism as a world religion as immigrants spread in transnational arcs across the globe.

## Content of Tradition

The process of transmission creates a sacred world that children learn to inhabit, a world that has recognizable content and shape. The diversity of Hindu groups and practices in India and in the United States makes it difficult to define that world exactly or to state what all Hindu children are supposed to know and how they are to behave. They are introduced to different images of god in various temples; they revere different holy men and women (gurus, sadhus, swamis, or *pujaris*) and follow different paths. Examples of differences are found in two organizations with extensive youth activities in America: first, the Chinmaya Mission, which focuses on knowledge (*jnanayoga*) in a philosophical tradition (Advaita of Shankara) with a lineage of teachers (*guruparampara*), in a Shaivite tradition that includes the current leader (Swami Tejomayananda) and, second, the Bochasanwasi Akshar Purushottam Swaminarayan Mission, which focuses on devotion (*bhaktiyoga*) based in a different philosophical tradition (Visishtadvaita of Ramanuja), with a different lineage of teachers that includes the current leader (Pramukh Swami), in a Vaishnava tradition that accepts Swaminarayan as a manifestation of god. Toleration of such diversity is taught as a

Hindu virtue. A new American Hinduism is taking shape, primarily in what is transmitted to the children and young people. It is being "made in the USA" but, like much of American culture, is "assembled in America using parts produced abroad." It is easier and, perhaps, more instructive to illustrate some common elements taught to American Hindu children than to explore the diversity.

Hindu teachers describe Hinduism and Sanatana Dharma as a way of life that implies a set of values and virtues. Bodhinatha Veylanswami, publisher of a popular Hindu publication, describes the basic qualities that parents should inculcate in children. The "ten restraints of Hinduism's Code of Conduct" (yamas) are noninjury, truthfulness, nonstealing, divine conduct, patience, steadfastness, compassion, honesty, moderate appetite, and purity. Veylanswami teaches that such self-control leads to self-mastery, enabling youth to be more successful in achieving personal goals. The "ten observances" (niyamas) are remorse, contentment, charity, faith, worship, attending to scripture, meditation, sacred vows, recitation, and austerity. These are nurtured by teaching the child to worship and pray at the home shrine or temple. Such pious conduct brings divine blessings.[27] In addition there are certain duties (dharma) appropriate to the individual according to status as son or daughter, child or youth, elder brother or younger sister, and student or householder, along with a sense of moral consequence of actions (karma). An individual's actions affect the future and, finally, establish status in future rebirths (samsara).

Most Hindu children will learn stories from the major epics and puranas: Ramayana, Mahabharata, and Bhagavata Purana. A handbook for Hindu teachers describes the story: "The Ramayana presents Rama as an ideal son, and ideal student, an ideal brother, an ideal husband and, above all, as an ideal king. Sita, the heroine of the Ramayana, the very embodiment of chastity, presents the highest ideals of Indian womanhood. She has become an unforgettable name for all Hindus and is respected as mother."[28] The Mahabharata, the world's longest epic poem, recounts a battle between good, personified by the Pandava brothers, and evil, personified by their cousins. One of the most important Hindu texts is a section of the Mahabharata called the Bhagavad Gita (Song of the Lord), which is a reflection on the three Hindu paths of knowledge, devotion, and action in a conversation between a Pandava warrior, Arjuna, and the god Krishna, in the form of his charioteer. The Bhagavata Purana contains stories of the life and exploits of Krishna, including childhood pranks and pious behavior, youthful relations with young women—especially his consort, Radha—and actions as a wise teacher and savior. These stories and dramas are enjoyed and interpreted at several levels, depending upon the age and devotion of the learner, as humorous stories, as adventures of heroes and demons, as moral guidance, or as deep philosophical reflection. Basic religious topics of creation, evil, honor, virtue, redemption, and salvation are revealed in story form.[29]

A young boy acting as guide to novice visitors at the dedication of a new Hindu temple in Aurora, Illinois, that houses many deities carefully explained that Hinduism teaches monotheism, "like Christianity and Judaism." That may be the linchpin for understanding diversity and unity in Hinduism. Gods in hundreds of forms coexist in the Hindu pantheon, and familiarity with the iconography, characteristics, and stories of the main deities are important in the education of Hindu children and youth. Vishnu and Shiva are the primary deities and they appear in many forms. The iconography of each deity is multiformed and the interpretation is multivalent, so the worshipper sees many deities understood at several levels of meaning. Hindu worship is not exclusive, and children are taught that all the images represent the divine; hence, the "monotheism" of the young boy's introduction to visitors corresponding to the monotheism of advanced Hindu philosophy.

Being Hindu involves knowing the appropriate words and gestures for rituals, which are learned at home, in temples, and in classes. The verses (*sloka* or *mantra*) used as chants or prayers in common rituals are in Sanskrit, so children and youth are taught the rudiments of transliteration and pronunciation of basic verses. Two common ones are the Gayatri Mantra and the Shanti Mantra. The Gayatri Mantra is chanted by many Hindus a part of morning *puja*: "AUM [a sacred syllable], the giver of life, remover of pains and sorrows, bestower of happiness, and creator of the universe, you are most luminous, pure and adorable. We meditate on you. May you inspire and guide our intellect in the right direction." The Shanti Mantra is repeated in many rituals as a prayer for peace: "AUM, may there be peace in heaven, peace across the waters. May there be peace on earth. May peace flow from herbs, plants and trees. May all the celestial beings radiate peace. May peace pervade all quarters. May that peace come to me, too. May there be peace, peace, peace." Children learn the appropriate verses for various ritual occasions.

Hindu education enables children and youth to pass through the veil of secularity and religious diversity of American society to enter, if only in passing, a sacred world where they are at home with parents, relatives, and other immigrants from India who share a common worldview. A sacred lunar calendar marks festivals and celebrations for Diwali (October/November, a festival of lights for New Year), Shivaratri (February/March, a day of fasting, repentance, and meditation on Shiva), Ramnavami (March/April, the birth of Rama and the birth of Swaminarayan), Krishna Janmashtami (August/September, the birth of Krishna, when temples are decorated and children stay awake until the time of birth at midnight), Navaratri (September/October, nine nights dedicated to the Durga, Lakshmi, and Saraswati), and Holi (February/March, a joyful festival of colors when people of all ages smear each other with colored water and powders). Other family, regional, or sectarian festivals celebrate events such as the birthday of a guru, the anniversary of the dedication of a temple, or a sectarian event.

Sacred people deserve special respect and reverence. Sadhus follow ascetic disciplines of renunciation of the world and are affiliated with specific lineages or groups (*sampradaya*). Some now live for long periods in temples and ashrams in the United States, but many more travel from India on regular tours to teach, lead conferences, and visit their followers. Leaders refer to "a new breed of swamis," some of whom were raised in Western countries, who are familiar with the issues faced by children in America and who can relate more closely with them. Families incorporate visits to gurus, sadhus, and other religious specialists during trips to India. Independent Brahman specialists visit homes to perform religious rituals. Temple priests (*pujaris*) are respected in their role as servants of the deities in the temples.

Children also learn a new sacred topography that begins at the local temple as sacred space. Some temples are related to pilgrimage sites in India. For example, Venkateswara temples in Pittsburgh, Pennsylvania, and Aurora, Illinois, are associated with the temple at Tirupati, Andhra Pradesh; the Meenakshi temple in Houston, Texas, is associated with the temple at Madurai, Tamil Nadu; and the Rama temple in Lemont, Illinois, is associated with the birthplace of Rama at Ayodhya, Uttar Pradesh. Some family vacations include visits to major Hindu temples in the United States. Each family and each group has an array of sacred places that are nascent in America and well established in India.

Individuals and families value and occupy different rooms in the Hindu house and experience various aspects of the Hindu worldview. Immigrant parents moved from India, where they were surrounded by cultural and religious institutions and practices that made the worldview part of the accepted structures of plausibility—what was taken for granted. That worldview is in many ways at odds with the dominant American culture, the influential religions, and the plausibility structures that support them. Hindu practices and institutions are constructing a new form of Hinduism as a minority option in the American cultural and religious landscape. Transmission of the tradition to children is a major aspect of that construction. Children and youth often feel that they are caught in the middle.

Hindu children in American are bicultural. They experience themselves as marginal in America but also in India when they return for visits. Youths joke among themselves about their marginal status—using humor with a bite. They call themselves "ABCDs," an acronym for American-Born Confused

Desis. (*Desi* refers to a compatriot.) The use of the two languages in the joke is intentional. An ABCD contrasts with new arrivals from India, known as "JOBS" (Just Off the Boat), who are still steeped in Indian ways. Young American Hindus say that they are "Coconuts" (brown on the outside and white on the inside).

Aditi Banerjee, a Yale Law School student, describes the experience of marginality of ABCDs':

> While I learned to speak Bengali before English, and while I bonded with the children of my parents' Bengali friends, what drew us together wasn't our ethnicity: it was our shared experience of being brown folk in a white world, of weekend get-togethers with other immigrant families and eating Indian food, of being dragged to pujas celebrated in local high schools rented out for the weekend. It was our shared experience of being perceived as the dorky nerds in school, of teachers and parents expecting us to excel in math and science and to be at the top of our class, of teachers and parents expecting us to be engineers or doctors, of being asked whether we spoke Indian. In short, what bound us together wasn't being Bengali American or even necessarily Indian American; it was the experience of being foreigners born in this country, a shared experience of alienation.[30]

Parents look to the network of Hindu institutions to help provide a secure identity and to shelter their children from the threats the parents perceive in American youth culture—disrespect for elders, rampant consumerism, individualism, addiction to alcohol and drugs, illicit sex, sexually transmitted diseases, and all the other horrors of popular culture they see portrayed in the media. Such challenges are addressed, and generational tensions are mediated in Hindu temples and organizations. Gurus and sadhus provide advice and counsel to individuals and families to help families keep open lines of communication, face the challenges, and be successful as Americans and as Hindus.

Rapid mobility and immediate media communication are creating transnational Hindu networks, stretching from India around the world. The open door to the United States continues to attract immigrants from India, who constitute a wealthy, well-educated, and influential component of transnational Hinduism. Mobility and media are defining elements of modernity that are shaping Hinduism. American Hinduism is being redefined by the impact of this modernity, and responses to the needs of American Hindu children is a process of determining what American Hinduism is and will be in the future, and it affects the character of transnational Hinduism in India and other countries as well.

## NOTES

1.  U.S. Census Bureau, "The Asian Population 2000 Census Brief," table 4, "Asian Population by Detailed Group: 2000" (February 2002), 9.

2.  Note that in the 2000 census, 88.4 percent self-identified as Asian Indian and 11.4 percent as Asian Indian in combination with another designation.

3.  U.S. Department of Homeland Security, Office of Immigration Statistics, "Persons Becoming Legal Permanent Residents during Fiscal Years 1820–2005 by Region and Country of Last Residence," in 2005 Yearbook of Immigrant Statistics, 11.

4.  2005 Kids Count Data Book Online, "Race and Child Well-Being, table 1, December 22, 2005, http://www.aecf.org/kindscount/sld/auxiliary/race_child.jsp.

5.  Vasudha Narayanan, "Rituals and Story Telling: Child and Family in Hinduism," in Religious Dimensions of Child and Family Life: Reflections on the UN Convention on the Rights of the Child, ed. Harold Coward and Philip Cook (Waterloo: Wilfrid Laurier University Press, 1996), 56.

6.  Prema Kurien, "Gendered Ethnicity: Creating a Hindu Indian Identity in the United States," American Behavioral Scientist 42 (January 1999): 661.

7.  L. A. Sroufe, R. G. Cooper, G. B. DeHart, and M. E. Marshall, Child Development: Its Nature and Course, 3rd ed. (New York: McGraw-Hill, 1996), 415.

8.  Williams, "Hindu Families in the United States," in American Religions and the Family, ed. Don Browning and David A. Clairmont (New York: Columbia University Press, 2007), 197–210.

9.  Sudhir Karkar, Inner World: A Psycho-analytic Study of Childhood and Society in India, 2nd ed. (Oxford: Oxford University Press, 1981), 153.

10.  Narayanan, "Rituals and Story Telling," 53.

11.  J. M. Farver, S. Narang, and B. H. Bhadhra, "East Meets West: Ethnic Identity, Acculturation, and Conflict in Asian Indian Families," Journal of Family Psychology 16 (2002): 340.

12.  Nawal K. Prinja, ed., Explaining Hindu Dharma: A Guide for Teachers (London: RMEP of Chansitor, 1996), 59.

13.  Krishna Yajur Veda, Taittiriya Upanishad 1.11.2.

14.  Diane Eck, Darshan, 2nd ed. (New York: Columbia University Press, 1996).

15.  Kurien, "Gendered Ethnicity," 653.

16.  Sadhu Amrutnandan Swami, personal communication.

17.  http://www.swaminarayan.org/satsangexams/detail.htm [12/30/05].

18.  Louis Dumont, Religion/Politics and History in India (Paris: Mouton, 1970), 37.

19.  V. P. Dhananjayan, "Lithe and Limber, Yogaville Dance Camp," Hinduism Today, November 1993, http://www.hinduismtoday.com/archives/1993/11/1993-11-16.shtml, December 20, 2005.

20.  Vasudha Narayanan, personal communication.

21.  Vasudha Narayanan, "Rituals and Story Telling," 75.

22.  Vasudha Narayanan, personal communication.

23.  http://www.hssus.org/, http://www.hindukids.org/, www.kytemple.org/, www.hindutempleofatlanta.org/,www.chinmayamission.org/, www.kids.swaminarayan.org/ [12/28/05].

24.  http://kids.swaminarayan.org/ [12/30/2005]

25. http://www.swaminarayan.org/dailydarshan/index.php#start [12/28/05].

26. http://www.swaminarayan.org/GuestBook/august2005.htm [12/28/05]

27. Veylanswami Bodhinatha, "Publisher's Desk: Nine Key Qualities to Cultivate in Children," *Hinduism Today*, September 2002, http://www.hinduismtoday.com/archives/2002/7–9/10–12_pub_desk.shtml.

28. Nawal K. Prinja, ed., *Explaining Hindu Dharma: A Guide for Teachers* (London: RMEP of Chansitor, 1996), 134.

29. See Narayanan, "Rituals and Story Telling," 72–77.

30. Aditi Banerjee, "Hindu-American: An Emerging Identity in an Increasingly Hyphenated World" (speech given at the Hindu Ideological Empowerment Seminar, conducted as part of the Human Empowerment Conference—2003, Chicago, November 1, 2003), http://www.indiapost.com/members/story.php?story_id=1896 2003–12–08.

# 10

# Buddhism and Children
# in North America

RITA M. GROSS

To speak of North American Buddhist views about childhood and the institutions specifically set up to nurture children by North American Buddhists in a single short book chapter is difficult because North American Buddhism is so diverse. It is also difficult because, though Buddhism is now quite popular among North Americans, it is not very well understood and is quite different from the dominant religions in many ways, including its various understandings of childhood. For one thing, though North American Buddhists do not always explicitly talk about rebirth, it is the assumed background of all traditional Buddhist discourse, which has important implications for the parent-child relationship. For another, Buddhism is not especially centered around the (nuclear) family and reproduction. In fact, because monasticism has such pride of place in traditional Buddhism, it has even been considered "antifamily" in more than one cultural context. Moreover, children became monastics quite frequently, and monastics have always had a large role in the education of children.

## Buddhist Diversity

Even within Asia, Buddhism is culturally extremely diverse, so diverse that the various forms of Buddhism had lost track of each other, and it was Western scholars who decided that Southeast Asians, Tibetans, Chinese, Japanese, and Koreans all practiced the same religion, which had originated in India. These Buddhisms do not look very much alike and some contemporary commentators claim that it would make as much sense to claim that Judaism, Christianity, and Islam are actually all branches of the same religion as to claim that all these forms of Buddhism represent one religion.[1] Had people from another planet or from Asia "discovered" the Western world, it is easy to imagine that they could have thought the three monotheistic religions were sectarian variations of the same religion; they are not much more different from each other than are various forms of Buddhism. Within each of these forms of Buddhism, there is also significant denominational diversity.

I make these observations only to emphasize the extreme diversity of North American Buddhisms, given that all forms of Asian Buddhism are now practiced in North America, both by Asian immigrants and by converts from other ethnic groups, though the immigrant and the convert communities have little contact with each other. What they share is some kind of choice. Buddhism is a relatively new religion in North America and most North Americans are unfamiliar with it. Immigrant Buddhists made the choice, for one reason or another but rarely because they were Buddhists, to come to North America. Many came as impoverished laborers or refugees seeking a better life, and they had little Buddhist education and few religious leaders initially. Convert Buddhists made the choice to abandon culturally familiar religions and to reeducate themselves radically in the time-consuming, demanding forms of Buddhism that stress meditation as the major discipline.

Students of North American Buddhism usually talk of two main groups of North American Buddhists—"immigrant" Buddhists, and "convert Buddhists." This terminology is inadequate. Some Asian American "immigrant" Buddhists have practiced Buddhism in North America for five generations, and a second generation of "convert" Buddhists has now grown up and members of this group are becoming leaders and teachers. Most scholars estimate that roughly four-fifths of the North American Buddhist population is Asian American, but convert Buddhists get most of the attention.

This is in part because convert Buddhists are usually well educated and articulate, but also because we are passionate practitioners who bring a questioning openness to our newfound faith. As a result, we have made significant contributions to Buddhist thought and scholarship, especially regarding gender equality, and are regarded as a vibrant and vital part of the Buddhist world by many Asian Buddhists. Some Asian Buddhist teachers, including one of my own teachers, Khandro Rinpoche, says that "secretly," she believes that the future of Buddhism lies in North America. Convert Buddhists have also had a significant impact on North American culture, well beyond their numbers, especially on the arts and on therapy techniques. Most of the literature on Buddhism one finds in the average bookstore was written either by Asian Buddhist teachers or by convert scholar-practitioners. Literature about or by Asian American Buddhists is difficult to find.

I am one of those scholar-practitioners. By 2006, I had practiced in the Tibetan Vajrayana tradition for thirty years with several Asian teachers. I have also studied Buddhism in Asia. Like many convert Buddhists of my generation, I have had relatively little contact with Asian American Buddhists. It seems that in that generation, though members of both communities made a life-altering choice, we are Buddhists for different reasons and that gap has proved difficult to bridge. In major urban centers and among younger convert and Asian American Buddhists, both of which groups are often educated in the same elite colleges, there is more interaction.

## Distinctive Buddhist Views of Childhood
## and the Parent-Child Relationship

To discuss Buddhist children in North America, we need to consider several topics. First, it is important to discuss some Buddhist views of children and the parent-child relationship. Although Buddhist practices and forms are remarkably different, I find an equally remarkable underlying consensus of view wherever I go in the Buddhist world. For Buddhists, this is as it should be. The Buddha taught eighty-four thousand different ways to understand reality, it is said, and diversity of practice is normal in the Buddhist worldview. It is extremely important to understand this underlying consensus of views about childhood first, even if the words are different in different contexts. Then, for North American Buddhists, it is important to look into two emerging bodies of literature. There is an emerging significant body of literature from the viewpoint of Buddhist parents, who have struggled very hard to learn how to raise Buddhist children as an extreme minority in a culture whose religious views are very different. Regarding this issue, I would argue that Buddhist parents are in a much more difficult situation than Jewish or Muslim parents; for these last two, at least there is a family resemblance with the dominant religious culture. Second, there is a much smaller emerging body of literature written in the voice of younger North American Buddhists. Fortunately, in both cases, the voices of both Asian American and convert Buddhists are expressed.

## Who Are Children? Buddhist Perspectives

Probably the biggest difference between culturally familiar ideas about children and Buddhist views about them concerns classic Buddhist teachings about karma and rebirth. In the Buddhist view, any birth is by definition a *rebirth*. To be born is to be reborn, without exception. Therefore, newborn children enter the world with a long, indeed an endless, past. In the Buddhist view, it is nonsensical to talk about an absolute beginning to linear time because, whatever the posited beginning may be, whether creation by a deity or the big bang, we simply always ask, "But what was there before that?" Individual lives do not *begin*. What seems to us to be an individual life is part of a beginningless and endless lifestream, interdependent with all other lifestreams, that will take continually changing forms until enlightenment.

It is difficult for many North Americans to imaginatively feel what it would be like to live in a cultural universe in which rebirth is taken for granted, but it is important to remember that most Asian Buddhists do. Buddhists may not talk about karma and rebirth in every sentence, but these core assumptions are always in the background of Buddhist discourse, just as assumptions about a creator deity and a personal immortal soul are always in the background of theistic discourse. Convert Buddhists may not take these beliefs literally, but their Asian teachers often do. Most North American Buddhist parents, whether convert or Asian American, would not assume that their children enter this life with a blank slate, and they certainly do not enter this lifetime as "innocent" beings. Taking rebirth requires a cause, and for Buddhists, that cause is a stream of energy called karma. Karma is often seriously misunderstood by outsiders, so it is important to try to keep in mind what Buddhists mean by this term. In its simplest meaning, karma relates to the fact that causes produce effects; therefore events, including any specific rebirth, are not random but are the result of the causes that set them in motion. However, it is crucial to understand that the reality of cause and effect does not negate freedom of choice, according to Buddhists. A present effect may be the unalterable result of previous causes, but my response to that present event, which is my own doing, becomes the cause of effects in the future. For example, if I choose to overeat as a response to crisis, in the future, I will gain weight, and perhaps health problems.

It is not possible in this context to delve deeply into the Buddhist worldview, but the implications of teachings about karma and rebirth for parent-child relationship are profound. The connection between a parent and a child is not simply biological or genetic. In the Buddhist view, conception requires three things, or perhaps four—an egg, a sperm, a karmic continuum seeking rebirth *and* attraction between parents and that karmic continuum. In Buddhist folklore, and even in doctrinal systems, conception is not the result only of a mechanical process; the consciousness seeking rebirth *chooses*, if it is well trained or, if it is not, is *compulsively driven* toward its next rebirth. The karmic heritage of a child both connects the child with its parents and separates that child from its parents. A particular parent and a particular child are drawn together because of previous interactions between them, but it cannot be assumed that this karmic interconnection is always positive, benign, or *what the parents want from the child*. The child also has its own karmic heritage, independent of what it may receive from these particular parents. Therefore, children cannot be construed as possessions of their parents or cultures.

These ways of thinking about rebirth and conception have interesting implications for some popular American notions about child rearing. Buddhist children really can't get away with the angry retort of some rebellious children: "I didn't ask to be born!" If one was born, one sought out that rebirth in some way. There is a consistent Buddhist emphasis that people should be grateful to their parents for providing them with a body and care when they were "young and helpless," as it's often put. However, because children have their own karmic inheritance independent of their parents' designs for them, parents really don't have the right to isolate children and reproduce in them their own cultural and religious prejudices. As consistently as Buddhists are told to be grateful to their parents for their bodies and for the care given to them when they were young, Buddhists are also told that, at least for serious practitioners, their true family is the spiritual family of their teachers and fellow practitioners, rather than their "blood" family. There is no assumption that the spiritual family and the blood family will consist of the same people.

Within the vast matrix of interconnected beings who are constantly dying and being reborn, rebirth as a human being is considered especially fortunate because it is much more likely that one can attain enlightenment as a human being than in any of the other forms in which one could have been reborn.[2] Therefore, especially in some forms of Tibetan Buddhism, one is urged to contemplate the preciousness of human birth and to use that birth wisely. However, among human rebirths, only a *fortunate* rebirth is truly useful. A *fortunate* human rebirth is one in which the opportunity for spiritual growth is present. Having a human body is relatively useless if the economic, emotional, and spiritual conditions for pursuing spiritual disciplines leading to enlightenment are not present. For this reason, mere biological reproduction has never been a central Buddhist value. Buddhists do not forbid controlling one's fertility and, in fact, would encourage it because only children who can be well cared for experience a truly *fortunate* rebirth. Buddhism may be the only major religion that neither requires its members to reproduce as a religious duty nor interferes with peoples' need to control their fertility if they are sexually active. Such attitudes toward biological reproduction are liberating for both adults and children. Adults are not pressured into reproducing and are not encouraged to reproduce beyond their ability or the planet's ability to provide adequately for children economically, emotionally, and spiritually. For Buddhists, the point of being alive is to become enlightened and to help all sentient beings, rather than promoting only one's own clan or family line, and having too many children detracts seriously from those tasks. If there is a basic commandment for Buddhists, it is "Save all sentient beings," not "Be fruitful and multiply." For children the benefits are also obvious. They get the care they need, which is impossible to provide if there are too many children, and also the freedom to live out their own karmic proclivities.

Children, like all beings, are more than bundles of karmic energy; they also are Buddhas who don't yet understand their true identity, though a *precious* human birth, properly nurtured, contains the possibility of awakening to that identity. Consistently across sectarian lines, Buddhists believe that the fundamental nature of beings is pristine, enlightened, and good, though not "good" versus "bad" in a dualistic sense. Mistakes, misunderstanding, and misdeeds are secondary, not primary, like clouds that temporarily block the sun, in an often-used analogy for the relationship between Buddhanature and temporary confusion. Nevertheless, unless enlightenment is attained, those temporary confusions persist from life to life, fueling the rebirth process, which is why the opportunity presented by a precious human birth is of such critical importance. However, in this context, the emphasis is on Buddhanature or basic goodness, the pristine nature of all beings, because not all Buddhists, especially convert Buddhists, believe in rebirth literally, whereas all Buddhists affirm that the basic nature of beings is unsullied and clear. Children, no less than any other beings, are endowed with this basic nature, according to Buddhists, and some would claim that it is closer to the surface in young children than in adults. Children do not have to be fixed or shaped by their parents or their culture. They only need to be nurtured and appreciated properly, so that their true nature can flourish.

Are children in some sense ideal practitioners? Most Buddhists would not quite agree with such a claim, for a child also possesses a great deal of ignorance, which it needs to outgrow through practicing the basic Buddhist disciplines of morality, meditation, and study. However, in Mahamudra texts, the example of a small child is used as one analogy for the ideal state of resting the mind in its essential nature. Mahamudra is the pinnacle of meditation practice in some forms of Tibetan Buddhism. It is part of Tibetan oral tradition, which means most of texts are not available to the general public, but this analogy of the child recurs in many contexts. The text reads: "Rest in meditation without grasping onto the existence of the clear aspect of mind, just like a small child gazing at a shrine hall." Khenpo Tsultrim Gyamtso, Rinpoche, one of the last great meditation masters to have been trained in Tibet, who teaches widely on Mahamudra, commented on the above passage in a very illuminating way—illuminating both about the child's experience and about the open, nonfixated, nonideological state of mind that is so prized by Buddhist meditators:

When a very small child who knows nothing about a shrineroom enters the shrineroom, he or she sees everything physically as clearly as anyone else does. But the child does not think, "Aha! That is Vajradhara and that is Vajrayogini, and he is blue and she is red." A child does not think that, and yet that does not in any way diminish the vividness of its perception of the colors and shapes and so forth. This analogy is an example of the fact that you do not need to conceptualize about what you are experiencing; you just need to look directly at the experience.[3]

Using children as examples of ideal practitioners is tricky, for sometimes the example is used to reinforce unexamined beliefs rather than to point to an uncomplicated natural state of mind. I remember vividly being taught as an older child about the New Testament notion that one needed childlike faith to be saved. "And what does that mean?" was the rhetorical question. "Little kids believe whatever you tell them. If you tell them that Santa Claus exists, they believe you. Your faith in God and Jesus should be like that." One wonders how the older child or the adult could discriminate between naive faith in Santa Claus and naive faith in God or Jesus, but such questions were not encouraged.

Note that in the Buddhist example, a state of openness, rather than any specific belief, is pointed to by the analogy of the small child. As the child grows, it inevitably starts to take on beliefs and opinions, which do a great deal to mar the basic open, clear, natural state of mind. Religious and cultural institutions can be among the worst offenders in trying to turn children into loyal party-liners rather than inquisitive, nonjudgmental adults.

## Childhood from the Perspective of North American Buddhist Parents

It is the job of Buddhist parents to work with the karma, the ignorance, and the openness of children to help them become moral, nondogmatic, happy adults. How to do this in North America has been a puzzle for both immigrant and convert parents, for different reasons. It is difficult in both cases because North American Buddhism lacks what has always been taken for granted in Asian Buddhist communities—the existence of a strong monastic community. The monastic community both provides religious education for everyone, children and adults, and is the vocation of those most serious about spiritual discipline. North American Buddhism is almost completely a lay movement, which constitutes a great experiment in the transmission of Buddhism from one culture to another, and from generation to generation.

In the late twentieth century, North American Buddhism experienced a growth spurt. Starting in the 1950s Japanese war brides who practiced Sokka

Gakai Buddhism quietly began group meetings in their homes. This form of Buddhism went on to become the most economically and racially integrated form of North American Buddhism. After changes in immigration laws in 1965, many immigrants and refugees from Southeast Asia brought their diverse forms of Buddhism to North America. Meanwhile, many young North Americans converted to Buddhism in the late 1960s and in the 1970s, partly as a spin-off of the countercultural movement that was so evident at that time. In an interesting historical convergence or as the outcome of major karmic tendencies, depending on whether one uses materialist or Buddhist analyses, many Asian Buddhist teachers came to North America at the same time. Japanese Zen teachers came to minister to Japanese American communities and wound up founding Zen centers that catered largely to convert audiences because their young American students really wanted to sit zazen, something that interested few Japanese American laypeople. Tibetan teachers in exile found a place where their endangered religion might be replanted as young Americans flocked to their fledgling meditation centers. Young Americans who would later start the Vipassana movement studied for years in India with Burmese and Thai meditation masters. Korean and Vietnamese Zen meditation masters, such as Thich Nhat Hahn, also had a major impact on emerging North American Buddhism.

For convert Buddhists, the dilemmas brought about when they eventually had children were intense because their model of Buddhist practice was essentially a monastic model, though they had never taken monastic vows and expected to have both North American careers and families and a serious Buddhist practice. For this comment to make sense, it is necessary to know something about how Buddhist communities throughout Asia, with the possible exception of Japan, have constituted themselves for many centuries, which at this point is not the way North American Buddhism is working, either for converts or for immigrants. In Asian Buddhism, there is a very practical division of labor between monastics and laypeople, who are completely dependent on each other. The Buddhist monastic vocation, which involves renouncing conventional family life and career to have time for other concerns, is not based on antisexual and anti-body prejudices, as is often supposed. Rather, it is based on the completely practical realization that there is not enough time in one lifetime for everything. Raising a family and having the economic basis to do so take a great deal of time. So do studying and mastering all the intricacies of Buddhist thought and practice. These two time demands are difficult to reconcile in one single day or one single lifetime. Thus, that one should do one or the other in this lifetime, or during a specific period of this lifetime, was the conclusion of most Asian Buddhists. Although the monastic vocation is revered, whether one takes the monastic or the householder path is primarily the result of one's own inclinations and tendencies. In the final analysis, it is better to take the path appropriate for oneself rather than to try to take the other path because of family pressure or other external forces. Either path, if done sincerely and ethically, will result in progress toward enlightenment. The most basic Buddhist practices for anyone, monastic or householder, are kindness and generosity; the householder lifestyle offers many opportunities to practice those disciplines.

But the alienated, well-educated, and childless young North Americans who converted to Buddhism in the 1960s and 1970s were drawn to intense, regular, and time-consuming meditation practices, which in Asia had been mainly a monastic pursuit, though lay meditation movements are gaining strength in Asia at present. Their Asian teachers were delighted because many of them were frustrated with the state of meditation practice in their Asian homelands and were eager to teach meditation to serious students. Daily meditation practice and long retreats became the norm for these enthusiastic convert Buddhists. Eventually, many of these rootless searchers married, settled down, got jobs, and began to have children. By the middle 1980s a disconcerted cry was being heard from these Buddhists, especially the women. How were they supposed to find time for formal practice while raising young children? Why hadn't they ever heard anything about how to raise children from their Buddhist teachers? How would they bring up their children as Buddhists in a largely Christian culture, given that at that time, convert Buddhist institutions had neither child-care facilities nor programs for educating children? As can readily be seen, this dilemma was specific to convert Buddhists. In the first place, the participation of so many laywomen in serious Buddhist practice was unprecedented in Asia. There Buddhist meditation has been so much a men's discipline that young Western women who asked to be taught meditation while traveling in Asia were often told that women were not capable of meditating. Second, most Asian Buddhists would not have expected to be able to raise a family and maintain a serious formal meditation practice at the same time.

Immigrant Buddhists did not face this problem. Most of them were laypeople and they honored the traditional division of labor between monastics and laypeople. Some, such as Japanese American Pure Land Buddhists (which is not a monastic form of Buddhism) had been in North America for several generations and had already established Buddhist institutions such as communal life, congregations, and Dharma schools for their children. One North American Pure Land Buddhist wrote of the importance placed on children's programs in that movement: "The adult members of our Jodo Shin temples place tremendous importance on the Dharma schools and recreational programs for their children. The programs and training for adults certainly take a backseat to the children's activities."[4] The same author noted that convert Buddhists were rarely attracted to that form of Buddhism, however.

Most other immigrant Buddhist communities have not been in North America as long as have Japanese Pure Land Buddhists, but as quickly as possible they have duplicated the institutional forms of their Asian homelands, including inviting resident monks from Asia as their leaders and teachers. As in Asia, the rhythm of events at the local temples and regular sermons and addresses by the monks present to the laypeople, both children and adults, the basic teachings of Buddhism. In presenting Buddhism to their children, immigrant Buddhists have several advantages over convert Buddhists. Often they live in ethnic neighborhoods, which means that their children can socialize with other Buddhist children more easily than the children of convert Buddhists who often do not live near other Buddhist families. And their children have Buddhist relatives, something that is quite rare for convert Buddhist children, who thus end up celebrating all major family holidays with their non-Buddhist family members. But immigrant Buddhists also have to deal with the typical immigrant experience of children who want to assimilate to the dominant culture; Buddhist identity can be one of the casualties of that assimilation process.

Convert Buddhists have developed significant rhetoric around their issues with child rearing. Sometimes they have criticized Buddhist traditions and institutions for not paying enough attention to the needs of families. If one takes account only of the literature most frequently studied in Asian Buddhist universities and meditation centers, that claim would be correct. Families are not at the center of that discourse. Furthermore, a Buddhism that did not include viable and valued alternatives to reproduction and family life would be unrecognizable as Buddhism, in my opinion. Because of its strong monastic tendencies and the fact that it offers a viable alternative to reproduction and family life, Buddhism has been viewed as not sympathetic to families in several cultural contexts, both Asian and North American. Those who want to pursue this line of discussion can easily point to the fact that the religion was founded by a man who abandoned his family in his quest for enlightenment. Buddhist sensibilities, however, revere that choice as renunciation leading to liberation for all humanity and as a necessary precondition for the Buddha's enlightenment. No Buddhist commentaries on the story suggest that the Buddha made a wrong or an unethical choice when he abandoned his family to seek enlightenment. Clearly for Buddhism, the family is not supreme. There are valued and viable alternatives to the family. For me, a single, childless convert Buddhist, one of the most important things about Buddhism is that it includes alternatives to reproduction and family life in the midst of religions and a culture that are relentlessly pronatalist, in the midst of a culture that honors no other lifestyle than that of the heterosexual nuclear family. Those convert Buddhists who claimed that Buddhism does not provide guidance about child rearing and family life were unfamiliar with the many examples of Asian Buddhist cultures in which lay Buddhists developed very workable ways of integrating family life and lay Buddhist practice. They also often expressed disapproval of the Asian division of labor between monastics and householders, seeing householders' forms of Buddhist practice as inadequate. About this issue, it seems that lack of information about Asian Buddhist models, rather than Buddhism's overall inattentiveness to the needs of families, was the cause of convert Buddhists' frustrations.

Their frustrations also led to important innovations. Because convert women did not want to delay serious formal practice until middle age or later, people began to insist on programs for children that would occur while adults were meditating, thus allowing parents to continue their formal practice even while they raised children. Such children's programs were especially needed at longer residential retreats, but many city centers now offer children's programs during the most popular weekly meditation period, which is often Sunday morning. These children's programs have the double agenda of providing adults with periods of formal meditation practice and of teaching Buddhism to children, thus approaching the model of the Jodo Shin temple, at which children's activities have higher priority than adults' programs.

Small changes have meant a lot to many parents. For example, at one residential meditation center with which I am familiar, morning chants, which are usually done during the first period of meditation, before breakfast, are now delayed until the beginning of the second period of meditation, after breakfast. Parents eat breakfast with their children, who then go off to the children's center, allowing parents to join the assembly for chants. One urban center, which constructed its own building, included members who insisted that one room in the new building be suited for children so that they could more easily come to activities at the center. Among those involved in the many experiments to include children in the activities of meditation centers and retreats, Thich Nhat Hahn and his students have perhaps gone the furthest in including children. His practice is described in the following words: "Children fully participate in the same practices as adults—sitting and walking meditation, precepts recitation, and dharma talks. Adults and children practice right alongside each other. The child in the adult and the adult in the child are equally honored. The only thing that differs is an understanding of the special energy needs of children and so children are encouraged to leave the meditation hall when they tire or are in need of active play."[5]

North American Buddhists, both converts and Asian Americans, also talk of integrating meditation into family life. Convert parents, predictably, have qualms about pressuring their children to meditate and there is some disagreement about the age at which children should begin to meditate. But by now, many who began meditating as children have grown up with the practice and been able as teenagers to complete practices and retreats that their parents did not do until many decades later in their lives. This more closely resembles Asian Buddhisms in which children—boys much more frequently than girls—received significant religious training at monasteries. Again Thich Nhat Hahn has taken the lead in encouraging family practice. He feels that because American Buddhism will be lay Buddhism for the foreseeable future, practicing Buddhism in families should be a priority, and he encourages letting children participate fully. His simple but profound meditation instruction focuses simply on mindfulness of breathing and smiling. He recommends that families have a special room, to be called the "breathing room," that is a place of refuge in the house. Family members retreat there to breathe and smile whenever they become angry and upset. In his words: "That little room . . . should not be violated by anger or shouting, but should be respected. When a child is about to be shouted at, he or she can take refuge in that room. Neither the father nor the mother can shout at him or her any more. He or she is safe on the grounds of the Buddha. Mommy needs that too. Sometimes she wants to take refuge in that room, sitting down, breathing, smiling, and restoring herself. Daddy also."[6] He also recommends turning mealtimes into a time of family mindfulness, beginning with taking three mindful breaths in silence. Then, "take a look at everyone around the table. You look at your child and you see him or her, really see them, like Mahakashyapa seeing the flower. You see deeply and it does not take a long time, just one or two seconds is enough. You look at your husband or wife in full awareness. That kind of awareness makes you happy and you look at the food for a few seconds."[7]

Another advocate of family meditation tells her own story. She, her new husband, and their five children were having many difficulties in getting their blended family to work. Although both adults had been meditating for years, they did not want to force their children to meditate, but finally decided that because meditation was the only thing that helped them cope with the difficult situation, it might also help their children. "So it was only out of desperation that we instituted our daily family meditation sessions. All five kids complained at first but soon got used to it and, believe it or not, some of them even came to *like* it. After only a year or two we found that not only had we survived the crisis, we were actually thriving."

At that point, the adults decided that the family meditation sessions were no longer mandatory, and all five children stopped coming to them immediately. Within two weeks, the parents noticed that family communication was deteriorating again, as the children became "grumpier, whinier, more selfish, and meaner. That's when we realized that our family meditation sessions were responsible for much of the peace and harmony we'd been enjoying." Needless to say, the parents decided to reinstate the family meditations, and they report that the kids didn't even argue when it was pointed out to them that they had been happier when the family meditation sessions had occurred. They bought the analogy that is often used in meditation circles to indicate the importance of regular meditation practice; it's just like flossing one's teeth. Flossing keeps the teeth clean and meditation keeps the mind healthy and happy.[8]

Perhaps the greatest innovation for North American Buddhists has been a dawning realization that child-care and parenting *themselves* can be forms of meditation practice. Perhaps the most passionate advocate of parenting as practice is Jon Kabat-Zinn, who has also pioneered using mindfulness practice to reduce stress levels in working with coronary patients. He writes, "It [mindful parenting] is a true *practice*, its own inner discipline, its own form of meditation. And it carries with it profound benefits for both parents and children."[9] This is not a radical claim for Buddhists to make. Every meditation teacher stresses that one's real meditation is one's life and that the reason to do formal practice is so that mindfulness and awareness can eventually inform everything we do. Nevertheless, all meditation teachers also stress that to reach that level of competence as a practitioner usually takes a great deal of formal sitting practice. It is not so easy to maintain the open, aware, nonfixated state of mind of the small child in the shrine room, especially in a culture that encourages the exact opposite of those qualities. The clash between parenting and meditation practice comes because children can be extremely distracting and demanding, and because for biological reasons, people usually undertake childrearing while they are still relatively young and may not have a mature enough meditation practice to be able to carry mindfulness and awareness into such a difficult situation. Of course, children who grew up meditating would have a head start on their convert parents, and future generations of North American Buddhists may have an easier time with mindful parenting.

In raising their children, "immigrant" Buddhists and "convert" Buddhists have come to resemble each other more, even though they usually gather in different groups. One group may emphasize community and the other may emphasize meditation, but the same kinds of programs work to introduce children to Buddhism. Not surprisingly these programs developed especially for children are not so different from those found in any other religion. Sunday schools, children's classes, alternative schools, rites of passage to mark critical points in growing up, youth programs, summer camps, less demanding meditation programs for young people, and conferences for Buddhists under thirty—one finds announcements for all of them on the pages of the many Buddhist newsletters and electronic bulletin boards now common in

North America. As a result, younger Buddhists have many of the same experiences, whether their parents were converts or immigrants, as we shall see.

## Representative Voices of Younger Buddhists

Until very recently, apart from talking with young Buddhists whom one might know, it was very difficult to hear from young Buddhists themselves about what it was like growing up Buddhist, whether in an immigrant or a convert home, or to hear from those who chose Buddhism as teenagers or young adults. Many younger Buddhists felt isolated and wondered where the other young Buddhists were, given that most dharma centers seemed to be peopled mainly by middle-aged Buddhists of their parents' generation. The older generation, especially among convert Buddhists, also wondered whether their bold experiment would burn out in one generation. But many among the twenty-something Buddhist generation are now checking in and becoming active in Buddhist communities.

One of these young Buddhists, who had grown up for eight years in a strict Zen community in New Hampshire, discovered while working in the kitchen of a meditation center that she really wanted to talk with other young Buddhists about the challenging life questions with which she was engaged, not just with Buddhists of her parents' generation, who were easy to find. She began collecting names of young Buddhists and corresponding with them. These conversations turned into two books filled with first-person accounts of being Buddhist written by young Buddhists of all kinds.[10]

Her conclusions? For one, that "we had certain questions in common. Should I consider life as a monastic, am I really a Buddhist, do I need a teacher, can I practice things from several traditions, should I try to learn an Asian language or go to Asia, can I just do meditation, what do my parents and friends think?"[11] She also concluded that the immigrant-convert divide that had been so central to her parents' generation was no longer as significant. Asian and non-Asian Buddhist young people had similar experiences and questions, went to the same schools, and often made the same decisions. She also found that, while many young people are hesitant to self-identify as Buddhists, young people are aware of Buddhism and are interested in exploring it. Buddhism has become known to North American culture to an extent that was almost unimaginable thirty or forty years ago, before so many Buddhists came to America and so many Americans became Buddhists. But most of all she was immensely impressed with the seriousness and thoughtfulness of her young Buddhist peers. She expects them especially to "be distinguished from those before us by our greater activity in socially engaged Buddhism and use of the dharma in professional capacities."[12] It is comforting to an older Buddhist to hear of these young people, as the generation of those of us who did so much to bring Buddhism to America, whether as converts or as immigrants, reaches old age and death.

## NOTES

1.  Richard H. Robinson, Willard L. Johnson, and Thanissaro Bhikkhu, *Buddhist Religions: A Historical Introduction*, 5th ed. (Belmont, CA: Wadsworth/Thompson Learning, 2005), xix–xxiii.

2.  Talking about some rebirths as more fortunate than others always provokes the question of "fairness," especially for Westerners. However, the question of fairness is not uppermost for Buddhists, who take comfort in having consistent explanations for why things happen as they do, just as Western theists take comfort in explaining that things happen as they do because that is "God's will." Neither explanation is inherently more logical, nor does either deal with questions of justice and fair play more adequately. For Buddhists, questions of justice and social justice are new and complex topics that cannot be discussed in this context. For my reflections on the relationship between karma and social justice, see Rita M. Gross and Rosemary Radford Ruether, *Religious Feminism and the Future of the Planet: A Buddhist-Christian-Feminist Conversation* (New York: Continuum, 2001), 163–182.

3.  Transcripts of oral instructions that have been privately circulated and are not available publicly.

4.  Ryo Imamura, "Good and Evil Are One," in *Dharma Family Treasures: Sharing Buddhism with Children*, ed. Sandy Eastoak (Berkeley, CA: North Atlantic Books, 1994), 200–201.

5.  Mobi Warren, "Partners in the Practice," in *Dharma Family Treasures: Sharing Buddhism with Children*, ed. Sandy Eastoak (Berkeley, CA: North Atlantic Books, 1994), 57–58.

6.  Thich Nhat Hahn, "Family Mindfulness," in *Dharma Family Treasures: Sharing Buddhism with Children*, ed. Sandy Eastoak (Berkeley, CA: North Atlantic Books, 1994), 99.

7.  Thich Nhat Hahn, "Practicing Mindfulness at Mealtimes," in *Dharma Family Treasures: Sharing Buddhism with Children*, ed. Sandy Eastoak (Berkeley, CA: North Atlantic Books, 1994), 229.

8.  Kerry Lee MacLean, *The Family Meditation Book: How Ten Minutes a Day Together Can Make Life Saner (and More Peaceful) for Even the Busiest Families* (Boulder, CO: On the Spot Books, 2004), 10–12.

9.  Myla Kabat-Zinn and Jon Kabat-Zinn, *Everyday Blessings: The Inner Work of Mindful Parenting* (New York: Hyperion, 1997), 25. While I was composing this chapter, a book on parenting and Buddhist practice written solely from a mother's viewpoint finally appeared. See Karen Maezen Miller, *Momma Zen: Walking the Crooked Path of Motherhood* (Boston: Shambhala, 2006).

10. Sumi Loundon, *Blue Jean Buddha: Voices of Young Buddhists* (Somerville, MA: Wisdom, 2001); Sumi Loundon, *The Buddha's Apprentices: More Voices of Young Buddhists* (Somerville, MA: Wisdom, 2006).

11. Loundon, *Blue Jean Buddha*, xvi.

12. Ibid., 218.

# 11

# Asian American Confucianism and Children

JEFFREY MEYER

In the Han Dynasty there was a man named Guoju whose family was destitute. His mother would often eat less of her own food so that she could give it to Guoju's three-year-old son. Guoju said to his wife: "We are so poor that we cannot give to mother the food she deserves. She has to share with our son. Should we not bury him?" When he had dug the grave about three feet deep, he uncovered a lump of gold, on which was inscribed: "No government official nor ordinary person can take it away."

Although it is a pervasive social and cultural influence, Confucianism is not considered an official religion in the People's Republic of China, Taiwan, or anywhere else in Asia. It is an ancient tradition that has shaped the ethical and social mores of the Chinese people for at least two thousand years and one that during the past millennium became firmly entrenched in the cultures of Korea, Japan, and Vietnam and other areas of significant Chinese settlement, such as Singapore and Malaysia. But as the story above, from the famous *Twenty-four Tales of Filial Piety*, makes clear, it traditionally included a strong religious element.[1] What Western readers might mistake for a merely ethical issue is in fact a matter of ultimate concern and commitment. As Abraham was asked to sacrifice Isaac as proof of a transcendent relationship to God, Guoju feels called to infanticide out of a transcendent relationship to his mother. In both cases what would normally be a heinous act of murder is transformed into an expression of highest virtue.

As an ethos that shaped the nature of the Chinese family system, Confucianism urged extreme forms of devotion to parents, who would one day become powerful spirits, living ancestors influencing the family in this world for good or ill. In many ways the honored ancestors of the family were considered more powerful after death than they had been in life, since the fortunes and success of the living depended upon their goodwill and earthly interventions. Although lacking some features of what we normally recognize as religion, Confucianism embodied at least unmistakable religious elements in its worship of the ancestral spirits and the ultimate nature of its central concerns. It determined what was worth dying for. And it was Confucianism, more than any other cultural influence, that developed enduring understandings of what it meant to be a child in East Asia.

As a cultural tradition, Confucianism had a number of important dimensions—social, religious, ethical, political—but in this chapter I will focus on just one of them, its function as shaper of the Asian family. In so doing I am confident that I am touching the heart and soul of the system, for the family was the central paradigm for all the rest of Confucian religious and political applications. In contemporary Asia, the religious dimension has been weakened and the connection with imperial systems of government attenuated, but the familial dimension of Confucianism remains strong. As Clark Sorensen and Sung-Chul Kim have pointed out, Korea has traditionally set filial piety (the linchpin of Confucian virtue) at the center of its ethical universe.[2] The same could be said for the other nations of East Asia. According to Tu Wei-ming, heaven has ordained the virtue of humanity (*ren*), an innate predisposition toward compassion and love for others that is universally and most convincingly expressed in one's love for one's parents.[3] Although the institution has its variations throughout Asia, the Confucian family system, with its emphasis on devotion to parents and self-abnegation for the welfare of the group, is what immigrants to America have brought with them and depended upon for strength and success in their new world. The emphasis of Confucianism is

> not on the individual but on the web of human relations . . . on a person's moral obligation to others, not on the individual's human rights. The fact that the Chinese language possesses an extraordinary number of kinship terms suggests an intense concern with family relationships; similarly, the rich body of ethical terms and concepts indicates China's preoccupation with moral values. The emphasis on kinship and familial relations bound nineteenth-century Chinese immigrants in the United States in ties of mutual reciprocity.[4]

To explore the idea of the child in American Confucianism, therefore, I will begin with the assertion that its concept of children is firmly embedded in its understanding of family. In every case, parents take precedence over children and the family as a whole over its individual members. The family's traditional purpose was corporate, to strengthen, preserve, and enhance itself in this world and the next. What Jean Lau Chin says of the Chinese family is applicable to East Asian families generally:

While family is important in most cultures, the emphasis on loyalty and obligation to the family in Chinese culture is unparalleled. In Chinese folklore and stories of the Confucian tradition, defiance of parental authority results in the admonition, punishment, or death of the transgressor. It is the benevolence of the parents that saves the child and enables them [sic] to achieve maturity and independence.[5]

And, as we see in the story of Guoju and his nameless son, if the "lifeboat" situation arises, it is the children, not the parents, who must be sacrificed.

## The Textual Sources of Filial Piety

What was the Asian/Confucian family? It was not the nuclear family, but an extended family system (da jiating zhidu), patriarchal, patrilinear, and usually patrilocal, tied together through each succeeding generation by the line connecting fathers and sons. Wives who married into the stem family were expected to give up their natal families and take on their husband's living parents and deceased ancestors as their own. The family was an entity separate from and superior to any of its individual members. The most significant virtue that united this corporate entity, the glue that held it together, was filial piety (xiao), greatly celebrated throughout Chinese history and still a powerful influence in Asia and wherever Asians have immigrated. "Central to all the virtues is filial piety: the duties of respecting and obeying one's parents, taking care of one's aged parents, striving to bring honor to the family name, and performing the ceremonial duties of ancestral worship."[6]

If I am correct that the Chinese family is the core unit of society and its main purpose to strengthen, preserve, and extend itself into future generations, then the corollary of this assumption is that the purpose of parenting is to produce offspring who excel in the virtue of filial piety. "A child's role and responsibilities can be summed up in one word: xiao."[7] I will attempt to define filial piety by reviewing the most influential texts that have promoted filial piety throughout Chinese history, then briefly survey its continuing presence in contemporary Asian cultures, and finally investigate how this virtue continues to influence child rearing among Asian immigrants in America.

The most ancient scriptural source of Chinese attitudes toward children is the Classic of Filial Piety (Xiaojing), which purports to be a discussion of virtue between Confucius and Zengzi, one of his most revered disciples and a noted exponent of filial piety. Were that true, the text would be about twenty-five hundred years old, but in fact it was likely written a few centuries later, becoming canonized as a "classic" during the Han Dynasty (206 B.C.E. to 220 C.E.). It seems to have been written as a primer for young boys, because of the limited vocabulary and gradually increasing level of difficulty through its eighteen chapters.[8] Its purpose was to teach boys the overwhelming importance of filial piety and to urge them toward filial practice. Chapter 10 contains a classic formulation of the parameters of filial piety:

> The filial child is one who serves parents in the following ways: when living at home with them, he goes all out to show his reverence to them; in nourishing them, he goes all out to cater to their pleasure; when they are sick, he carries to the utmost his expressions of distress; when they die, he carries to the utmost his grief; when sacrificing to the spirits, he carries to the utmost his attitude of awesome respect. When these five things have been done perfectly, he may then be said to have truly served his parents.[9]

Throughout the centuries this quotation has been taken to express the essence of filial piety.[10]

A second important writing on this virtue is the *Family Rituals* (*Jiali*) of Zhuxi, the great twelfth-century expositor of a renewed Confucianism. His work represents a codification of ritual practice for his own time, with specific directions for performing four rites of passage: capping (for boys) and pinning (for girls), weddings, funerals, and ancestral worship. It was an idealized text and probably at first applied only to wealthy and prominent families, but later began to exert its influence on less powerful families as they strove to emulate their "betters." While not a theoretical treatise on filial piety, it was a manual that inculcated virtue by ritual performance, since the spirit of the whole work created a system of symbolic behaviors that validated reverence and respect for parents and elders in a hierarchy of persons, both living and dead. By later centuries the *Family Rituals* became the standard by which a family's practice of filial piety was judged, and its use as a model of family ritual practice deeply influenced Vietnam, Korea, and Japan. A French missionary reported in the early eighteenth century that the *Family Rituals* was second in popularity only to the *Analects* of Confucius.[11]

And finally, there are the collections of popular stories of filial piety that were told and retold throughout the centuries, the best known of which is the collection from which the story of Guoju was taken, *Twenty-four Tales of Filial Piety* (*Ershisixiao*). These famous stories were "influential in Chinese childrearing, analogous to books by Dr. Benjamin Spock."[12] They provided dramatic accounts of young paragons of virtue, some otherwise famous and some not, who had served their parents with extreme expressions of filial love and devotion. Reading these stories and being doubly removed from their context (neither Chinese nor traditional), they strike the contemporary reader as exaggerated, ridiculous, incredible, or even disgusting. Yet if the Asian/Confucian family is unique in its strength and resilience, if its powerful influence still supports Asian Americans and has enabled them to succeed as immigrants, I believe that the clue to its success lies in enduring ideals implied in these stories. If not the literal stories themselves, the values so dramatically conveyed by them are what Asian parents have sought to convey to their children, inspiring in them behaviors that would carry on the long tradition of family even in the inhospitable contemporary world of a foreign country.

There is, for example, the story of a paragon of filial piety named Wang Xiang, who, despite his stepmother's unfair criticisms and cruelty to him, continued in his perfect obedience and filial service to both of his parents. This same stepmother had an unusual fondness for fresh fish, but because it was winter, her craving seemed impossible to satisfy. So Wang Xiang hit upon an idea. He flung off his clothing and threw his body on the frozen surface of the nearby river, hoping to thaw the ice and catch a fish for his demanding mother-in-law. High heaven responded to this extreme expression of filial virtue, a hole opened up, and two fish leapt out and landed on the ice. Wang Xiang delightedly took the fish back to his family home and gave them to his stepmother to eat. This kind of full-hearted filial piety is rare, notes the compiler of the story.

Heaven responds to high virtue with miracles. In another story a young man wants to make a soup for his mother out of bamboo shoots, but it is dead winter. He goes to a bamboo grove, embraces the bamboo, and cries because he cannot fulfill her request. Heaven and earth respond: the bamboo shoots suddenly break through the frozen ground.[13] The Guoju story with which I began makes the same point. The lump of gold he digs up is not just a lucky accident. It carries the miraculous inscription honoring his filial piety, which (unlike the gold) no one can take away from him.

Another significant story, called "The Grieving Heart Tastes Excrement," features Yu Qianlou, who exhibits unexcelled filial devotion. Yu has become a high official in the imperial government and is sent to an important post. One day he suddenly feels his tongue twitch wildly and his body pours out cold sweat. Knowing this is a bad omen, he hastens home to find that his father is near death. The doctor says that the only way to find out what is wrong with him is to taste his excrement. If it tastes bitter, it will be easy to cure him; if it tastes sweet, his illness will be hard to cure. As soon as he hears this, Yu tastes his father's excrement from the night soil pot and finds it is the latter, so he is deeply grieved. That evening, he lights the incense and worships heaven, kowtows to the spirit of the Big Dipper, and asks heaven to take his life in place of his father's. We are not told what happens, but the point is that Yu Qianlou exhibits great filial devotion in abandoning his official post and tasting his father's excrement, and especially in being willing to give up his own life to save his father's.[14]

These stories of filial piety, however incredible or disgusting they may sound to outsiders, affirm the central importance of filial piety in Asian cultures. They demonstrate the paramount virtue that men and women are supposed to exhibit, no matter at what cost to themselves. The religious dimension of filial piety is revealed, not only in the sacrifices to the ancestors in the other world, but also in the ultimate sacrifices of self that are required, whereby individuals endure any pain, and even death itself, to be a filial son or daughter. When heroic filial piety is practiced, heaven responds with miracles.

## Children and Filial Piety in Contemporary Asia

The quaint and idealized stories just recounted should not deceive us. Without being literalistic, they express values that continue to be influential, but often in entirely new forms. Family life and filial piety have undergone dramatic changes in Asian societies throughout the twentieth century, especially during the past fifty years. Some of the factors propelling these changes are the decay of the extended family system and its practice of coresidence; the decline of parent-arranged marriages; shrinking birthrates and the preponderance of smaller families generally; aging populations with longer life expectancies; geographic mobility; higher divorce rates; and a whole host of economic changes, including industrialization, new job opportunities, state welfare programs, and the decline of land as the major source of a family's wealth.[15]

All these factors have brought changes in the concept and practice of filial piety and a corresponding change in the understanding and upbringing of children. Filial piety appears to continue to be important but the manner of its practice has changed and the scope of its influence has been reduced. Generally speaking, the last two requirement of filial piety demanded by the Xiaojing—rites of mourning and sacrifice to ancestral spirits—have been curtailed, while the first three requirements, though modified, have remained nearly as important as they had been in earlier times.

Perhaps the most direct Asian assault on familial values and filial piety was made in the People's Republic of China (PRC), where the tradition was initially condemned as feudal, patriarchal, and injurious to the equality of women. Radical forms of social engineering were attempted. Government ideologues attacked the family and attempted to create a commune system in which children were taken away from the parents and nourished and educated by the state. These draconian experiments failed, and after the chaos of the Cultural Revolution had dissipated, the government went back to a more traditional view of the family, again reaffirming the filial obligations of children to their parents. Still, prohibitions against burial, in favor of cremation, and restrictions on the sumptuary expenditures of sacrificial rituals continue to restrict the two final Xiaojing requirements. Although those prohibitions against the pieties of death and burial have been somewhat relaxed—there has been a notable increase in burial over cremation, with its attendant geomantic rites, especially in rural areas—it is doubtful that the old expressions of piety will ever regain their traditional fervor.[16]

Long-term effects on child-rearing practices and children's experience will also result from China's one-child policy. Current statistics in the PRC show that there are 117 boys born for every 100 girl babies. Although the one-child family is more prevalent in urban areas, it is certain to fundamentally modify the practice of filial piety and change the experience of children everywhere. On the other hand, various adaptations have occurred in the PRC that alter traditional practice yet allow the continuation of some forms of filial piety. As fewer married children wish to live with their parents, those in one rural village have developed the practice of "ritualized" coresidence with parents for a brief period after their marriage. The young can thereby express their filial piety and the old can "maintain face."[17] The old male-centered, elder-son practice of filiality has been replaced by a system in which daughters are playing an equal role, with "much feminized filial figures" emerging in the official discourse.[18] Generally speaking, filial piety in the PRC now means children of either gender taking care of their elderly parents.

The situation in Korea and Japan is similar. Not subjected to such drastic forms of social engineering as those of the PRC, modernization has been the major agent of change in these nations. Yet research indicates that in Korea, "the cultural understanding of indebtedness to parents has not disappeared." Many elderly parents still live with their children's families, daughters now contribute more actively to the care of elderly parents, differential shares of inheritance still are related to expectations of filial care, and various national campaigns to revitalize filial piety as a moral code indicate a continuing awareness of this obligation.[19] Other findings suggest that while the content of old customs has been modified to fit modern circumstances, and obedience to parents has suffered some deterioration, in most respects Koreans have maintained the value of filial piety by reinterpreting it for modern society and by pragmatically adjusting performance standards to new circumstances.[20]

The same dynamics noted above may be documented in Japan. Despite changes in family structure, declining birthrates, an aging population, and all the other social changes noted above, the ideal of filial piety "has for the most part remained relatively unscathed," although the discourse now is likely to emphasize the child's debt of gratitude toward parents rather than the child's obligation to serve. Furthermore, the old authoritarian father figure has been displaced. Today's children, when asked about their ideal image of parents, overwhelmingly say that they want their parents to be "like friends."[21] Yet despite the changes of modernization, the impact of training in filial piety on today's children is still enormous. Japanese children are still taught from their earliest days the quality of obedience, so that they may attain the ideal of the "good" Japanese child, training that is reinforced in preschool socialization, for example, where teachers will have children verbalize their gratefulness to their mothers and fathers for giving them lunch. As the child grows older these teachings are transformed into expectations of diligence and high achievement, represented in the willingness to work hard to get good grades, pass exams, and be accepted into good schools.[22]

In Asia, although the parameters of the virtue have changed to some degree, children in Confucian societies are still inculcated with most of the values of filial piety and feel the weight of parental expectations throughout their lives. Thus being a child in East Asia means being shaped by the expectations of filial piety, with all the advantages and disadvantages that these may bring. Such expectations are a source of both conflict and strength.

## Confucian Children in America

The early years in the life of an Asian child are generally rather carefree, and this pattern has continued in America. Mothers maintain a close physical connection with their children, attending to all their physical needs rather than talking to them and pushing them toward verbalization. Toilet training takes place rather early but in a stress-free manner. Parents conceptualize early childhood moral development in two distinct stages: the age of innocence and the age of understanding. During the first stage, children are indulged, and parents are tolerant and lenient in their expectations. This leniency may reflect the long-held Chinese conviction that all human beings are born good—there is no concept equivalent to the Christian idea of original sin.[23] Then, when children are about to enter school, the situation changes abruptly; strict discipline is imposed because the child is judged to have reached the age of understanding, capable of distinguishing right from wrong.[24] It is then that the shaping of the child, by parents and educators, toward accepted notions of filial piety, takes place. The mother generally maintains a closeness to her children, whereas the father often becomes distant and remote, as the family disciplinarian. This developmental pattern seems to be very ancient, as evidence for it may be found in Zhu Xi's *Family Rituals*: "Before the seventh year, children are called youngsters; they can go to sleep early, get up late, and eat whenever they wish. Beginning in the eighth year, however, whenever they enter or exit through a doorway or whenever they sit down to eat, they must wait their turn, which will come after all those who are older. At this age they begin to learn modesty and yielding."[25] Learning to grow up means learning one's specific place in the extended family.

Here we must consider gender. Were this chapter dealing only with filial piety in traditional Asia, it would have been impossible to speak generi-
cally of "children," because the expectations for boys and girls would have
been so different. Even today, in both Asia and America, the understanding of the filial education of boys and girls, weighed down by centuries of
traditional attitudes, is often quite different, though these differences are
narrowing. Even so, there were common perceptions and practices and I will
begin by outlining the most important of these before going on to look at
the gender differentials.

Stated without nuance, the Asian child is seen first and foremost as
a part of a larger and more important entity called "the family," while the
child of Western culture is first and foremost an individual. The cultural
conditioning of Asian children, rather than stressing their uniqueness and
separateness, first seeks to develop an embedded identity. The child is a
part of a group. As has often been pointed out, when stating one's name in
Asian languages, one begins with the surname; for example, Wang Jianguo
would be a member of the Wang family with the given name Jianguo. This
practice is clearly indicative of the primary importance of the family group
over the individual. This clue about Asian identity is reaffirmed in countless
other aspects of Asian cultural conditioning. Children are unambiguously
located in a family hierarchy and, where possible, in a hierarchical extended
family. They are taught not only to address their fathers and mothers with
the appropriate designations, but also to address uncles and aunts with
their proper titles—Aunt So and So, Uncle So and So—their elder siblings as
Gege (older brother) and Jiejie (older sister) and even unrelated friends of
their parents with relational terms of respect. Chinese immigrants are often
appalled to hear American children call members of senior generations by
their first names.[26]

In such a system of group dominance, the appropriate filial virtues for
both boys and girls are those that affirm their place within the family hierarchy, maintain harmony, inculcate responsibility, and advocate the sacrificing of individual needs for the welfare and integrity of the family. Great
emphasis is placed upon the need for obedience and a high compliment for
Chinese children is that they *ting hua*, that is, they obey or "listen to what
their superiors say." While American children are often taught to speak up
for themselves, Asian children are taught to get along, fit in, and place others' needs before their own. Numerous Chinese sayings teach the values of
blending and conforming with the group and point out the perils of doing
the opposite: "The nail that sticks up gets pounded down," and "The tallest
trees catch the strongest winds."

In contrast, the status of the child is elevated by the fact that the child-
parent relationship is considered more important than that of husband and

wife. However, this higher status has a greater impact on the psychic development of boys, whose connection to parents results in the continuation of the family line, while the connection of girls is severed when they move into the family of their husbands. Gender differentials in traditional Asia were rather stark. As a "small happiness" to their families, young girls were born, as the saying goes, "facing out." That is, they were destined to leave their natal family and be married into another, one in which their primary filial duties were directed toward their husband's parents. A boy's birth was a "great happiness" and they were born "facing in," with their chief duties being toward their birth parents. Therefore family resources were generally reserved for the education and advancement of sons rather than daughters. The eldest son in particular had the heavy responsibility to support his parents in old age, bury them with appropriate ceremony, and report to them regularly through the medium of regular offerings and sacrifices throughout the year. Along with these duties came significant resources, with the eldest son receiving all or most of the family property as well as the prestige of being the family head. Today, however, even in Asia, with the rise in the prevalence of the nuclear family and the decline in coresidence, the situation is sometimes exactly the reverse. Being the eldest son can be a detriment rather than an advantage. "Being born first, particularly if one is male, has taken on something of the character of a curse in contemporary Japan." At a time when industrialization and mobility have made family land in rural areas less attractive as compensation, many potential spouses simply do not want to be burdened with the responsibility of caring for their husband's parents in their old age.[27] The same situation holds in America, where land inheritance is not a significant factor.

Generally speaking, gender differentials have narrowed in Confucian societies of East Asia as well as in America. As the prestige of the eldest son wanes in both places, the role of females in being filial to their own natal parents has broadened. Chinese American fiction of the past two decades has in fact focused on the continuing (if problematic) relations of mothers and daughters, as we see in the novels of Amy Tan and Maxine Hong Kingston. Education is no longer the exclusive province of male children, and many families are quite as happy with daughters as with sons. In fact, among those in Asia and America who have absorbed the messages of individualism and freedom, a growing number of couples in both Asia and America are choosing not to have children at all.

In traditional China, one of the few avenues to independence and authority for women was religious life as nuns in Buddhism or Daoism. While that door is still open in Asia, it is hardly possible in the United States unless the Chinese in question are Christians. However, because of various factors mentioned above—the demise of the patriarchal extended family, easier transportation and communication, and other factors—young girls no longer face the loss of their natal family. They often have even more filial obligations, now not just to their husband's parents, but also to their own. As the gender differential has narrowed, it may be said that the female child's obligations of filiality have increased. This is a gain for women in both Asia and American, but it comes with a price.

There is a wide range of Confucianism that shapes children, running the gamut from very conservative and traditional to very Westernized. Some would have been subject to the dictates of a stern and remote father, while others have grown up in a household in which parents are more like "friends." Just like its counterpart in Asia, the "Confucian child" in America is living in a time of significant change. Up until the 1960s, the East Asian population in the United States was aging, and a majority had been born in this country. Now because of liberalized immigration laws, large numbers of Chinese have arrived, first from Hong Kong and Taiwan, and then from the PRC. Currently, nearly two-thirds of Chinese Americans have not been born in this country and something like 80 percent speak Chinese in their homes, and thus attitudes toward children reflect present conditions in the countries of origin. One would think, therefore, that these understandings would be more conservative and more resistant to acculturation. And it is true that, as with other ethnic groups covered in this volume, Chinese in the United States have established many language schools for their children, whose purpose is to help "the younger generation to preserve and appreciate [traditional] culture." There are now some three hundred member schools of the Chinese School Association in the United States with an enrollment of more than sixty thousand students.[28] But counteracting this conservative tendency is the fact that the new immigrants have tended to be from the more monied and educated classes and thus more liberal in their views toward family, children, and filial piety.[29] The educated Chinese from Taiwan and the PRC would probably share more values than either group would with rural dwellers in their own country of origin.

What remains is, among other things, the continuing attempt to shape children to appreciate the values of a closely knit family. The 2000 census revealed that 81 percent of Chinese American families are two-parent families.[30] Implicit in this family cohesiveness is an array of other values transmitted to children: a need to place the welfare of the familial group above the self; a bond between child and parent; care for aging parents; an emphasis on the value of sacrifice, discipline, and hard work; and a drive for education and success as a measure of family well-being. These are the qualities that have made the Chinese and other Asians into "model immigrants" in America, both a source of pride and at the same time a burden. If we take just one of these cultural values, education, it is evident that Asian

American parents have succeeded in pushing their children to a level of success far out of proportion to their numbers. While making up only about 4 percent of the American population, Asian Americans make up 14, 12, and 24 percent of the undergraduate populations at Yale, Harvard, and Stanford, respectively.[31] Asian Americans have found the same level of achievement in graduate education. This success is not the result of superior genes, as one scholar notes, but of "Asian cultural values, which place a high priority on education, hard work, and family honor." He also notes that Asian educational success derives from "cultural capital"—in one study 85 percent of high-achieving Chinese Americans had fathers who had earned graduate degrees, 71 percent of which were doctorates.[32] In any case, it is clear that educational success is one facet of filial piety. Children strive to succeed not so much for themselves, but for the family.

The idea of Asians as ideal immigrants, rooted in familial values, was both a strength and a burden. The same factors that preserve and advance the family are often the source of individual problems for those children who have been most influenced by the dominant American culture. As one Chinese American psychiatrist writes, most of the problems she sees in the Asian Americans she counsels are rooted in family.[33] As they struggle to establish themselves in a society that prizes independence, young boys feel torn between two cultures: the American one, stressing individuality, and the traditional one, emphasizing obedience and submission to parents. For young girls, the process of growing up may be even more difficult. They have been trained in attitudes of modesty, humility, and submissiveness and to take a backseat to their brothers.

Despite losses and modifications in their practice of filial piety, the Confucian child is, so far, no vanishing species in America. The ethnic identities of the majority of Chinese American children may be classified as "bicultural." In a recent study of such children in Chicago and Los Angeles, 83.5 percent were identified as either "mostly Chinese" (11.5 percent) or "bicultural" (72 percent) as opposed to "mostly American" (16.5 percent). Although most were first-generation Americans, the study makes clear that there has been no sudden shift in ethnic identity.[34] The residual effects of the religious roots of filial piety are still evident in the enduring family values that continue to guide parents as they raise their children. It is possible to imagine a time when, through relentless acculturation to majority values, Asian American children will be indistinguishable from their dominant-culture counterparts. But not yet. For the time being, many of the old values first outlined in the *Xiaojing*, the *Family Rituals*, and even the *Twenty-four Tales of Filial Piety* persist, and will continue to shape Asian American children in a different mold. They will be sufficiently different as to require special attention by educators, counselors, and social workers who seek to understand and help them. The roots of their separateness are Confucian—a strong sense of family and a self-understanding more corporate than individual, an identity more participatory than independent. This sense of self will continue to give them a unique identity. It will offer them the promise of security and a sense of belonging, but will also be the source of tension for those who attempt to accommodate to the Western/modern values they may acquire from their peers. This tension will likely be a consistent factor in the lives of Asian American children for the foreseeable future.

## NOTES

1.  Zeng Wenzheng, ed., *Siti baijia xing, zengtu ershis xiao* (Taizhong, Taiwan: Zengwen, 1968). My translation.

2.  In Charlotte Ikels, ed., *Filial Piety: Practice and Discourse in Contemporary East Asia* (Stanford: Stanford University Press, 2004), 153.

3.  Tu Wei-ming, *Centrality and Commonality: An Essay on Confucian Religiousness* (Albany: State University of New York Press, 1989), 50–51.

4.  Benson Tong, *The Chinese Americans*, rev. ed. (Boulder: University Press of Colorado, 2003), 7.

5.  Jean Lau Chin, *Learning from My Mother's Voice: Family Legend and the Chinese American Experience* (New York: Columbia University Teachers College, 2005), 148.

6.  Amy Lin Tan, *Chinese American Children and Families: A Guide for Educators and Service Providers* (Olney, MD: ACEI Press, 2004), 17.

7.  Ibid., 43.

8.  Herrlee Glesner Creel, ed., *Literary Chinese by the Inductive Method*, 2nd ed., vol. 1, *Hsiao Ching* (Chicago: University of Chicago Press, 1948), 36.

9.  Ibid., 47. My translation.

10. Ikels, *Filial Piety*, 3.

11. Patricia Buckley Ebrey, ed. and trans., *Chu Hsi's Family Rituals* (Princeton: Princeton University Press, 1991), xiii.

12. Chin, *Learning from My Mother's Voice*, 18.

13. Zeng Wenzheng, *Siti baijia xing*, 45.

14. Ibid., 21, 23, 31.

15. Charlotte Ikels, introduction to *Filial Piety: Practice and Discourse in Contemporary East Asia*, ed. Charlotte Ikels (Stanford: Stanford University Press, 2004), 7–12; and Hong Zhang, "'Living Alone'" and the Rural Elderly: Strategy and Agency in Post-Mao Rural China"; Roger L. Janelli and Dawnhee Yim, "The Transformation of Filial Piety in Contemporary South Korea"; Akiko Hashimoto, "Culture, Power, and the Discourse of Filial Piety in Japan: The Disempowerment of Youth and Its Social Consequences," all in *Filial Piety: Practice and Discourse in Contemporary East Asia*, ed. Charlotte Ikels (Stanford: Stanford University Press, 2004), 63, 140, 183.

16. Ole Bruun, *Fengshui in China: Geomantic Divination between State Orthodoxy and Popular Religion* (Honolulu: University of Hawaii Press, 2003), 117.

17. Danyu Wang, "Ritualistic Coresidence and the Weakening of Filial Practice in Rural China," in *Filial Piety: Practice and Discourse in Contemporary East Asia*, ed. Charlotte Ikels (Stanford: Stanford University Press, 2004), 33.

18. Ibid., 25.

19. Janelli and Yim, "The Transformation of Filial Piety in Contemporary South Korea," 146, 150.

20. Clark Sorensen and Sung-Chul Kim, "Filial Piety In Contemporary Urban Southeast Korea: Practices and Discourses," in *Filial Piety: Practice and Discourse in Contemporary East Asia*, ed. Charlotte Ikels (Stanford: Stanford University Press, 2004), 175.

21. Hashimoto, "Culture, Power, and the Discourse of Filial Piety in Japan," 183.

22. Ibid., 185–186.

23. There had been an early disagreement between Mencius (385?–312? B.C.E.) and Xunzi (310?–219? B.C.E.) about whether human nature was, at its beginning, good or evil, but the Confucian tradition decisively chose the position of Mencius—that humans were born good.

24. Tan, *Chinese American Children and Families*, 56–57.

25. Ebrey, *Chu Hsi's Family Rituals*, 32.

26. May Paomay Tung, *Chinese Americans and Their Immigrant Parents* (New York: Haworth Clinical Practice Press, 2000), 6–10; Tan, *Chinese American Children and Families*, 31–32.

27. John w. Traphagan, Curse of the Successor: Filial Piety vs. Marriage Among Rural Japanese," in *Filial Piety: Practice and Discourse in Contemporary East Asia*, ed. Charlotte Ikels (Stanford: Stanford University Press, 2004), 198–216.

28. http://csaus.org.

29. Tong, *The Chinese Americans*, 239.

30. Tan, *Chinese American Children and Families*, 33.

31. Ibid., 73.

32. Tong, *The Chinese Americans*, 182.

33. Tung, *Chinese Americans and Their Immigrant Parents*, 1.

34. Zhuojun (Joyce) Chen, "Chinese-American Children's Ethnic Identity: Measurement and Implications," *Communication Studies* 51, no. 1 (2000): 74–95.

# 12

## Immigrant Parochial Schools

### Religion, Morality, Citizenship

PAUL D. NUMRICH

Established in 1974, the Islamic Foundation is one of metropolitan Chicago's largest and most successful immigrant mosques. Located in affluent DuPage County, the tenth-wealthiest U.S. county in terms of median household income, the Islamic Foundation opened an elementary school in 1988, moving eventually to a full K–12 program. The Islamic Foundation School is accredited and recognized for its excellence by the state of Illinois.

Asked to describe the most significant challenge facing its student body, one school administrator explained, "For the students, the biggest challenge is the struggle and temptation that they see around them in mainstream society. I mean, they are Muslims, and our aim is to produce Muslim identities. We want to produce clear Muslim identities, but American citizens as well who would be totally comfortable in mainstream society but not lose their identity. This is easier said than done."

This statement anticipates several key topics in this chapter. First, immigrant parents and community leaders often worry about the struggles and temptations their children face in a new (for the immigrants) society, particularly in the public school setting. Immigrant congregations often perceive the larger society as inherently threatening or corrosive to the religious identity and moral standards of the immigrant community, typically addressing this tension with the larger society through general educational programming. Some immigrant congregations take the significant next step of establishing a parochial school, that is, a full-time school operated by a religious group or organization as an alternative to government-sponsored public education for grades K–12 or some portion thereof.

Yet, second, establishing a parochial school does not necessarily signal an immigrant congregation's radical separation or retreat from positive civic engagement with the larger society. Note the school administrator's references to "mainstream society" above. The Islamic Foundation School seeks to produce Muslim American citizens who will maintain their distinctive religious identities and moral standards without succumbing to the perceived pitfalls of the larger society, but also without opting out of society altogether. This is the mark of what can be labeled "mainstream" immigrant parochial education, across all religious traditions and throughout American history. As we shall see, this kind of parochial education considers itself a transformative or redemptive influence on society.

Third, parochial school education is certainly "easier said than done." We will examine the challenges and difficulties faced by those immigrant congregations that establish parochial schools. Not all immigrant congregations desire to do so, while some with the desire lack the institutional resources, at least in the short term. Moreover, some immigrant communities have established significant parochial school movements, while others have not. We will examine such patterns to see what can be learned about immigrant parochial education generally. We will also consider larger lessons about the education of children in America, both immigrant and nonimmigrant.[1]

## Education in the Immigrant Context

In a classic essay, historian Timothy L. Smith asserted that "migration was often a theologizing experience" for American immigrants and that this theologizing included strong moral overtones. Uprooted from their home countries and replanted in a new society, religious immigrants of all traditions tend to become preoccupied with "the ethical dimension of faith," Smith explained. "Once in America, immigrants uniformly felt that learning new patterns of correct behavior was crucial to their sense of well-being." The resulting "immigrant Puritanism," Smith wrote, invoking Marcus Hansen's phrase, is "a predictable reaction to the ethical or behavioral disorientation that affected most immigrants, whatever the place or the century of their arrival."[2]

In a sense, much of what any congregation does can be considered "faith-based education," that is, instruction in how to remain faithful to the worldview, practices, and, especially, the moral standards of an inherited religious tradition. Rituals, sermons, social activities, informal conversations—these and other components of common congregational life carry important didactic content. Additionally, congregations typically establish more formal educational programming, such as the "religious education" or catechetical instruction found in Christian contexts. These include children's programs of various types, such as Sunday or weekend schools, weekday after-school and evening classes, short-term retreats and camps, preschool and other child-care programs, youth groups, and parochial schools (detailed below). The purpose of all such faith-based education, in immigrant congregations even more than in nonimmigrant ones, is "inescapably particularistic," to borrow sociologist R. Stephen Warner's insight.[3] That is, it applies the wisdom and insights of the inherited religious tradition to the contemporary social, cultural, and moral contexts of the local congregation.

Religious identity and morality are intertwined in immigrant (and all) congregations, as seen in the following excerpts from an English *khutba* (sermon) preached at the Islamic Foundation in the Chicago area:

> Most respected Brothers and Sisters, I just recited from the Book of Guidance [the Qur'an]. This book is a complete guide, whether it relates to individual behavior, community affairs, or international problems. It contains the basic rules and regulations for certain situations. Allah [God] tells us that these are the things He likes, and these are the things He doesn't like. . . . We must spend time to educate our children, teach them in their beginning stages. Within a few days, a bird can start flying, functioning, but the human child Allah has given sixteen or seventeen years to learn how to live in this world, to learn what Allah likes and dislikes. It is the responsibility of the parents and leaders of the *umma* [the whole Islamic community] to tell them and to establish educational institutions.

Immigrant congregations often express severe criticism of the moral status of the larger society. "Across the gamut of recent immigrant religions, concern is raised about the secular and material enticements of modern American society," I wrote previously in a survey of immigrant religious views on the family, continuing:

> To summarize the content of the conservative critique coming from many new immigrant religious groups, America has abandoned its original moral compass, and dissolute Americans today give in to passions and proclivities fueled by modern ideologies like individualism, feminism, secularism, and materialism. . . . The fears of the immigrant generation find intense focus in efforts to protect their American-born offspring from these social ills by inculcating traditional Old World values through educational, cultural, and religious programs.[4]

Such moral conservatism is fueled partly by a growing religious conservatism in the immigrants' home countries today, but also by the inherent migration dynamics identified by Timothy Smith. Immigrant groups may vary in the specific objects of their moral concern because of socioeconomic, doctrinal, or other variables, but moral concern is pervasive, particularly among parents with regard to the well-being of their children.[5]

## Parochial Schools in the Classical Period of American Immigration

Parochial schools have been around since colonial times and have played a significant role in American immigrant history. In the classical period of American immigration that ended in 1924, Lutherans and Catholics stood out as the torchbearers of parochial education. In the century between 1840 and 1940, driven by huge waves of German and Scandinavian immigrants, nearly three thousand Lutheran schools arose in what one Lutheran historian calls "the major Protestant educational undertaking during two centuries."[6]

The Catholic initiative was even more impressive. In 1924, Catholic elementary school enrollment passed the 2 million mark, with more than seven thousand schools.[7] A Catholic historian calls the Catholic elementary school system "one of the greatest achievements in U.S. religious history."[8] A massive University of Notre Dame study in the 1960s described the American Catholic educational system as having "no parallel anywhere in the world."[9]

The philosophies driving Lutheran and Catholic parochial education are similar in basic respects. Parochial education is viewed as holistic, integrated, and superior, supplying the religious and moral content that the public school system not only lacks but has replaced by unacceptable secular norms and values. This has important civic implications for the nation—parochial education at once withdraws students from a secular and morally flawed society in order to prepare them to be positive change agents of that society.

As summarized by Walter Beck,

> The *primary objective* of Lutheran parochial schools has at all times and in all synods been the inculcation of Christian doctrines and principles of life and their coordination with the entire curriculum of the school. It is the long-established conviction of the Lutheran Church that education and religion must go hand in hand; that a nation cannot make the right kind of citizens by a godless education and bringing in religion afterward. Most Lutheran bodies have held that this can be achieved only by means of the full-time parochial school, and they accordingly at some time in their history fostered schools and promoted the movement.[10]

Note here the tension of being a moral voice both apart from and a part of the larger society.

The Catholic school movement began in earnest in the nineteenth century largely out of concern that the public school system would erode the
faith of the growing numbers of immigrant Catholics because it was dominated by non-Catholic ideologies, whether Protestantism or later secularity.[11] Given the larger context of anti-Catholic (and related anti-immigrant)
sentiment in the nineteenth and twentieth centuries, Catholic educators
needed to stress the assimilationist or Americanization function of their
parochial schools. The church's twofold purpose in parochial education was
"to preserve the faith in the immigrant and to prepare him for American
citizenship."[12] This dual religious and civic focus continued beyond the classical period of Catholic immigration: "The central consideration, therefore,
is . . . how does the Catholic school carry out the mandate to provide religious training, while at the same time serving the purposes which are those
of education for life in the United States at this period in its history?"[13] Here,
again, religion offers the value added that is missing from public school
education and needed in the public square: "Thus one can discern a marked
continuity of thought in the declarations made by the teaching authority of
the Church on the subject of education. Because man is endowed by his Creator with rights that in turn impose duties, moral training in the rational use
of those rights and in the performance of the duties that accompany them
is inseparable from education; and religion provides the only light in which
the significance of moral action can be adequately understood."[14]

The Buddhist and Jewish cases during the classical period of American
immigration provide counterexamples to the Lutheran and Catholic ones.
Immigrant Buddhists experienced social marginalization comparable with
that of their Catholic counterparts, yet they established a minuscule number
of parochial schools. Many Japanese Buddhist temples established so-called
language schools that taught Japanese culture, values, and Buddhist tenets
in addition to the Japanese language.[15] These schools usually convened outside public school hours and became a focal point of the contentious Americanization debates of the time. In the early 1900s, the head of the Honpa
Hongwanji Mission saw the two school systems—public and Buddhist—as
complementary, together stressing citizenship, family values, and morality,
familiar concerns of parochial educators generally, as we have seen.[16]

If immigrant Japanese Buddhist temples promoted educating their
children in this way, then why not through full-time parochial schools
that would provide an alternative to the public school system, particularly
when the latter was hostile to Japanese culture in general and to Buddhism
in particular? Three factors seem most salient. First, immigrant Japanese
Buddhists lacked the social and financial resources to establish full-time
parochial schools. But this was not a sufficient impediment, since parochial
schools did not arise in significant numbers even when the community

prospered in later generations, and to this day. A second, and more significant, reason for the lack of parochial schools was the strong desire to assimilate into American society rather than to exacerbate tensions with the majority population by opting out of the public school system. Assimilation accelerated with the growth of the Nisei (second) generation after 1920.[17] In the throes of the decades-long Americanization controversy in Hawaii, many Nisei parted ways with their elders and opposed even the part-time language schools at temples.[18] A third reason for the lack of parochial schools has to do with the individualist orientation of Buddhist education, which emphasizes personal morality rather than a collectivist religious identity.

The majority of immigrant Jewish children during the classical period of American immigration attended public schools, largely for the second reason noted above in the Buddhist case, namely, as a means of assimilation into American society. Jewish "day schools" (parochial schools) were found mostly among the Orthodox, at least until recently, as some liberal Jewish groups have become concerned that part-time Jewish education programs are insufficient to retain students' Jewish identities.[19]

## Parochial Schools in the Current Period of American Immigration, with Special Attention to Islamic Schools

Of the three largest non-Christian religious groups in the current (post-1965) wave of American immigration—Muslims, Buddhists, and Hindus, in order of size—only Muslims have established a significant parochial school presence. I know of no immigrant Hindu parochial schools in the United States. One Hindu group in Hawaii reported the sentiment among Hindu youth that parochial education could address the issues they face in their lives: "Most students thought that Hindu parochial schools could solve the problems, harmonizing education and religion, giving a sound knowledge of Hinduism. Then, as adults, they felt they could stand strong on the foundation of understanding and talk intelligently with their Christian and Jewish peers in a pluralistic society."[20] This echoes the rationale for parochial education we have seen across religious groups. But, as we found earlier regarding Buddhists, mitigating factors have been more powerful among immigrant Hindus, including a more individualist than collectivist religious identity and remarkable success (at least in some strata) in assimilating into American society.[21]

Extrapolating from data in the Mosque Study Project report, slightly more than 20 percent of immigrant mosques nationally operate Islamic parochial schools, which would put the total number at around 185 by 2001.[22] The scholarly literature on the Islamic parochial school movement is still scant, but we know enough to make two generalizations about this movement.[23]

First, many immigrant Muslim parents have ambivalent feelings about their children's religious and academic needs. In their benchmark study, Haddad and Lummis described the parental dilemma: "The tension comes in reconciling the desire for an academically excellent education, which is possible in some American institutions both public and private, with the fear that such exposure to different value systems may lead their children away from the principles of Islam."[24] Fully 40 percent of the respondents in that study answered "Not important" to a question about providing a mosque-based Islamic school as an alternative to the public schools.[25] As noted by Haddad and Lummis, among several reasons for parental resistance to Islamic schools, there is a primary one: "The most commonly expressed fear of those who indicated they would not send their children to Muslim schools . . . is that it would isolate them from American society."[26]

A parent at the Islamic Foundation School in the Chicago area expressed her ambivalence. Referring to the public school system, she said:

> There is so much more out there. When you look at private education versus public education, there are a lot of things that are lacking in the private. I think in the academic sphere, you don't have all those bells and whistles that you'll find in public schools. But at the same time, the environment here is so healthy, I feel, and so nurturing. I think that the psychology of little ones especially is so important, to foster this healthy mind, this happy mind. They should feel secure and be able to charge the world [face it confidently]. So I am very comfortable with my choice of Islamic Foundation for my child for K through five. But maybe after she reaches middle school, I might choose a different environment just because academics might play a bigger role at a different stage in life. But right now I think that it serves our needs wonderfully.

Second, we can generalize that religious or moral concerns, or both, usually tip parental decisions in the direction of an Islamic education for their children, particularly in situations in which the public schools do not offer a superior academic alternative. In a survey of research, Karen Leonard discusses the motivations of immigrant Muslims for establishing Islamic schools. These include, on the negative side, "a major concern about sex and violence in American schools" and objections to sex education curricula and coeducational activities. On the positive side, motivations include "teaching Islamic subjects and fulfilling the ideal of pan-ethnic Islamic unity in the *umma*: "Many Muslims see the establishment of Islamic schools in multi-ethnic America as a step in bringing the international umma into being."[27]

Many Muslim observers emphasize the negative motivations for offering an Islamic education in a non-Islamic and secular society. Louay Safi writes:

> While Muslims have been impressed by the vibrant American culture, and hence willing to learn from its strengths, they have been equally alarmed by its downside. Particularly of concern to Muslims is the increasing moral laxity of the American society, reflected in sexual promiscuity, violence, pornography, drug abuse, and other social ills that have been on the increase. The perceived moral laxity has prompted many Muslim parents to search for alternative schooling and social activities for their children, and hence brought them closer to Islamic centers, and highlighted the importance of community.[28]

Safi contends that a secular educational philosophy has created the current moral crisis in America and lays out a philosophy of holistic Islamic education to address this crisis: "The mission of Islamic education is to reintegrate the fragmented consciousness of modern man by once again repositioning divine revelation at the core of human consciousness, the binding and nurturing core which the secular project has managed to destroy."[29] Islamic education will work hand in hand with the political maturation of the American Muslim community, which stands ready to transform America: "American Muslims, I contend, could contribute profoundly to the restoration of the spiritual and moral core of modern civilization which has been fading away with the advancement of hardcore secularism. Indeed, American Muslims are in a position to restore the spiritual and moral dimensions of modern life while continuing to be faithful to the true spirit of liberalism."[30]

In the view of Necva Ozgur, most Islamic schools in the United States see their mission as providing "quality academic education in an Islamic environment."[31] Curricular offerings include both a nonreligious component, compliant with state education requirements, and an Islamic component, the religious "value added" of a parochial education. "The Islamic Foundation School [in Chicago] is committed to the education of each child as a *whole*," explains the school's Web site, its emphasis on this final word serving as a critique of the putatively incomplete education offered by the public school system. Parochial courses include "Qur'anic studies, Hadith [traditions about the Prophet Muhammad], Prophet's *seerat* [biographies], Prophet's companions, Islamic teachings, Islamic morals, Islamic history, Arabic reading and language, and the rights and obligations of each individual Muslim to himself/herself, to the parents, to our community in this country and all over the world, and to all humanity."[32]

At Averroes Academy, a parochial school housed at the Islamic Cultural Center of Greater Chicago, in a northern suburb, "the Islamic Education curriculum is aimed at nurturing the development of Islamic scholars and promotes the learning of traditional Islamic sciences such as Arabic, *Fiqh* [Islamic jurisprudence] and Qur'an recitation and memorization." This religious grounding is intended to promote academic and social success: "Averroes Academy will give a high priority to the Islamic education of our children as we prepare them to achieve high academic standards thereby preparing them to excel for future successful and prosperous avocations and careers (*InshaAllah*) [God willing]."[33]

Averroes Academy was established by the North Shore Education Foundation (NSEF), a group consisting of local Muslim leaders. "Because NSEF believes that being American is clearly compatible with being Muslim," explains its mission statement, "this school will provide a balanced approach to education both academically and socially." Moreover, "NSEF believes that this institution can make a positive contribution in this society by promoting justice and truth. . . . This school, God willing, will produce exceptionally educated children with positive moral and ethical values who will go on to succeed in higher education and will make positive contributions to American society, including the Muslim community."[34]

Averroes Academy, like the Islamic Foundation School, clearly provides an Islamic alternative to the public schools, but not an extreme alternative. The school's founders made a conscious decision to resist a disturbing trend they perceived in Islamic school circles, as noted in a posting about a 2001 fund-raising event on the school's Web site. The posting argues that the "gravest" challenge to the growing number of Islamic parochial schools in the United States has nothing to do with minimal resources, as many might think, but rather is the "lack of intellectual vision on the role and the function that Islamic education should play in a non-Muslim society. This lack of vision is manifested in an isolationist Islamic education where Muslim children are being taught in a closed environment, hardly exposed to the American culture, which is portrayed as a threat to the Islamic values and beliefs." Much of this isolationism stems from the immigrant generation confusing ethnic culture with Islam. "Averroes Academy has been trying . . . not to fall into this traditional pattern," the posting explains. According to the fund-raiser's organizer, the president of the Council of Islamic Organizations of Greater Chicago: "Averroes Academy achieved a great goal for a small school only two years old, that is to provide Islamic education while being in touch [with] the American society."[35] Without more research, it is difficult to assess the extent of the isolationist trend identified in this posting, but it certainly does not represent mainstream Islamic parochial education in the United States.[36]

In an earlier report, Nimat Hafez Barazangi took great pains to establish "the contrast between the Islamic and Western worldviews" and how these fundamentally different worldviews "impinge strongly on the ways in which their respective philosophies of education are set forth."[37] Given the fact that American-born or -raised Muslim children identify more with Western values than with Islamic ones, Barazangi asserted that Islamic parochial schools must make an "educational intervention" that features explicit and critical comparisons between the two value systems.[38] Significantly, Barazangi sought thereby "to preserve the Islamic identity in an integrative manner within the pluralistic Western society."[39] "The term *integrative*," Barazangi explained, "is used here to indicate the ability to maintain the Islamic belief system at its central concept level, tawhid [divine unity], and to objectify this belief system in the Western secular environment without (1) compromising the Islamic principles, (2) sacrificing national/ethnic group attachment, (3) living dual, but separate lives (Islamic and Western), or (4) withdrawing from the outside society."[40] This statement epitomizes the inherent tensions between Islamic education and the larger society, again without resort to extreme isolationism.

Indicators of increasingly positive civic engagement between mainstream Islamic parochial education and the larger American society abound. Ozgur concludes a presentation on the "top ten hot issues for Islamic schools" to the 2005 Education Forum sponsored by the Islamic Society of North America with the following advice: "Creating an Islamic community for our children is a step in the right direction. However, we must not let that community become isolated from the rest of the educational world. We need to find ways to outreach to and network with other schools and professional organizations so that we may benefit from their experiences and knowledge." This is specified with an admonition to join national education associations such as the National Association of Independent Schools, the Association for Supervision and Curriculum Development, and the National Association for the Education of Young Children.[41] This kind of networking can be seen in the Council of Islamic Organizations of Greater Chicago's Full-Time Islamic Schools Coordination Committee, which is committed to using "its access and goodwill to seek and provide consultative services from the Public and Parochial school systems of metropolitan Chicago."[42]

The Islamic Foundation School's participation in the cooperative Muslim Scouts of Greater Chicago program also illustrates positive civic engagement. This program's Web site and its links reveal a close interweaving of Islamic and Scouting philosophies. Clearly, the goal here is to nurture upstanding Muslim American citizens. As we read in one place, "Girl Scouts is the pre-eminent organization *Where Girls Grow Strong!* You can help today's Muslim girls become tomorrow's leaders inshaAllah [God willing]."[43] The same intersection—with its inherent tensions—between civic and religious identities that we have noted with regard to Islamic parochial schools can be heard in a statement by one of the local Muslim Scout organizers: "There's a big cry [from the Muslim community] not to be isolated but to keep our Muslim identity. . . . We're trying to do it without offending anyone. We're trying to do it to bridge our communities."[44]

To summarize, like mainstream parochial education generally, Islamic parochial education attempts to shelter students from society's negative influences while training those students for faith-informed citizenship and social success in that same society. As Asma Gull Hasan puts it, Islamic schools "focus on helping students strike a balance between Islam and American culture."[45] Islamic educators sometimes bemoan the weakness of the religious "value added" component of Islamic parochial education, given the reliance on public school standards and curricula, an irony not lost on proponents of a parochial alternative to the public schools.[46] As the principal of the Islamic Foundation School explained, Islamic schools "constantly walk a fine line" between parental factions—on one side, those whose disdain for the negative elements of American society overshadows any concern about the quality of education offered by Islamic schools; on the other side, those who place quality of education over Islamic content.[47]

An article posted on the Web site of the Islamic Society of North America draws out the parallels between the Catholic and Islamic parochial school movements:

> Muslims have objected to public schools on both the grounds that motivated Catholics to establish a separate school system. Firstly, on philosophical grounds, it can be argued that Islamic education is not compatible with secularism since the "revealed knowledge" found in the Qur'an and Hadeeth literature supersedes scientific knowledge. Secondly, anti-Muslim rhetoric and bigotry has also been identified in the public schools and their texts. . . . In fact, the goals for establishing Islamic schools are not much different [from Catholic schools]: Firstly, to promulgate the teachings of the religion and secondly to safeguard the students from such evils of society as drugs, racism, and premarital sex.[48]

Hasan also discusses the parallels between Islamic and Christian (especially Catholic) parochial education, including the inherent tensions in being a religious citizen: "Islamic schools are similar to Catholic schools or other parochial schools in emphasizing the importance of one's own religion. An Islamic school has the same goals as does a Catholic school—to create an environment that is still very American but is sheltered from influences that work against Islam and Catholicism or that make kids feel 'weird' and different being a Muslim or Catholic."[49]

Some in the Muslim community wonder just how successful Islamic schools can be in producing good Muslims in today's society. As an administrator at one school in Chicago explained, the very discipline problems and immoral behaviors that Muslim parents feared in the public schools are increasing in this school: "I foresee these will become bigger problems in the future because this is reality. I mean, these children are living in this society; we will see these types of things coming up. We don't expect that all children who attend our school are perfect angels and that they will be doing everything which is Islamic and appropriate and they do not make any mistakes. That's not gonna happen."

Another interviewee who attended both this Islamic school and public schools pointed out that a parochial school education is only one factor in the lives of its students. Regarding a classmate who attended Islamic school through high school: "If you saw her, you wouldn't think she would have come from Islamic school. She did not change at all, even though she went to school and everything. So I mean, it depends if the person wants to change, too. Environment can only do so much."

Another alumna of Chicago Islamic schools commented on both the ideals and the realities of Islamic education, specifically with regard to gender separation. For practical reasons, most Islamic schools compromise the ideal by mixing students in the classroom while emphasizing the inappropriateness of socializing outside it.[50] "Yeah, right," scoffs Khadijah Abd'l-Haleem. "Let me tell you, a lot can happen in three minutes of chaotic herding [between classes], not to mention unlimited after-school time." She felt liberated scholastically when she transferred to an all-girl school, where she could study "unhindered by the subconscious awareness that they [boys] are in the room, aware of your every move." She does not fall into the opposite kind of idealism, thinking that such segregation can ever be complete for this age group. Still, she was thankful to be relatively free of the "dynamics of intermingling" during school hours.[51]

## Religion, Morality, and Citizenship in the Education of American Children

Faced with perceived threats to their religious identities and moral standards, immigrant congregations educate their children in the ways of the faith and the traditions of the community. When religious and moral tensions with the larger society reach a critical level, some immigrant congregations establish parochial schools to supplement their regular educational programming, as an alternative to a public school system that represents the larger society's problematic norms, values, and ideologies. As we have seen, other factors can influence the decision to establish a parochial school—congregational or community resources, the relative strength or weakness of a tradition's collectivist identity, and the quality of the public schools (this last related to the perceived tension with the larger society).

Clearly, the level of tension between the immigrant congregation/community and the larger society typically plays the greatest role in determining the presence or absence, as well as the vitality, of a parochial school movement. A relative lack of tension, or at least a desire to overcome tensions through assimilation into the majority American culture, made parochial schools counterproductive for Buddhists and Jews during the classical period of American immigration, and to Hindus in the current period. Among Lutherans, only the sectarian Missouri Synod held forth as other denominations abandoned the field of parochial education by the mid-twentieth century.[52] Catholic parochial education was headed in the same direction by that time. Jesuit sociologist Joseph Fichter's study of one urban (nonimmigrant) Catholic school in the 1950s suggested that parochial and public schools were more alike than independent private schools were like either of them.[53] Michael Cieslak predicts that the Catholic school movement will look different in the twenty-first century, "if for no other reason than because Catholics have been well integrated into society and no longer need the social isolation that Catholic schools offered."[54]

Yet the tension with the larger society is never fully resolved in mainstream immigrant parochial schools, as it is likewise never fully resolved in mainstream nonimmigrant parochial schools. We have seen the striking similarities between the immigrant Lutheran, Catholic, and Islamic parochial school movements. They seek to inculcate their respective, distinctive religious identities and moral standards in their children. They consider parochial education holistic, integrated, and morally legitimate, in contrast to the public schools. They seek to shelter their students from the perceived threats of the larger society. But these movements do not advocate extreme separatism from society. In fact, they train their students for faith-informed participation in society, to be positive change agents for the greater good. On the whole, mainstream immigrant parochial schools function more as bridging institutions to the larger society than as bonding enclaves for their own communities.[55]

Two final insights derive from the foregoing discussion. First, we can understand the presence or absence of nonimmigrant parochial schools also as a function of tensions with the larger society. For instance, although it perceives the same threats from American society as the immigrant religious groups discussed in this chapter, the Church of Jesus Christ of Latter-day Saints (the Mormons) has not established a parochial school movement, because this religion so dominates the local culture of the Western states where it is concentrated.[56]

Second, we can predict that public school initiatives such as Character Counts will help to mitigate the motivations for parochial schools. Such public initiatives address at least some of the moral concerns of religious parents and groups.[57] The question remains, however, of just how important are the specifically religious concerns that the public schools cannot address.

## NOTES

1. Portions of this chapter derive from a draft chapter in Fred Kniss and Paul D. Numrich, *Sacred Assemblies and Civic Engagement: How Religion Matters for America's Newest Immigrants* (New Brunswick: Rutgers University Press, 2007). Field data are drawn from the Religion, Immigration and Civil Society in Chicago Project, funded by The Pew Charitable Trusts and housed at Loyola University Chicago.

2. Timothy L. Smith, "Religion and Ethnicity in America," *American Historical Review* 83 (1978): 1175, 1176.

3. R. Stephen Warner, "The Place of the Congregation in the Contemporary American Religious Configuration," in *American Congregations*, vol. 2, ed. James P. Wind and James W. Lewis (Chicago: University of Chicago Press, 1994), 65.

4. Paul D. Numrich, "Immigrant American Religions and the Family: New Diversity and Conservatism," in *Families and American Religion: Comparative Family Ethics and Strategies of the Major American Faiths*, ed. Don S. Browning and David Clairmont (New York: Columbia University Press, forthcoming).

5. Helen Rose Ebaugh and Janet Saltzman Chafetz, *Religion and the New Immigrants: Continuities and Adaptations in Immigrant Congregations* (Walnut Creek, CA: AltaMira Press, 2000), 433.

6. Walter H. Beck, *Lutheran Elementary Schools in the United States: A History of the Development of Parochial Schools and Synodical Educational Policies and Programs*, 2nd ed. (St. Louis: Concordia, 1965), vii.

7. J. A. Burns, Bernard J. Kohlbrenner, and John B. Peterson, *A History of Catholic Education in the United States: A Textbook for Normal Schools and Teachers' Colleges* (New York: Benziger Brothers, 1937), 145.

8. James T. Fisher, *Communion of Immigrants: A History of Catholics in America* (New York: Oxford University Press, 2002), 79.

9. Reginald A. Neuwien, ed., *Catholic Schools in Action: A Report; The Notre Dame Study of Catholic Elementary and Secondary Schools in the United States* (Notre Dame: University of Notre Dame Press, 1966), 9.

10. Beck, *Lutheran Elementary Schools*, 408; emphasis in original.

11. Burns, Kohlbrenner, and Peterson, *A History of Catholic Education*, 109–110; Vincent P. Lannie, "Catholics, Protestants, and Public Education," in *Catholicism in America*, ed. Philip Gleason (New York: Harper and Row, 1970), 45–57.

12. Burns, Kohlbrenner, and Peterson, *A History of Catholic Education*, 176.

13. Neuwien, *Catholic Schools in Action*, 2.

14. Ibid., 19.

15. Louise H. Hunter, *Buddhism in Hawaii: Its Impact on a Yankee Community* (Honolulu: University of Hawaii Press, 1971); Tetsuden Kashima, *Buddhism in America: The Social Organization of an Ethnic Religious Institution* (Westport, CT: Greenwood Press, 1977).

16. Hunter, *Buddhism in Hawaii*, 97–98.

17. Gurinder Singh Mann, Paul David Numrich, and Raymond B. Williams, *Buddhists, Hindus, and Sikhs in America* (New York: Oxford University Press, 2001).

18. Hunter, *Buddhism in Hawaii*, 148, 172–173.

19. My thanks to Elliot Dorff for these insights; see his chapter in this volume.

20. "Dharma Suffers in US Schools," *Hinduism Today*, August 1987, http://www.hinduismtoday.com/archives/1987/08/1987–08–01.shtml.

21. See Raymond Williams's chapter in this volume.

22 Ihsan Bagby, Paul M. Perl, and Bryan T. Froehle, "The Mosque in America: A National Report" (Washington, DC: Council on American-Islamic Relations, 2001). Available lists and tallies of Islamic schools in the United States tend to be imprecise, making it difficult to distinguish immigrant from nonimmigrant schools and parochial from other types of educational programs. See, for example, http://islamicvalley.com/prod/entitySearch.php/t/oBK; http://www.msa-natl.org/resources/Schools.html; Asma Gull Hasan, *American Muslims: The New Generation.* 2nd ed. (New York: Continuum, 2002), 145; Mohamed Nimer, *The North American Muslim Resource Guide: Muslim Community Life in the United States and Canada* (New York: Routledge, 2002), 54–55; Richard Wormser, *American Islam: Growing Up Muslim in America* (New York: Walker, 1994), 54; "Directory of Masjids and Muslim Organizations of North America 1994/1415" (Fountain Valley, CA: Islamic Resource Institute, 1994). See also Jane I. Smith's chapter in this volume for a general discussion of Islamic education in America.

23. See Yvonne Yazbeck Haddad, "Make Room for the Muslims?" in *Religious Diversity and American Religious History: Studies in Traditions and Cultures*, ed. Walter H. Conser Jr. and Sumner B. Twiss (Athens: University of Georgia Press, 1997), 237n134; Karen Leonard, *Muslims in the United States: The State of Research* (New York: Russell Sage Foundation, 2003), 112, 114.

24. Yvonne Yazbeck Haddad and Adair T. Lummis, *Islamic Values in the United States: A Comparative Study* (New York: Oxford University Press, 1987), 168.

25. Ibid., 49–51.

26. Ibid., 51.

27. Leonard, *Muslims in the United States*, 113.

28. Louay M. Safi, "The Transforming Experience of American Muslims: Islamic Education and Political Maturation," in *Muslims and Islamization in North America: Problems and Prospects*, ed. Amber Haque (Beltsville, MD: Amana, 1999), 37.

29. Ibid., 43.

30. Ibid., 33.

31. Necva Ozgur, "Top Ten Hot Issues for Islamic Schools," http://www.isna.net/conferences/educationforum/2005downloads.html.

32. http://www.ifsvp.org.

33. http://www.averroesacademy.org. Averroes Academy opened in 1999, offering grades K–5. It is named after the noted medieval Islamic intellectual Ibn Rushd, known in the West as Averroes.

34. http://www.averroesacademy.org.

35. Ibid.

36. For an isolationist example, see the Qur'an recitation school described in Garbi Schmidt, *American Medina: A Study of the Sunni Muslim Immigrant Communities in Chicago* (Lund, Sweden: University of Lund, 1998), 104–107.

37. Nimat Hafez Barazangi, "Islamic Education in the United States and Canada: Conception and Practice of the Islamic Belief System," in *The Muslims of America*, ed. Yvonne Yazbeck Haddad (New York: Oxford University Press, 1991), 157, 158; cf. Safi, "The Transforming Experience of American Muslims."

38. Ibid., 169, 171.

39. Ibid., 172.

40. Ibid., 174n20; emphasis in original.

41. Ozgur, "Top Ten Hot Issues for Islamic Schools."

42. http://www.ciogc.org.

43. http://www.chicagomuslimscouts.org; emphasis in original.

44. Jon Yates, "Muslim Scouts Blazing Own Trail," *Chicago Tribune*, 12 January 2003, sec. 4 (TribWest), 1. According to spokespersons for the Boy and Girl Scouts of America cited in this article, in 2003 there were fifty-eight Boy Scout units sponsored by mosques in the United States and "at least a handful" of Girl Scout units.

45. Hasan, *American Muslims*, 145.

46. E.g., Schmidt, *American Medina*, 95–96; Freda Shamma, "The Curriculum Challenge for Islamic Schools in America," in *Muslims and Islamization in North America: Problems and Prospects*, ed. Amber Haque, 273–295 (Beltsville, MD: Amana Publications, 1999).

47. Stephen Franklin, "Growing Pains: It's Not Easy Being Muslim in America, but It Is Getting Less Lonely," *Chicago Tribune Magazine*, 18 March 2001: 16.

48. Matthew Moes, "Islamic Schools as Change Agents," http://www.isna.net/library/Papers/education/IslamicSchoolsAsAgents2.htm.

49. Hasan, *American Muslims*, 146–147.

50. See Franklin, "Growing Pains," 16.

51. Khadijah Abd'l-Haleem, "Islamic Schooling in the Rear View Mirror," *Chicago Muslim*, July 2001, 5–6.

52. Francis X. Curran, *The Churches and the Schools: American Protestantism and Popular Elementary Education* (Chicago: Loyola University Press, 1954), 118–119.

53. Joseph H. Fichter, *Parochial School: A Sociological Study* (Notre Dame: University of Notre Dame Press, 1958), 428–429.

54. Michael Cieslak, "The Lack of Consensus among Catholics for Establishing New Elementary Schools," *Review of Religious Research*, 47, no. 2 (2005): 185.

55. On these concepts generally, see Mark Chaves, *Congregations in America* (Cambridge: Harvard University Press, 2004), 96–97.

56. Cf. David Dollahite's chapter in this volume.

57. My thanks to Elliot Dorff for bringing this to my attention. See http://www.charactercounts.org

# 13

## The Law's Influence over Children's Religious Development

EMILY BUSS

Our nation was founded, almost exclusively, by mainline Protestants who could not have anticipated how religiously diverse the United States would become. There was enough diversity among them, however, to make the protection of religious liberty an important aim when they drafted the Constitution. How far the right to religious liberty should reach has been an ongoing source of debate among lawmakers, as our citizenry has become increasingly diverse.

At the heart of this debate is how control over children's development should be divided between the government and a child's parents. On the one hand, the government has a strong interest in protecting all children and ensuring that they are raised and educated in a way that will allow them to function successfully as adults in a democratic society. On the other hand, parents have a strong interest in raising children to embrace their own religious faith. The interests of the government and parents are often compatible, but when they are not, the issue generally comes down to a legal question: Can the state enforce a law, such as a compulsory attendance law or mandatory vaccination law, that it enacted to serve children's welfare, or do the parents have a right to avoid the law's effect because it conflicts with their own religious beliefs?

A great deal hinges on the answers to these legal questions for parents, religious communities, children, and the state. For parents, their ability to meet their religious obligations and raise their children as they wish may be at stake. For religious communities, their ability to attract and retain members in the future, or even their survival, could be at issue. For children, the range and nature of their opportunities for work, faith, and relationships may hang in the balance. For the state, the trade-off will often be between the preservation of pluralism, on the one hand, and the development of common social values, on the other.

## Parents' Right to Control Their Children's Religious Upbringing

In the early years of the twentieth century, many states were concerned that recent immigrant groups were not doing enough to assimilate into mainstream American society. Of particular concern was a growing trend among immigrants to educate their children in a manner that maintained their distinct language and religious communities. In an attempt to compel assimilation, states enacted laws forbidding instruction in languages other than English, and even, in some circumstances, requiring all children to attend public schools. At their worst, these laws reflected hostility toward immigrants, and most particularly Roman Catholics. At best, they reflected America's commitment to fostering a common community among all citizens.

The Supreme Court of the United States is the highest authority on questions of constitutional law and, in that role, determines whether state laws offend rights established by the United States Constitution. Exercising that authority, the Court struck down these state assimilation laws, ruling that they violated teachers' and parents' right to "liberty" protected by the Constitution. In two cases, *Meyer v. Nebraska*[1] and *Pierce v. Society of Sisters*,[2] the Court embraced the right of parents to exercise control over their children's education and warned against state attempts to eradicate pluralism by making all children the same. Parents, the Court explained, had both the right and "the high duty" to direct their children's destiny and to "prepare them for additional obligations."[3]

While these cases did not expressly consider the parents' religious motivation for their school choices, the Supreme Court made clear in the subsequent case of *Wisconsin v. Yoder* that parents' right to control their children's upbringing is at its strongest when it is motivated by religious conviction.[4] In that case, several Amish parents challenged Wisconsin's attempt to prosecute them criminally for removing their children from school two years earlier than the compulsory attendance law allowed. According to the Amish parents' beliefs, removing the children from school at fourteen was necessary to protect them from the corrupting influences of the high school curriculum and non-Amish peers and to prepare them for life as self-sufficient Amish farmers. In ruling that the state's prosecution of the Amish parents violated their rights under the Free Exercise Clause of the Constitution,[5] the

Court stressed two things: first, that the parents' views were based on deeply held religious beliefs and, second, that deferring to their views might be necessary to assure the survival of the Amish community. Thus, in the context of protecting individual parents' right to control the upbringing of their children, the Court suggested that parents play an important, and legally protected, role in the preservation of their religious communities.

In ruling for the Amish parents, the Supreme Court recognized that Wisconsin had a compelling interest in ensuring that children were adequately educated to develop into self-sufficient citizens capable of participating in our democratic system of government. It nevertheless concluded that it did not serve this interest to require Amish children to stay in school until they were sixteen, because the Amish had a long history of self-sufficiency and noninvolvement in the democratic process. In its analysis, the Court assumed that it was proper for parents to determine the religious identity of their children and that it was relatively unlikely, if raised as their parents wished to raise them, that Amish children would choose to leave the Amish community.

In a dissenting opinion, Justice William O. Douglas criticized the court majority for failing to take into account the Amish children's views about their education and religion. Citing developmental literature for support, Douglas argued that these fourteen-year-olds were mature enough to understand the issues involved and to form their own views on the subject. While there was no evidence in the case that the children disagreed with their parents, Douglas suggested that the Court should not have proceeded without first asking all the children involved whether they shared their parents' religious commitment to end formal schooling at the age of fourteen. The level of control *Yoder* gives to parents to prevent their children from choosing a different faith or way of life has made the case a subject of ongoing controversy.

Since *Yoder*, there have been many cases in which parents have successfully asserted a right to avoid a general legal requirement in order to raise their children in keeping with their religious faith. Moreover, state legislators have changed state laws to reflect these broad rights of parental control. One example of such legislative change—the legalization of homeschooling—is of particular importance to certain religious communities.

Not long ago, the homeschooling movement was considered a short-term, "fringe" movement that states actively sought to control through stiff regulations and some criminal prosecutions. But the numbers of homeschooled children continued to grow, and this eventually tipped the political balance in favor of homeschooling. Homeschooling is now legal in all fifty states, and some estimates put the number of homeschooled children at more than 1 million. A majority of those who homeschool their children do so for religious reasons. Particularly among conservative Christians, there is growing concern about the values conveyed in the schools through curriculum and peer interactions, and there is an increasing commitment within families to exercise greater control over what and how their children learn.[6]

Even homeschooled students, however, are subject to some state control over their education. This is generally accomplished through legal requirements regarding curriculum, teaching qualifications, and student academic performance. The law does not, however, give the state any authority to limit parents' control over their children's peer associations. When parents send their children to private schools and, to a much greater extent, when they educate their children at home, they control their social networks. If parents wish to prevent their children from interacting with anyone who does not share their religious beliefs, homeschooling protections now make it possible to do so legally.

As this discussion of parental control in the context of education makes clear, the law's deference to parents' religiously motivated child-rearing choices is considerable, but not absolute. Parents have even more control over other child-rearing choices, such as how children spend their nonacademic time and how children are cared for and disciplined. Unless parents are putting their children at serious risk of harm through abuse or neglect, the state has no authority to interfere in these matters.

One important implication of this parent-deferential approach is that no state has ever attempted to outlaw the use of corporal punishment. Among child development professionals, there is a growing consensus against the use of corporal punishment as a form of discipline. Among many religious faiths, however, physical discipline under certain controlled circumstances is encouraged. "Spare the rod, spoil the child" is probably one of the most widely known biblical directives. Because corporal punishment is accepted among many American communities, it is unlikely that our laws will move in the direction of Sweden's, for example, which have outlawed all use of corporal punishment as a form of discipline. If the findings of social scientists ever convinced a legislature to enact such a law in the United States, however, the law would surely be challenged in court as a violation of parents' constitutional right to raise their children pursuant to the teachings of their faith.

In one context, the abuse and neglect laws explicitly protect religiously motivated parenting choices that may put their children at serious risk. All fifty states grant an exemption within their definition of medical neglect for parents who refuse to secure conventional medical treatment for their children for religious reasons. These laws still give states the authority to intervene in an emergency to protect children from serious illness or death, but in shielding their parents from prosecution, these exemptions are criticized by those who believe they improperly favor parents' interests over the well-being of their children. Note that these exemptions are probably not compelled by the Constitution, as parental rights can be limited where children's health and safety is at stake. Rather, these laws were enacted by state legislatures as part of the democratic lawmaking process. Those critical of the laws suggest that they reflect the power of certain religious lobbies, rather than the views of a majority of voters.

None of this is to suggest that the mere fact that abuse occurs in a religious context, or is perpetrated by religious figures, would shield the perpetrator from prosecution. Where the alleged conduct is in no way linked to religious teachings, as in the sex abuse scandals within the Roman Catholic Church, the law in no way lessens the sanctions that can be imposed on the perpetrators. That being said, enforcement of those laws against religious organizations and individuals raises complicated issues of church-state relations that some believe have inappropriately shielded religious figures from the full effect of the law.[7]

In sum, the law shows considerable, if not absolute, deference to parents' child-rearing choices, and the law shows the greatest deference to those choices where they are grounded on the parents' religious beliefs. Those who support this parent-deferential legal system point to its value to children (parents are generally intensely devoted to securing their children's well-being) and to society as a whole (we nurture pluralism by giving this control to parents). Those critical of the current legal regime question whether the law does enough to protect children's health and well-being and to nurture children's opportunity to make their own choices about how they wish to live their lives. Some critics also contend that the level of protection afforded to parents varies with the religion involved, with the greatest protection afforded to religious communities, such as the Amish, whose relationship with mainstream American society has been uncontentious.[8]

## The Prohibition against Government Involvement in Religious Upbringing

Where the Free Exercise Clause of the Constitution protects private religious exercise, including child rearing, from government intervention, the Establishment Clause limits the government's participation in religion.[9] Under this clause, controversies affecting parents and children arise when the state exposes children to public displays and expressions of religion, particularly in the public school setting. Commonly, parents align themselves on both sides of the controversy, some seeking to encourage opportunities for their children's religious expression in school and others seeking to shield their children from any such government involvement in religious matters.

A number of different standards have been identified to describe the scope of the establishment prohibition. The traditional test prohibits government action that has the primary effect or purpose of advancing a religion or that excessively entangles the government with religion. More modern analyses prohibit government action that has a coercive effect on those who do not share the religious beliefs espoused or that appears to endorse the religious expression in question. Because children are thought to be particularly vulnerable to pressure from peers and authority figures, the Supreme Court has imposed greater limitations on religious activity in the school setting than in settings frequented by adults.

As a general matter, the Establishment Clause has been interpreted to greatly limit communities' opportunities to cultivate children's religious practices or beliefs in school. In 1962, the Supreme Court outlawed prayer in public schools,[10] and in 1968, the Court struck down a ban on the teaching of evolution, concluding that the ban was impermissibly grounded on religious belief.[11] In both these areas, however, there is continuing public pressure to find lawful ways to circumvent the Court's rulings, by reshaping the activity from public prayer to private meditation and by supplementing the teaching of evolutionary theory with theories consistent with the Bible's account of creation. Thus far, no such alterations have been found legally sufficient by the Supreme Court, but the persistence of the efforts over the decades is testament to the strength of the convictions of those who believe that children are disserved by a sharp church-state divide.

The Supreme Court has shown considerably greater willingness to protect public displays and recitations of religion that are conceived as insignificant, nondenominational, or "civil." For example, although it has not yet ruled on the issue, the Supreme Court has suggested that leading schoolchildren in a recitation of the Pledge of Allegiance that includes the words *under God* is lawful, despite the fact that this reference conflicts with the beliefs of polytheists such as Buddhists and of atheists. Currently in the United States there is strong political support for the inclusion of the *under God* language in the pledge. Some of this support derives from those who are committed to identifying the United States as a Judeo-Christian (or even a Christian) nation, a commitment that is hard to justify in light of the Court's interpretation of the Establishment Clause in other contexts and in light of the diversity of American religious faiths, as reflected in this volume. Others support inclusion of the language because it is conceived as traditional and harmless. While there are no studies tracking the effect of invoking this language repeatedly in school on children's religious development, some studies suggest that young children understand the Pledge of Allegiance to be a prayer.[12]

Another strand of the Supreme Court's Establishment Clause doctrine addresses the extent to which the state can provide financial assistance to parochial schools that have undertaken to meet the educational needs of a considerable percentage of American children.[13] The Supreme Court has allowed payments for buses, texts, and other nonreligious educational expenses. More recently, the Court upheld a school voucher program that allowed parents to pay for their children's education at a religious school (among other options) with public education dollars if they were dissatisfied with the education offered in the public schools.[14] Note that those expenditure programs that have been authorized to support parochial education have been justified in spite of rather than because of their religious educational mission.

Read together, the Free Exercise and Establishment Clauses provide considerable protection for the individual child-rearing choices made by parents for religious reasons and impose considerable restrictions on the state's engagement in children's religious upbringing. At times the two clauses are perceived to clash, as when parents and their children are prevented from sharing religious messages with others in the context of school activities. In one such recent example, a kindergarten student brought gifts with a message about Jesus to school to distribute to his classmates during a school-sponsored gift exchange.[15] When the school refused to let the child distribute the gifts, his parents sued. The school argued that schoolchildren, particularly such young children, would likely assume that the religious message was endorsed by the school. The parents invoked the Free Exercise Clause to assert their right, and the right of their child, to share their religious message with their child's classmates. The court ruled in favor of the school, ruling that the state's legitimate interest in avoiding the appearance of religious endorsement outweighed any right the family had to express their religious beliefs in this manner.

## Children's Independent Religious Rights

Complicating the legal picture even further is the fact that children, too, have constitutional rights, and these rights will sometimes trump the religious rights of their parents. Children, for example, have a right to free speech in schools, a right to obtain an abortion, and a right to be protected from unreasonable searches of their property and person. Children's rights are modeled after the rights of adults, but in most instances, they are modified to reflect children's immaturity and their dependence on their parents. Thus, their speech in school can be controlled in ways that adult speech cannot; they can be required, unlike adults, to obtain someone's permission before having an abortion; and they can be searched under circumstances that would be deemed unreasonable for adults. Children also have religious rights, though the lack of litigation in this area has, to date, left these rights poorly defined.

Parents frequently assert their children's religious rights along with their own religious rights in lawsuits against the government. But in most such cases, the children's religious claims are entirely dependent on the parents' claims and in no way change the nature of the claims asserted. In a smaller number of cases, however, the primary or exclusive rights asserter is the child, and from these cases we can get a rough sense of the scope of children's religious rights.

The most common context in which minors have asserted religious rights is the medical context, in which a doctor has recommended some medical procedure and the minor has refused the procedure on religious grounds. The state is generally powerless to force a competent adult to undergo medical procedures that she or he clearly opposes. But in the case of children, if the state determines that a procedure is necessary to protect the child from serious illness, impairment, or death, it will seek a court order to compel it. Unless the court finds the child sufficiently mature to act in her or his own best interest, the court will order the child to undergo procedures it deems medically necessary, even if the child believes the procedure violates her or his religious obligations. Note that these claims only arise when the child and parent are aligned in opposing the procedure, for parents have broad authority to compel their children to undergo medically necessary procedures without state intervention.

When children assert religious claims that are consistent with the religious views of their parents, it is difficult to ascertain to what extent the child holds an independent, authentic religious view. This generally will not matter if a child's life is in danger, as the denial of the rights claim will hinge on this threat to life, rather than on the authenticity of the child's claim. In other contexts, however, the independent view of a child may be important, as Justice Douglas suggested it should be in the *Yoder* case. Where the child's view is relevant to the rights analysis, the authenticity of the child's views, as distinct from those of the parents, becomes significant.

Ascertaining the "true" religious views of a child is likely to be difficult, and in some cases impossible. Frieda Yoder's testimony in *Wisconsin v. Yoder* helps to illustrate this point. In *Yoder*, three fathers' decisions to remove their children from school were at issue, but only one child, Frieda, was asked whether she agreed with her father's religious conviction that her schooling should end at fourteen. Frieda's testimony consists of single word answers (mostly yeses) to the leading questions of lawyers, all done in the intimidating context of a court of law and in front of her parents, church leaders, and other members of the Amish community. Unless

Frieda was prepared to face serious negative consequences in her home
and in her community, she had every reason to go along with the views of
her parents. This is not to suggest that she actually disagreed with their
views, but, rather, that she was in no position to opine freely about them,
if she did, in fact, disagree.

Where children actually do disagree with their parents' religious views,
they rarely pursue those religious differences in court. Rather, they generally
view these issues as private and personal, to be kept to themselves or discussed with their friends, family, and community. But even if children wished
to invoke the help of the courts in resolving religious differences, they would,
in most circumstances, not have a direct claim against their parents. Because
our constitutional rights are rights against the state, a child would only have
a legal claim if the state somehow cooperated with her or his parents in their
refusal to protect the child's independent religious beliefs.

Perhaps the most famous example of such a claim was asserted by Walter Polovchak, a twelve-year-old boy who sought to remain in the United
States when his parents returned to the Soviet Union to live. Walter applied
for asylum, asserting that he was a Baptist, and, as such, would face persecution in the Soviet Union. The case worked its way slowly through the courts
and was not finally disposed of until just before his eighteenth birthday. In
recognizing Walter's independent religious claim, the Court of Appeals for
the Seventh Circuit emphasized how children's religious (and other civil)
rights grow as they approach adulthood:

> The subject of the departure control order is a person who, though a
> minor, has constitutional rights that the government must respect. . . .
> [Even if Walter's private interests were considerably less than his
> parents when he was twelve,] Walter's rights have evolved over the
> past five years, and facts and circumstances relevant to such a bal-
> ancing have changed. At the age of twelve, Walter was presumably
> near the lower end of an age range in which a minor may be mature
> enough to assert certain individual rights that equal or override
> those of his parents; at age seventeen (indeed, on the eve of his eigh-
> teenth birthday), Walter is certainly at the high end of such a scale,
> and the question whether he should have to subordinate his own
> political commitments to his parents' wishes looks very different. The
> minor's rights grow more compelling with age, particularly in the fac-
> tual context of this case. . . . As the child grows, his parents' influence
> over him weakens, and the time his parents have in which to guide
> him grows shorter. The district court may be correct that parents
> "have the right to bring their children up as atheists or Communists,"
> but it is surely relevant that Walter has decided that he does not want

to be a communist or an atheist and that his parents have only the few remaining days of his minority to try to change his mind.[16]

This sliding-scale approach makes a great deal of sense and at least roughly reflects the courts' approach to children's constitutional rights in general. Because there are so few cases in which children assert a right to practice a religion that conflicts with their parents', it is impossible to determine how the sliding scale would be applied to resolve any particular religious issue at any particular age.

Far more common than children's assertions of religious rights are their assertions of other rights that conflict with parents' religious commitments in the upbringing of their children. In such contexts, parental deference is sometimes significantly, but not completely, diminished to protect the developing rights of their minor children. The most controversial example of this reallocation of authority from parent to child occurs in the context of abortion. In all states, children have the right to obtain an abortion without their parents' permission if they can prove to a court that they are mature enough to make the decision on their own or that the abortion is in their best interest.[17]

A final issue that bears on children's religious rights goes to the state's role in preparing children to make independent choices about their religious identity, a theme already touched upon in the first section of this chapter. Some have argued that in *Yoder*, the Supreme Court misconstrued the state's interest in keeping children in school until they were sixteen by overemphasizing the values of self-sufficiency and orderly government and underemphasizing the value of developing children's ability to act autonomously. There is some evidence to conclude that what the Amish parents most feared about high school was that it would encourage their children to develop critical reasoning skills and exposure to alternative life choices that might inspire them to question their Amish faith. Although the Amish and many other Christian denominations discussed in this volume practice adult baptism to ensure that members enter the church by choice, these denominations advocate child-rearing practices that steer children away from the knowledge and experiences that might inspire children to make other choices. Some champions of children's autonomy believe that it is the state's obligation to counter these choice-restricting parental influences. In their view, *Yoder* improperly favors parents' rights over children's rights by giving parents too much control over children's ultimate exercise of choice into adulthood.

## Choosing between Parents' Faiths

In the case of an intact family, both the Free Exercise Clause and the Establishment Clause prevent the state from intervening in parents' choices about the religious upbringing of their children, and states will refuse to entertain the request of one parent to compel another parent to cooperate in her or his efforts at religious upbringing or even to fulfill a promise to raise a child in a particular faith. When parents divorce, however, the court becomes involved in overseeing the terms of that divorce, and this task sometimes involves the court in resolving religious disputes. Parents' constitutional right to control the religious upbringing of their children has been interpreted to limit the extent to which parents' religious choices can affect the court's custody determination or the terms of visitation. There are circumstances, however, in which the court determines that parents' religious practices are having a sufficiently adverse affect on the children to justify imposing some limitations.

The general rule in custody cases is that religiously based behavior cannot serve as a basis for denying custody, unless the behavior can be shown to cause the children harm. Thus, in most states, religiously motivated behavior that strikes the court as unusual, or extreme, cannot, for that reason alone, be counted against that parent in the "best interest" calculus, even though the same behavior could count against the parent if not justified in religious terms. If the religious belief or behavior can be shown to cause physical or psychological harm, however, including an alienation of the child's affections for the other parent, then a court can justify assigning custody to the other parent on the basis of these effects.

Similarly, the Constitution generally prevents a court from identifying a single religion as the religion of a child or from restricting either of the divorced parent's attempts to influence the child's religious upbringing. This is true regardless of what prior agreements were reached between the parents regarding their children's religious upbringing and identity.[18] This is also true regardless of how custodial authority is divided between the two parents. Thus, even a parent with modest visitation rights, whose religion is different from the custodial parent's, is permitted to spend as much of the visitation time as she or he wishes involving the child in religious education and observance that comports with the parent's beliefs.[19]

The court may limit a parent's authority to expose her or his child to that parent's religion if the other parent can show that the exposure is causing the child actual harm. Many courts have concluded that evidence that a child is somewhat confused about her or his religious identity, or how the religious views of the parents fit together, does not constitute harm. However, evidence that one parent was telling his children that the other parent was damned and going to hell for her beliefs, and that these comments were provoking anxiety in their children, was found to be enough to justify a finding of harm and an order directing the father not to make any comments, or take the children to any religious services, that taught that those who did not accept Jesus Christ as their savior were destined to burn in hell.[20]

In determining with whom children should live, and what sort of visitation should be ordered, courts are generally required to solicit the views of older children. This means that children are sometimes given the opportunity to express their religious views in the custody context. While a child's expression of religious identity sometimes helps a court to ascertain in which household the child will feel more comfortable, it rarely justifies a curtailing of the other parent's authority to influence the child's religious upbringing. Because a parent's right to influence her or his child's religious upbringing is defined as fundamental, courts have determined that it survives separation and even diminution of overall authority over a child.

## Conclusion

Our government enacts laws to protect children from harm and to foster their healthy development. At the same time, the law, in the form of individual rights, puts limits on government's authority to intervene in matters such as child rearing and religion that are deeply personal and private. The challenge, for our law, is to strike the right balance for children between intervention and restraint, to ensure their successful upbringing as members of a family, a community, and a nation.

### NOTES

1. 262 U.S. 390 (S.Ct. 1923).
2. 268 U.S. 510 (S.Ct. 1925).
3. *Id.* at 535.
4. 406 U.S. 205 (S.Ct. 1972).
5. For the Free Exercise Clause of the Constitution, see U.S. Constitution, amend. 1.
6. See Bartkowski and Ellison's chapter in this volume.
7. See Beste's chapter in this volume.
8. Supporting this skepticism is the Supreme Court's ruling in *Prince v. Massachusetts*, 321 U.S. 158 (S.Ct. 1944), a case decided three decades prior to *Yoder*. In *Prince*, the Court denied constitutional protection to a child's guardian charged with violating child labor laws when she let her nine-year-old niece sell religious pamphlets on a public street in fulfillment of her religious obligations as a Jehovah's Witness. While the Court suggested that its decision rested on the state's strong interest in protecting children from the dangers of nightlife on the streets, it is far from obvious that the harm Massachusetts was seeking to avoid in prohibiting this conduct (particularly when carried out within view of her guardian) was greater than the harm Wisconsin was seeking to avoid in requiring schooling through the tenth grade.
9. U.S. Constitution, amend. 1.

10. *Engel v. Vitale*, 370 U.S. 421 (S.Ct. 1962).

11. *Epperson v. Arkansas*, 393 U.S. 97 (S.Ct. 1968).

12. Eugene H. Freund and Donna Givner, "Schooling, the Pledge Phenomenon, and Social Control" (paper presented at the 1975 meetings of the American Educational Research Association, April 1975), 12; Robert D. Hess and Judith V. Torney, *The Development of Political Attitudes in Children* 19 (Garden City, NY: Doubleday, 1967).

13. See Numrich's chapter in this volume.

14. *Zelman v. Simmons-Harris*, 536 U.S. 639 (S.Ct. 2002).

15. *Walz v. Egg Harbor Twp. Bd. of Educ.*, 342 F.3d 271 (3d Cir. 2003).

16. *Polovchak v. Meese*, 774 F.2d 731, 736–37 (7th Cir. 1985).

17. *Bellotti v. Baird*, 443 U.S. 622 (S.Ct. 1979).

18. *In re Marriage of Weiss*, 42 Cal. App. 4th 106 (1996).

19. *Zummo v. Zummo*, 394 Pa. Super. 30 (Pa. App. 1990).

20. *Kendall v. Kendall*, 426 Mass. 238 (1997).

# CONTRIBUTORS

JOHN P. BARTKOWSKI, a professor of sociology at the University of Texas at San Antonio, has published on religion, family, gender, youth, and social welfare. His most recent book is *The Promise Keepers: Servants, Soldiers, and Godly Men* (2004), which charts the rise and fall of the Evangelical men's movement. He is currently completing two books, one on the contours and effects of Latter-day Saint teen religiosity and the other on faith-based initiatives across various policy domains.

MARGARET BENDROTH is the executive director of the American Congregational Association in Boston, Massachusetts, and the director of the Congregational Library. She is the author of *Fundamentalism and Gender, 1875 to the Present*, and *Growing Up Protestant: Parents, Children, and Mainline Churches*.

JENNIFER BESTE is an associate professor of theological ethics at Xavier University in Cincinnati, Ohio. She is author of *God and the Victim: Traumatic Intrusions on Grace and Freedom* (2007). She is presently conducting a qualitative research study interviewing Catholic second graders about their first experiences of the Sacrament of Reconciliation.

DON S. BROWNING is Alexander Campbell Professor of Religious Ethics and the Social Sciences, Divinity School, University of Chicago, emeritus. He is most recently the author of *Christian Ethics and the Moral Psychologies* (2006) and coeditor of *Sex, Marriage, and Family in the World Religions* (2006).

RAYMOND BUCKO is a professor of anthropology, the chair of the Department of Sociology and Anthropology, and the director of the Native American studies program at Creighton University. He is the author of *The Lakota Ritual of the Sweat Lodge* (1998) and "Peter the Aleut: Sacred Icons and the

Iconography of Violence," in *Boletín: The Journal of the California Mission Studies Association.*

**EMILY BUSS** is the Mark and Barbara Fried Professor of Law and Kanter Director of Policy Initiatives at the University of Chicago Law School. Buss's research focuses on children's and parents' rights and the legal system's allocation of authority and responsibility between parent, child, and state. As Kanter Director, she heads a project aimed at improving the legal system's treatment of children aging out of foster care.

**DAVID C. DOLLAHITE**, PhD, is a professor of family life at Brigham Young University. He has been a visiting scholar at the University of Massachusetts–Amherst; Dominican University of California; and the M.S. University of Baroda, India. He coedited *Helping and Healing Our Families* (2005) and edited *Strengthening Our Families* (2000), both on Mormon family life.

**ELLIOT N. DORFF**, rabbi, PhD, is rector and Distinguished Professor of Philosophy at the University of Judaism in Los Angeles. His twelve books include *Love Your Neighbor and Yourself: A Jewish Approach to Modern Personal Ethics* (2003), which contains a chapter on how Jewish sources and modern Jews perceive parent-child relationships.

**CHRISTOPHER G. ELLISON** is the Elsie and Stanley E. Adams Sr. Centennial Professor of Sociology and Religious Studies at the University of Texas at Austin. His previous work on Evangelicalism and child rearing has appeared in the *American Sociological Review*, *Social Forces*, the *Journal for the Scientific Study of Religion*, and numerous other outlets.

**CHERYL TOWNSEND GILKES**, John D. and Catherine T. MacArthur Professor of African-American Studies and Sociology at Colby College, is the author of *If It Wasn't for the Women: Black Women's Experience and Womanist Culture in Church and Community* (2001). She is an ordained Baptist minister, and her published sermons have appeared in the *African American Pulpit*.

**RITA M. GROSS** is a scholar-practitioner who has specialized in issues relating to gender and religion. Her best-known book is *Buddhism after Patriarchy: A Feminist History, Analysis, and Reconstruction of Buddhism* (1993). She has also participated widely in interreligious discussions.

**ROGER IRON CLOUD** is a former federal employee, child development specialist, and community organizer. He is a member of the Oglala Lakota Tribe from the Pine Ridge Indian Reservation in South Dakota. Mr. Iron Cloud currently lives in Virginia.

**JEFFREY MEYER** is a professor of religious studies at the University of North Carolina at Charlotte. His books include *The Dragons of Tiananmen: Beijing as a Sacred City* (1991). He has written extensively on moral education in the elementary and junior high schools of the People's Republic of China and Taiwan.

**BONNIE J. MILLER-MCLEMORE** is E. Rhodes and Leona B. Carpenter Professor of Pastoral Theology, Vanderbilt University Divinity School, and the author of several books on religion and family, including *Let the Children Come: Reimagining Childhood from a Christian Perspective* (2003) and *In the Midst of Chaos: Care of Children as Spiritual Practice* (2006).

**PAUL D. NUMRICH** is an associate professor and chair of the Program in World Religions and Inter-religious Dialogue at the Theological Consortium of Greater Columbus, Ohio, and affiliate research associate professor at the McNamara Center for the Social Study of Religion, Department of Sociology, Loyola University Chicago.

**JANE I. SMITH** is associate dean for faculty and academic affairs at Harvard Divinity School. She is the author of *Muslims, Christians, and the Challenge of Interfaith Dialogue* (2007); *Muslim Women in America* (coauthor, 2006); *Becoming American: Immigration and Religious Life in the United States* (coeditor, 2004) and *Islam in America* (1999).

**RAYMOND BRADY WILLIAMS** is LaFollette Distinguished Professor in the Humanities emeritus at Wabash College. Among his books on Hindus and immigrants are *An Introduction to Swaminarayan Hinduism* (2001), *Williams on South Asian Religions and Immigration* (2005), and *Religions of Immigrants from India and Pakistan in the United States* (1988).

# INDEX

Abd'l-Haleem, Khadijah, 205, 209n51
abortion, 26, 38, 72; children's rights and, 216, 219
Abyssinian Baptist Church (Harlem, New York), 97
adoption: in American Islam, 134; Native American, 120, 121, 132, 125
African Americans: baptism and baby dedication, 87; Black Church and children, 9, 21, 85–101; childhood crisis, 93; children and music in worship, 90, 91; children and racial oppression, 98, 101n30; and Christianity, 85, 86, 87, 99n1, 100n12; culture, 93, 101n22; denominations, 100n8; family, 96; and Islam, 133, 137, 141, 142, 143, 144, 145, 147n15; spirituals, 88; Sunday school, 89; urbanization, 97
agency, 3, 8, 67, 87, 94, 97, 192n15; individual, 106; moral, 64, 65, 66, 103, 106, 110
Allen AME Church (Queens, New York), 97
*Amar Chitra Katha* (Hindu picture books for children), 157
American Academy of Religion, 8, 9
American-Born Confused Desi (ABCD), 161–162
American culture: African American identity within, 85–101; Asian American identity within, 180–193; Bible as primer, 94; Catholic identity within, 56, 61; Hindu identity within, 148–164; Islamic identity within, 133–147, 201, 202, 204; Latter-day Saint identity within, 112, 114; Native American identity within, 119–132; and parochial school movement, 206; religious view of, 4, 26, 28, 29
American Sociological Association, 8
Amish, 211, 212, 214, 217, 219
*Analects* (Confucius), 183
Andrews, Dale, 93, 100n21
anthropology, 3, 7, 8, 9, 22n13, 132n27
'Aqiqa ceremony, 135
Ashkenazim, 79

Asian Americans: Buddhists, 166, 167, 168, 175; Confucians, 180–193
assimilation, 174, 198, 199, 206; laws and, 211
Association for Supervision and Curriculum Development, 203
Averroes Academy (Chicago), 201, 202, 208n33

Banerjee, Aditi, 162, 164n30
Baptists, 28, 88, 100n7, 218; Abyssinian Baptist Church, 97; African American, 89, 100n8; conventions, 95; Shiloh Baptist Church, 97; Southern, 89
Barazangi, Nimat Hafez, 202, 203, 209n37
bar mitzvah. *See under* Jewish Americans
Bartkowski, John, 5, 6, 16, 17, 23n22, 54nn1–4, 54n12, 54n15, 55n18, 55nn20–22, 55n25, 55nn27–28, 221n6
Beck, Walter, 197, 207n6, 207n10
Bendroth, Margaret, 5, 6, 15, 22n18, 23n21, 25–40, 53, 55n31
Benedict XVI (pope), 76
Beshir, Sumaiya, 143
Beste, Jennifer, 5, 6, 56–70, 221n7
Bethel AME Church (Baltimore), 97
*bhajans* (sacred Hindu songs), 154
Bible: and childbirth issues, 73; child discipline in, 45, 54n13; Christian, 17; inerrancy of, 29, 42, 43, 49; Jewish, 71, 78, 80; and literacy; 94; memorization of, 42; and Mormons, 118n12; and pedagogy, 35; Protestant, 29
Bloom, Harold, 104, 118n10
Bochaswansi Akshar Purushottam Sanstha (BAPS) Swaminarayan Group, 150; mission, 157, 158
Book of Mormon, 17, 106, 111, 118n12
Braxton, Toni, 92
*Breach of Trust, Breach of Faith* (Canadian Conference of Bishops), 65, 70n30, 70n33
Brigham Young University (BYU), 104
Browning, Don S., 24n30, 118n16, 163n8, 207n4